Steel Shadows

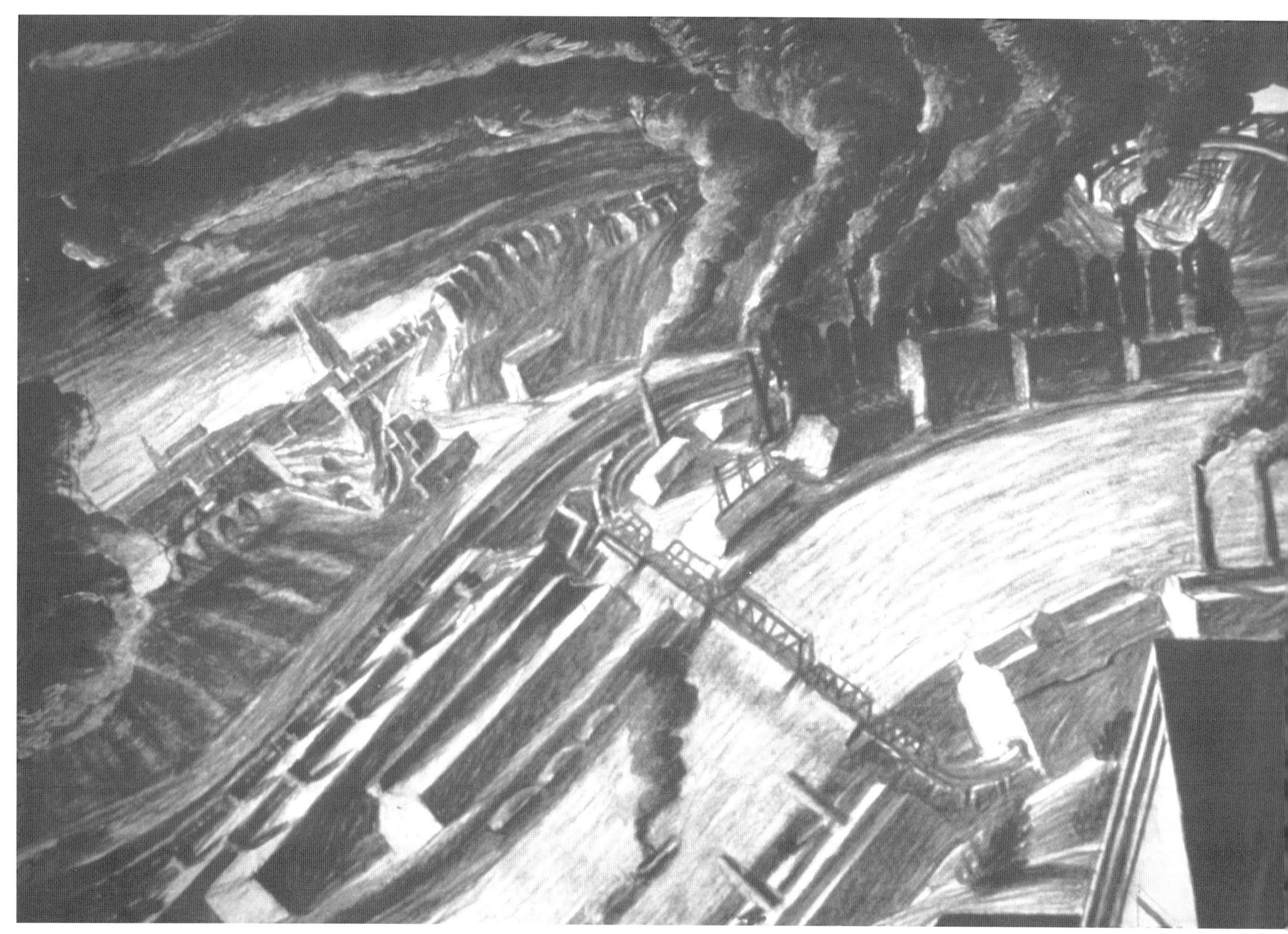

Jones and Laughlin Iron Mill. The Senator John Heinz Pittsburgh Regional History Center Mural, 1992–1993.

Douglas Cooper

Steel Shadows

Murals and Drawings of Pittsburgh

University of Pittsburgh Press

Manufactured in the United States of America
Printed on acid-free paper

10 9 8 7 6 5 4 3 2 1

Text and cover design by Kachergis Book Design,
Pittsboro, North Carolina.

For my mother, who sometime in 1952 or so painted a mural, in my bedroom. It is the first memory I have of the pictorial world.

For my two children, Laura and Sarah, who have been kind and discerning critics.

For my very patient and supportive wife, Meg.

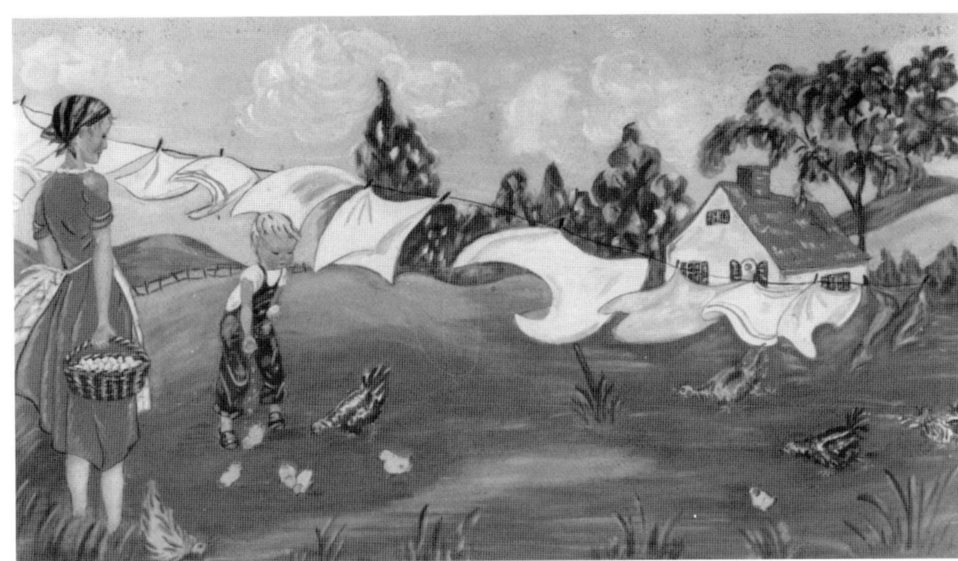

Mural painted by my mother, Martha Smith Cooper, circa 1952. *(Photo: Pamela Picher.)*

Blackest place I ever saw. At my hotel everything was black; not black to the eye, for the eye teaches itself to discriminate colors even when loaded with dirt, but black to the touch. On coming out of a tub of water my foot took an impress from the carpet exactly as it would have done had I trod bare footed on a path laid with soot.

—Anthony Trollope, on a visit to Pittsburgh, 1862

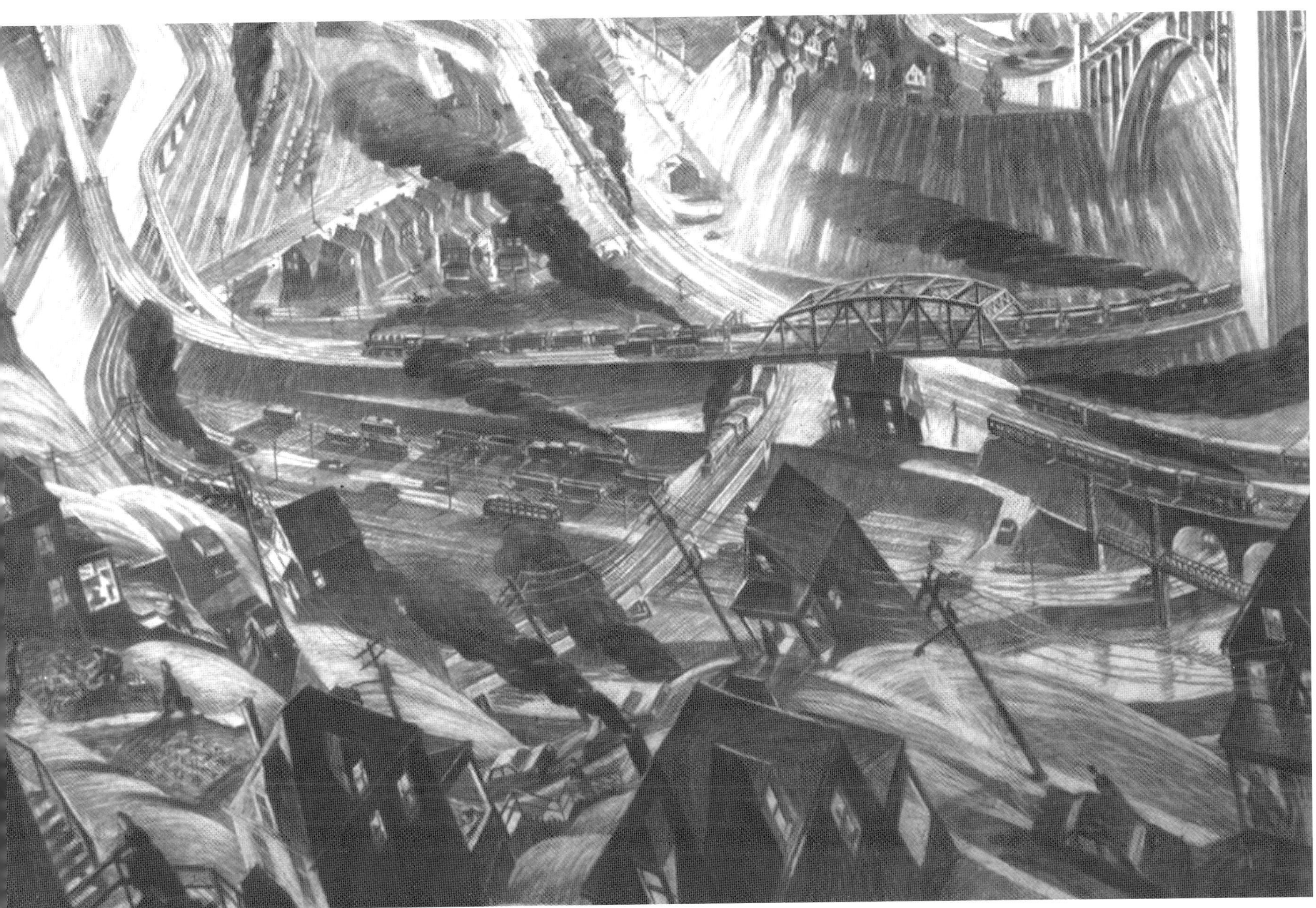

Morning Arrivals in Turtle Creek. (Private collection.)

Contents

Foreword

The Pittsburgh Doug Cooper shows us is a captivating amalgamation of memory and reality, a great city seen and recollected from many vantage points. These sketches and murals derive their visceral impact from their detail, for Cooper trains an inquisitive and omnivorous eye on the built and inhabited environment around him. Trained as an architect, Cooper has been a practicing artist throughout his career. Just as he changes perspectives within a drawing to dramatize terrain and emphasize certain sites, Cooper mixes past and present to enrich his geographic accounts. Cooper's work manifests his ideas about drawing as a means of recall and as an act of independent creation: his work consistently accommodates a representational reality that is both fact and fantasy. As he puts it, his drawings report on the visual world, rather than just a visual field. The roiling pictorial space he achieves mirrors Pittsburgh's hilly topography while supporting a host of literal and diagrammatic narratives. Cooper reckons that the art of drawing records data from an upright position, combining plane and elevation views in one expression. The plan provides both a sense of location and the specifics of place, while the elevational surfaces yield profiles. His preferred mode is elevational: he makes recognizable landmarks—physical and psychological.

The rivers that so frequently course and coil through Cooper's drawings not only help situate the knowing viewer but also underscore Pittsburgh's location astride the Monongahela and the Allegheny as they join to form the Ohio. We are reminded that rivers are the carriers of civilization, the lifeblood of discovery and commerce. Cooper's close observation of Pittsburgh suffuses his drawings, lending them a striking credibility. He knows, and can conjure, its hills and valleys and waterways, its streets and peculiar orders of neighborhoods. As he remembers, Cooper studied architecture in order "to imagine how a place might be." As an artist, he gives form to that imagination.

RICHARD ARMSTRONG
The Henry J. Heinz II Director
Carnegie Museum of Art, Pittsburgh

Acknowledgments

The work shown in this book began with a drawing assignment given to me by Kent Bloomer when I was studying architecture at Carnegie Tech. In a real sense, these works are late submissions to that assignment. But there are other people I could not acknowledge in the text of this book who have also helped along the way. My parents and my three wonderful sisters, Carolyn, Barbara, and Pamela, gave me a sense in earliest childhood that I could accomplish something with art if I stuck with it. Two teachers at the Choate School in Wallingford, Connecticut, Don Hickman, who taught art, and John Joseph, who taught Latin, still give me inspiration through my memory of their words.

I shifted careers from architecture to art while Meg and I were living in Germany. The interest of my employer Herbert Ohl in my work played a big role in that decision. I am also forever grateful to my many Frankfurt friends and colleagues who encouraged me with their comments, interest, and early purchases of my work.

During the years I have taught drawing at Carnegie Mellon University, fine arts deans Akram Midani and Martin Prekop and department heads Robert S. Taylor, Omer Akin, John Eberhard, and Vivian Loftness have always given me great support. Architect Syl Damianos helped organize a key exhibition of my work at the AIA national headquarters in Washington, D.C., in 1989. In 1991, Steve Mendelson of the Mendelson Gallery put on a show of my work that helped immensely in interesting the Carnegie Museum in the first Pittsburgh mural. At the museum Bay Hallowell, Vicki Clark, Mark Francis and Annegret Nill were early supporters of that project. Architect Stefani Ledewitz arranged my first contact with Vintage, the center that worked with me on that mural. Stephanie Johnston, Bob Grom, and Frely Shea helped me find much-needed studio space to complete the mural away from the museum. Ann Wardrop was very helpful with the second show at the Carnegie Museum. Mary Rawson and Nancy Lavin at WQED produced the wonderful documentary, "A Map of Memories," that presents that mural, and John Herbst and Kathleen Wendel pushed hard to ensure that it would be permanently displayed at the Heinz History Center.

So many were helpful with the Carnegie Mellon mural that there is no way I can name them all. Former president Robert Mehrabian commissioned the mural right away when the idea was originally presented to him by the fine arts dean, Martin Prekop. Provost Paul Christiano remained supportive all the way through the project, even when it looked as though one of the buildings that figured prominently in the mural might never be built. All the while I was working on the mural (and ever since), the members of Local 95 Operating Engineers, the owners of the building where I have my studio, were the most companionable landlords I could imagine. Steve Calvert made sure the mural was photo-graphed before it was installed, and Ted Fenton's interview with me led to my keeping notes about some of the technical aspects of its production. Dan Boxx served as my contact at architect Michael Dennis's office throughout the process of producing and installing the mural. After it was completed, Virginia Schatz was instrumental in making a very fine video about the entire project. Her husband, Ed, had been so helpful to the project by making sure proper lighting and a protective rail would be installed. Sadly, he died during the fall before the work was finished, and was never able to see it.

In the background, my colleague Bruce Lindsey at Carnegie Mellon offered some key observations about my work at the time I began doing drawings of Pittsburgh after a trip to Bryce Canyon. Leon Arkus, director emeritus of the Carnegie Museum of Art, and current director Richard Armstrong have been constant supporters of my work. Several of my former CMU teachers, William

S. Huff and Raymond Gindroz, and colleague Marsha Berger have been hugely generous with professional contacts. My good friend New York architect Andy Tesoro has always been a great booster and has helped with other commissions in New York. Over the years of doing murals, Ross Kronenbitter, John Trivelli, and later Rob Johnson have served as my installation team. More directly for the production of this book, David Demarest, Martha Estabrook, Judy Kampert, David Lewis, and my sister Pamela Picher read early drafts and made many helpful comments. Marilyn Kraitchman helped me get back in contact with the people I had worked with at Vintage for permissions. David Lewis has also been so helpful in tracking down the painting by Alfred Wallis that appears in this book. Midway in the process, Joanna Schultz offered critical structural suggestions, and she made the final edit before I sent the manuscript off to the University of Pittsburgh Press. Finally, all uncredited photos were taken by me.

In the beginning was the land. This, Nature's first and richest gift to Pittsburgh, required 500 million years to prepare. What would one day be Pittsburgh was the highest of a series of stone terraces created from sediment and the fossilized remains of plant life that grew and decayed in the various shifts of the Atlantic Ocean, when periodically the Pittsburgh district would be dry and periodically flooded in a vast swamp that extended throughout the Midwest. Between the layers of sandstone, limestone, and shales, Nature stored away natural gas, some of the world's purest oil, and coal in greater abundance than anywhere on earth. Finally and almost by caprice, Nature pushed up the Allegheny Mountains about 120 million years ago to ensure that Pittsburgh would mature by self-reliance in isolation from Philadelphia and the East Coast. Fortunately, Pittsburghers knew how to use the land, first growing crops on it, later exploiting the fossil deposits and minerals of western Pennsylvania to fuel its industries.

—Franklin Toker, *Pittsburgh: An Urban Portrait*

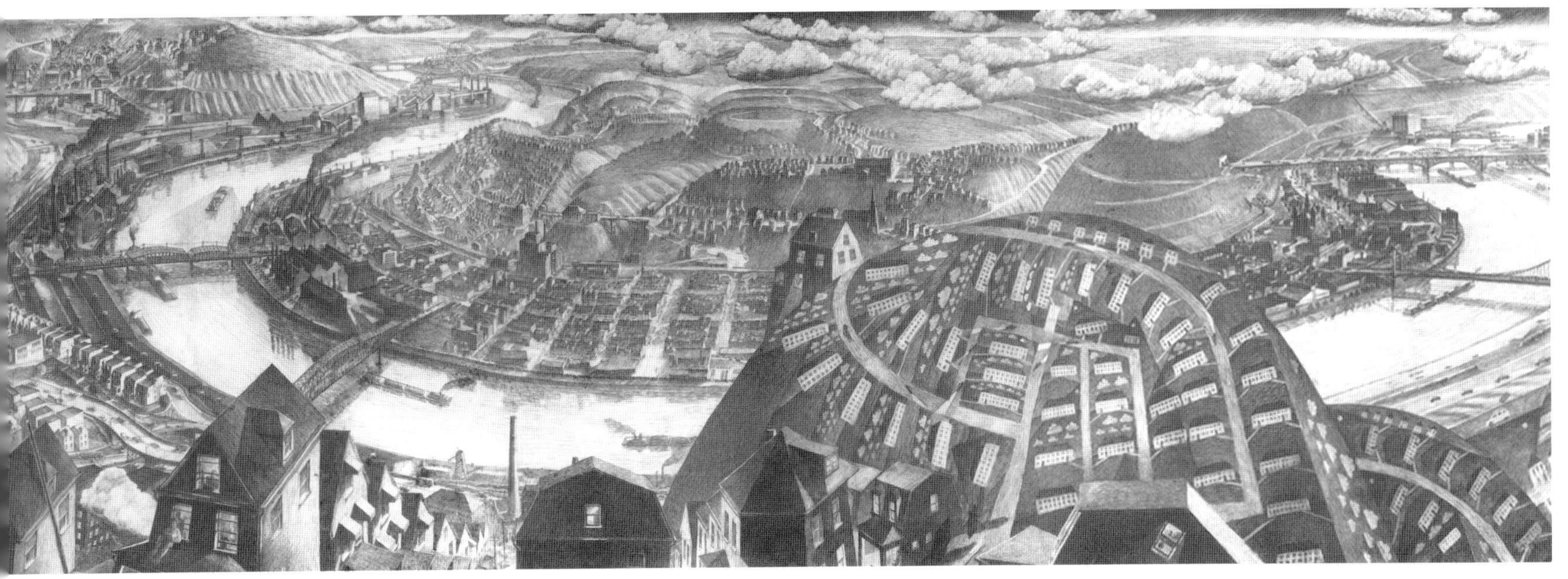

Southside panorama. University Center Mural. (Photo: Ken Andreyo.)

Part 1

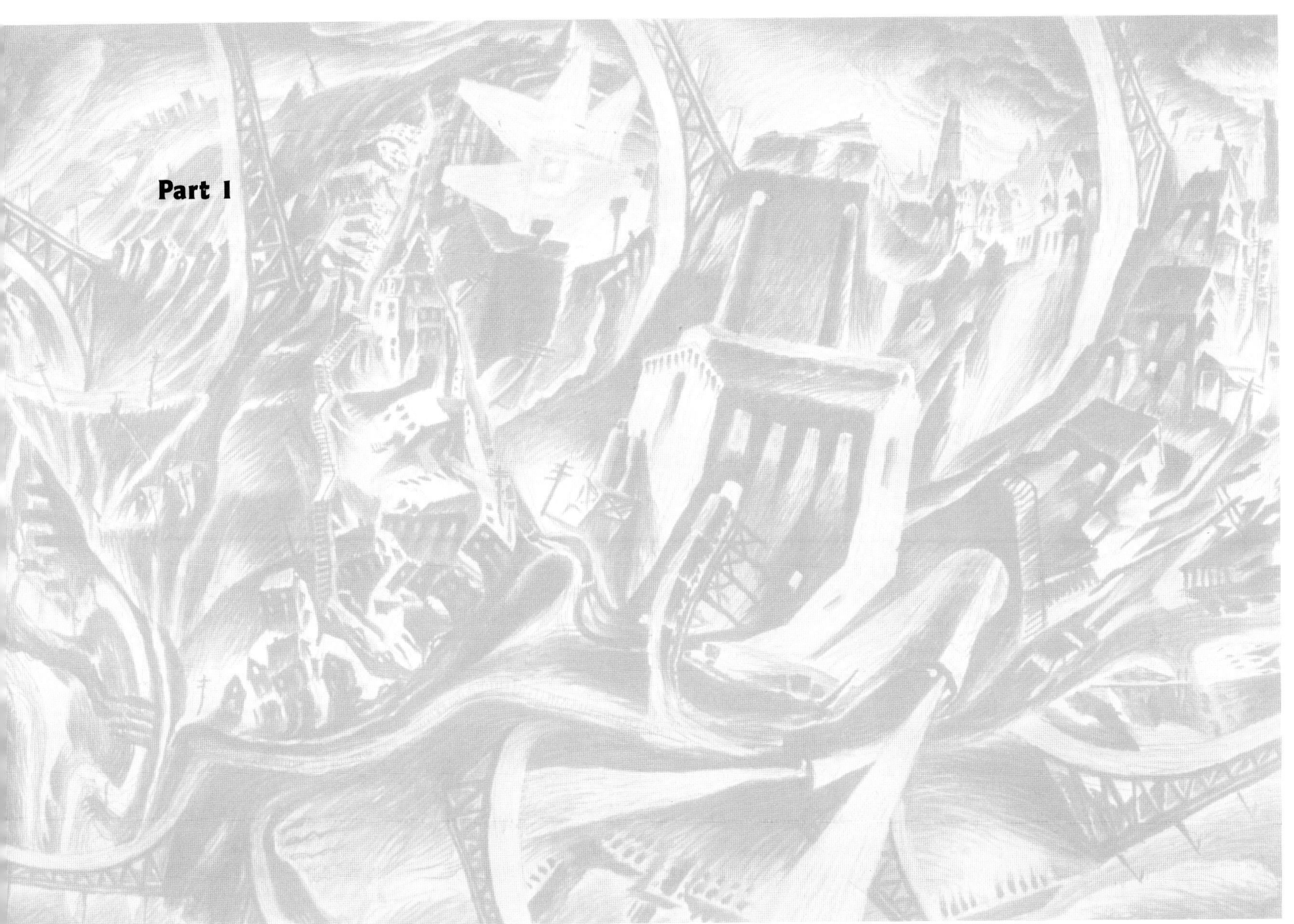

Between Shadow and Light

I *was not born in Pittsburgh*. During most of my childhood, my family lived in Connecticut. But in August 1953, when I was six, I decided my true home was Pittsburgh. It was the year after my grandfather had died of cancer. My father often came to Pittsburgh on business, and he brought me with him, on the night train, to visit my grandmother.

I lay awake most of the night watching the world pass by the lower-berth window. My first views of Pittsburgh were of its periphery and, in half-light, the Horseshoe Curve, steam trains pulling coal cars out of the night: views with reflected moons and clouds skimming the Connemaugh River leading to the mills at Johnstown. It was an incremental sense of the city, not the sudden introduction one gets today arriving by plane. It was as though the elements that made up Pittsburgh's approaching chemistry were laid out for inspection, one by one in sequence: first the hills, then the coal, then the valleys, then the water, and finally the fire.

We passed under the Westinghouse Bridge while we were in the dining car. Below us and alongside Westinghouse Airbrake, Turtle Creek flowed a color yellow I had never seen before. "There's a story about this bridge." All of a sudden my father spoke over his coffee. "When they were pouring the concrete, one of the workers fell into the form. You can't get them out during a pour. They leave them in. He's still in there." I imagined him still in there, still drowning in the concrete, still trying to swim to the top of the pour.

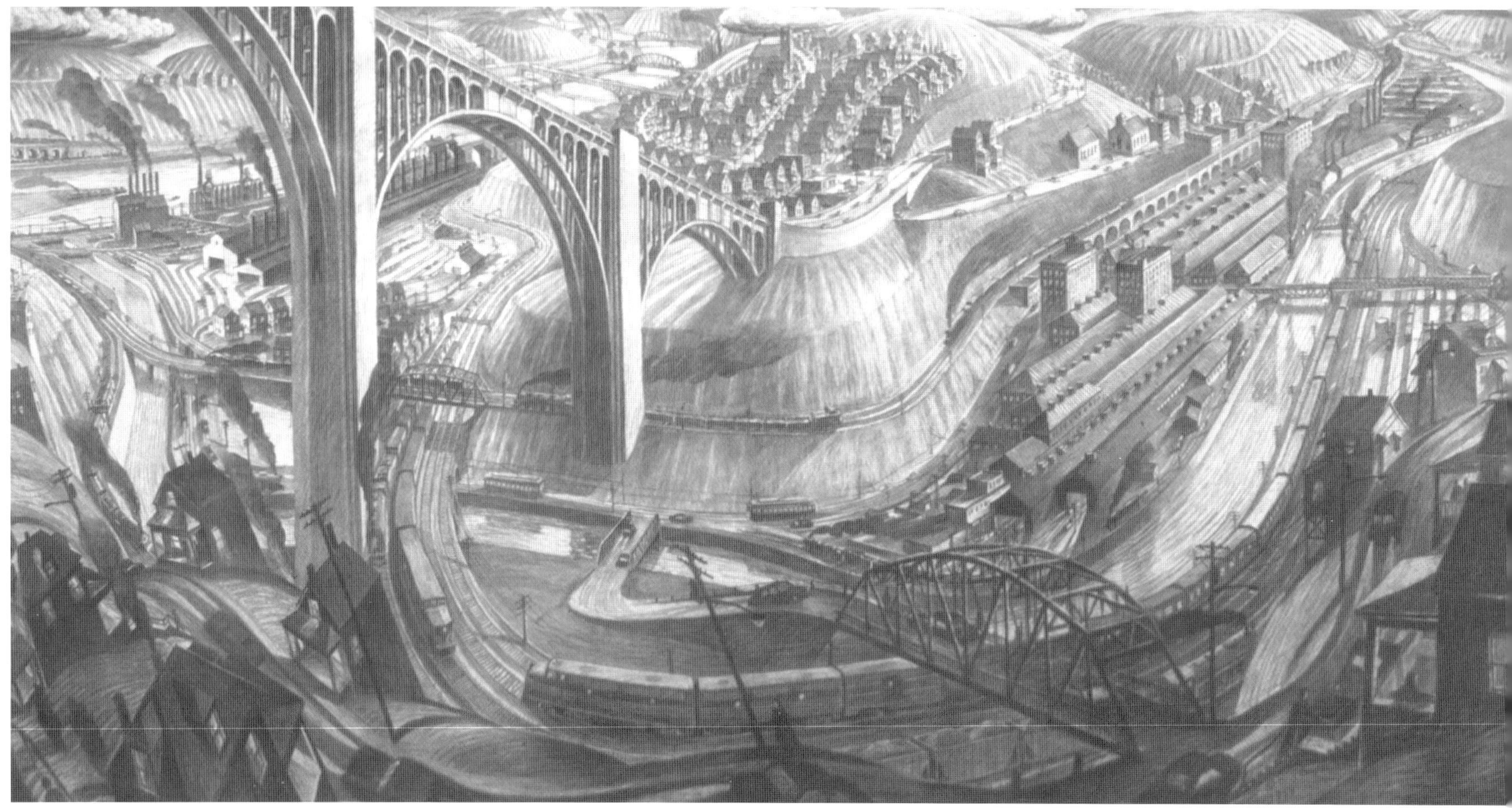

Morning Train under the Westinghouse Bridge, 1999.
48″ x 96″.

"There's a story about this bridge," all of a sudden my father spoke over his coffee. "When they were pouring the concrete, one of the workers fell into the form. You can't get them out during a pour. They leave them in. He's still in there."

Then the valley widened, and as the train rounded the bend overlooking Braddock, the smoke and fire plumes of the Edgar Thomson steelworks rose beside us. It was a layered scene, rust-brown haze and red heat in the foreground, with dark, stacked profiles behind. Peek-a-boo morning light reflected past the sheds and furnaces from the distant Monongahela River. Gas jets fired overhead. Then, just as quickly, the view closed again as the train turned into the cut through Swissvale. House-house-house-house-house–street, house-house-house-house-house–street, the rhythm gained speed on the long straightaway through Wilkinsburg but could not dull my sense of awe for this fire land where people were buried drowning in concrete.

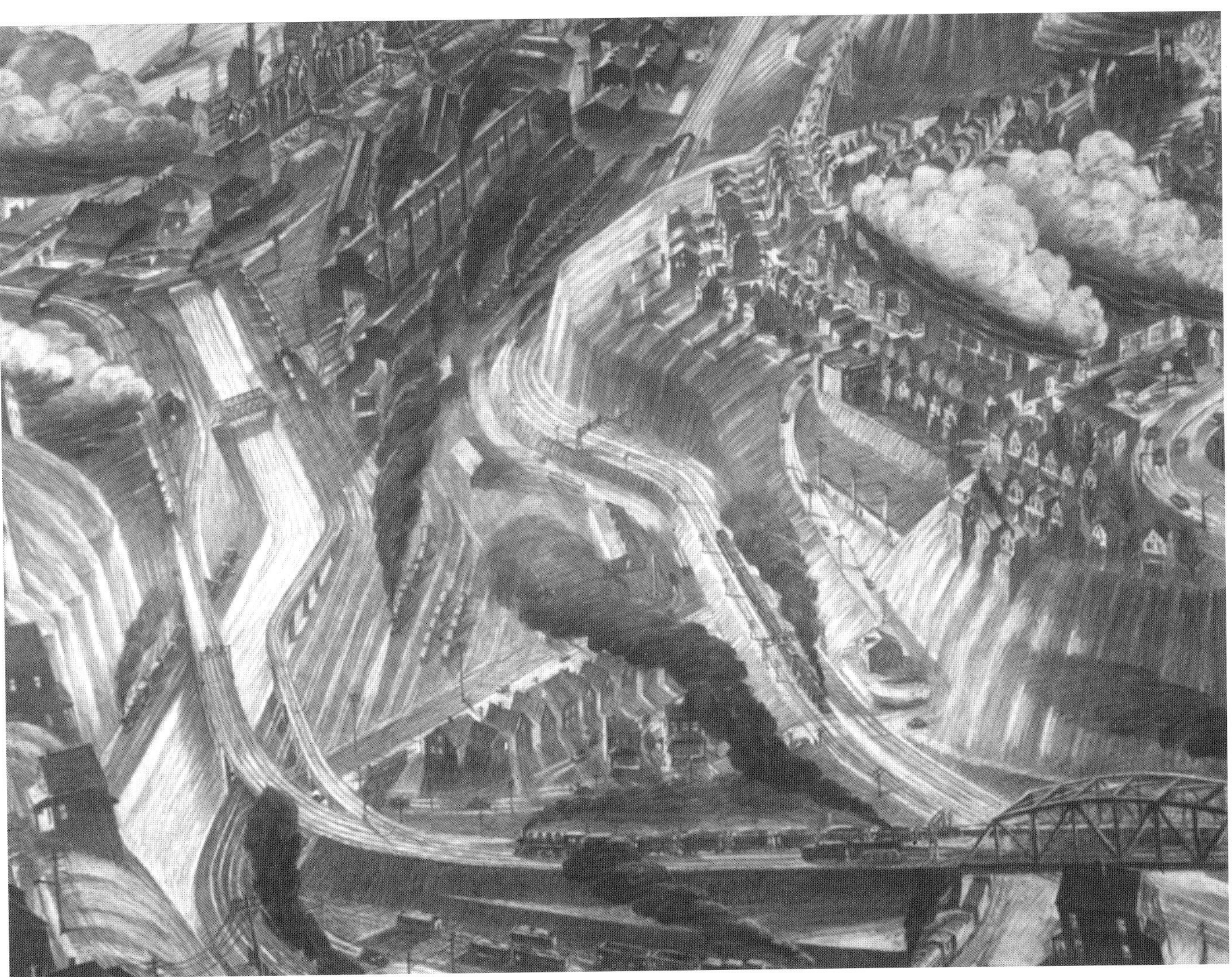

Morning Arrivals in Turtle Creek

Then the valley widened, and as the train rounded the bend, the smoke and fire plumes of the Edgar Thomson steelworks rose beside us.

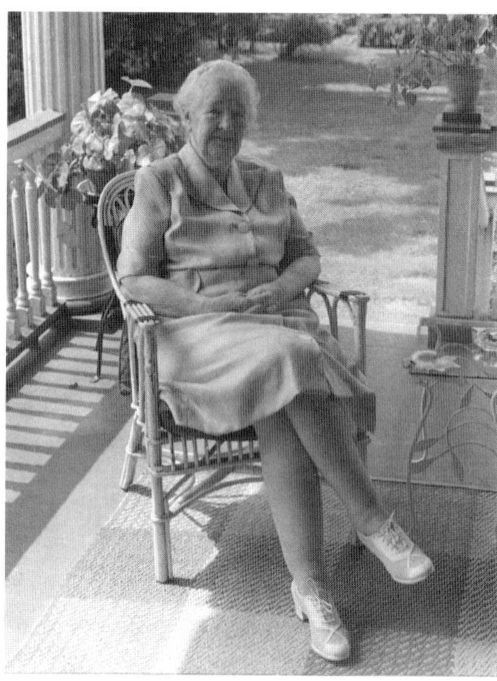

Mema, circa 1958.

My grandmother's name was Mema (pronounced Meema). While my father stayed in Pittsburgh for work, I was picked up at the Pennsylvania Station by my Aunt Mary and taken to Mema's, a big white clapboard house with a hipped roof and a Palladian window in the upstairs bathroom. Afternoons we spent on her porch under green canvas awnings.

Mema had scrapbooks from a trip she had taken with my grandfather to Eastern Europe during the 1930s and she brought these out to the porch to show me. It was on this trip, in a mine in Bulgaria, Mema used to say, that my grandfather had "caught" the cancer that would kill him years later. But that afternoon, looking at the scrapbook, Mema was remembering only the romance of their trip. She had difficulty seeing, so she used a large rectangular magnifying glass held close to her face to look at the pictures. From my view this had the wonderful effect of enlarging her features and skin. Her face was lined and fallen, and all that was fallen wiggled with each word. The bridge at Budapest, she told me, connects two cities, Buda and Pest, that sit on opposite banks of the Danube. And she held out a picture of a chain suspension bridge with great stone piers, which I see to this day whenever I meet people who have dual natures.

Evenings we listened to Pirate games on the radio. Mema had been orphaned at an early age but was taken in and raised by relatives, the Ernst family, and grew up living an almost idyllic childhood in the Park Slope section of Brooklyn. Her Uncle Will's family had a box at Ebbets Field, and that was but a short trolley ride away. The unfortunate Brooklyn teams of the century's first decade had given Mema the patience and loyalty necessary for the Pirates' teams of the early 1950s. The 1953 team, although a slight improvement over the one from 1952, would still lose 104 games. Mema scored as many of their games as she could. On the top row of the bookshelf of the upstairs sitting room, where we listened to the games, were stacks of spiral-bound score books filled with losses.

Mema knitted while we listened, putting her knitting down to record each play. The inning ledgers were printed in pale blue, and the squares to record the outcome of each player's at bat contained small baseball diamonds. Mema had a singular way of scoring, directed as much at the feel of the play as at its outcome. When the Pirates were at bat, she indicated the direction and character of their hits and outs. In this way line-drive outs could enter the record as might-have-been hits. This was a necessary habit for her continued optimism. It fascinated me that she recorded these faraway events. Not knowing yet of her earlier life in Brooklyn, I assumed that Mema had never actually seen a baseball game; I imagined that, for her, the games existed only in Rosey Rowswell and Bob Prince's descriptions and the score books she used to record them.

From the trip back to Connecticut, I remember only two things: that the train oddly was called the "Clevelander" and that I tried unsuccessfully to stay awake until the Braddock mills.

The next spring, on my school playground, I traded Mickey Mantle's 1953 baseball card even up for an obscure 1952 Pirate pitcher named Paul LaPalme. LaPalme's record that year was one win and two losses. Mantle had his second straight good year in what would become an illustrious career, and that card in good condition today would be worth a small fortune. But it was a good trade and a decisive one. From that day forward, I felt I was from Pittsburgh. Though I would not know the depth of my roots until years later, I knew I came from there: the land of hills, coal, water, and fire.

Pittsburgh, as it was during my week with Mema, and Pittsburgh, as it was when I later went to Carnegie Tech, still burns at the center of my memory, still draws me to its shadow and light. Though the land has been savaged, it has been good for me to live near the fire where things were made. I still see the poured slag rolling down the valleys and lighting the rows of houses and the hillsides in reflected afterglow. As in the pulse of summer lightning, the houses and the land seem to have but two natures: either they are shadow and material or they are light.

Scientists write that in the beginning there was light and that the material of the universe and the earth itself cooled out of the primal bang. Material is congealed light. Material and light are paired opposites; the one came from the other.

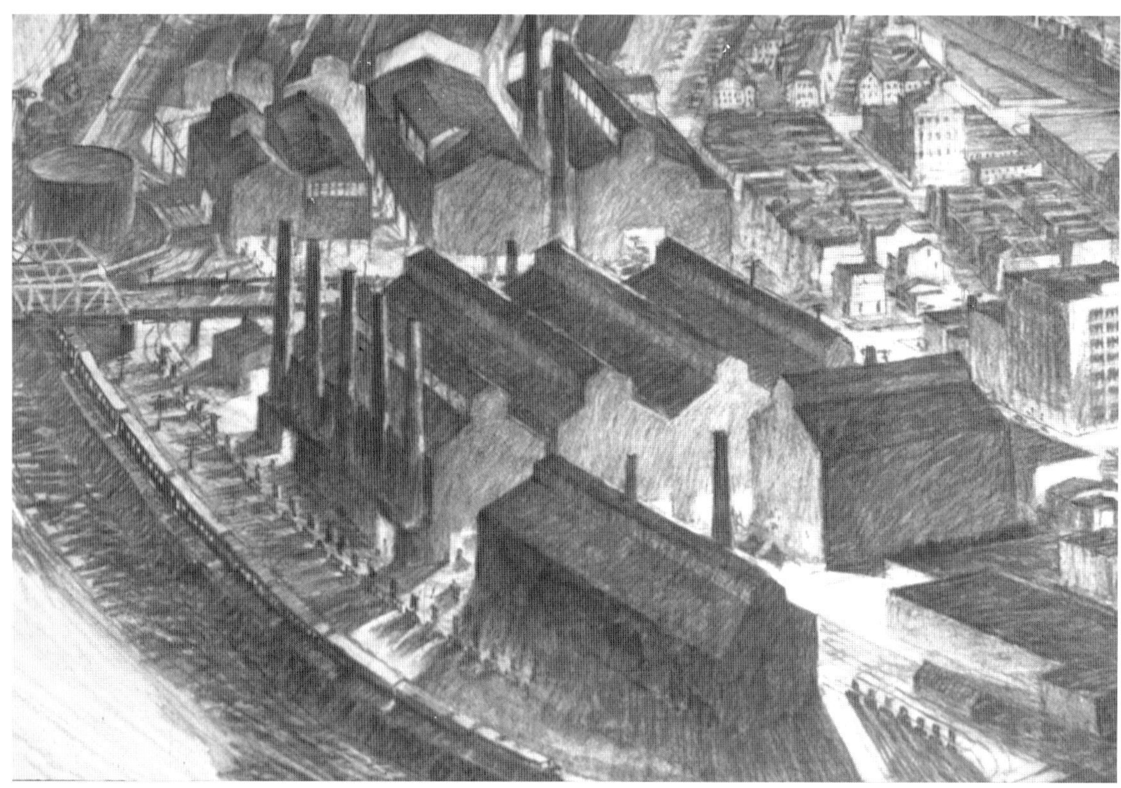

Jones and Laughlin Southside Works. Carnegie Mellon University Center Mural.

. . . as the Bessemer is turned, as the slag is poured, as the furnace is tapped, when the shadow and light flare out and the world is transfixed by the transforming fire.

For years now I have drawn Pittsburgh in charcoal murals. Charcoal is burned wood. It is fire that was. I use the charcoal for the shadows. I use the white of the paper for the light. And it has been this one moment between shadow and light that thrills me; as the Bessemer is turned, as the slag is poured, as the furnace is tapped, when the shadow and light flare out, the world watches transfixed by the transforming fire.

A Sculptor's Drawing Assignment

Someone once shared with me a way I could know in advance if people were insane. "Just look into their eyes," he advised. "If you see white all around the iris, they're nuts." When I was a freshman studying architecture at Carnegie Tech in 1965, Kent Bloomer (now a professor at Yale) was our drawing teacher. On the first Friday of the semester and within five minutes of beginning his introductory talk, Bloomer showed the full white of his eyes several times. Bloomer used an odd assortment of gestures while talking. With one he used to cock his head sidewise while arching his back and pulling back on his shoulders. This action had the effect of raising his eyelids, and, suddenly, his blue eyes went into free-float.

The drawing assignment Bloomer gave us that first day seemed no less odd than his person. He asked us to draw everything in our studio and, in the same drawing, everything outside as well. As offhanded as his assignment seemed at first hearing—Bloomer had thought it up on his way to school that day—it has meant a career for me.

Bloomer was and is a sculptor, and I have come to think that his assignment had much to do with his trade. As a sculptor, he brought a natural skepticism about drawing to the class. Accustomed to considering his work in the round and from all aspects, he distrusted the

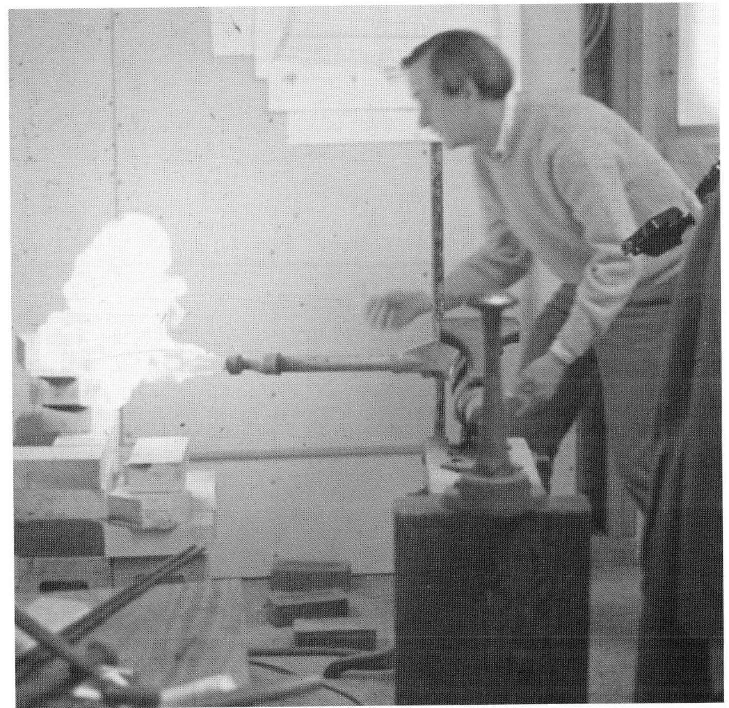

Kent Bloomer at work at his Southside studio, circa 1965.

(Photo: Pat Lewis.)

Bloomer was and is a sculptor.

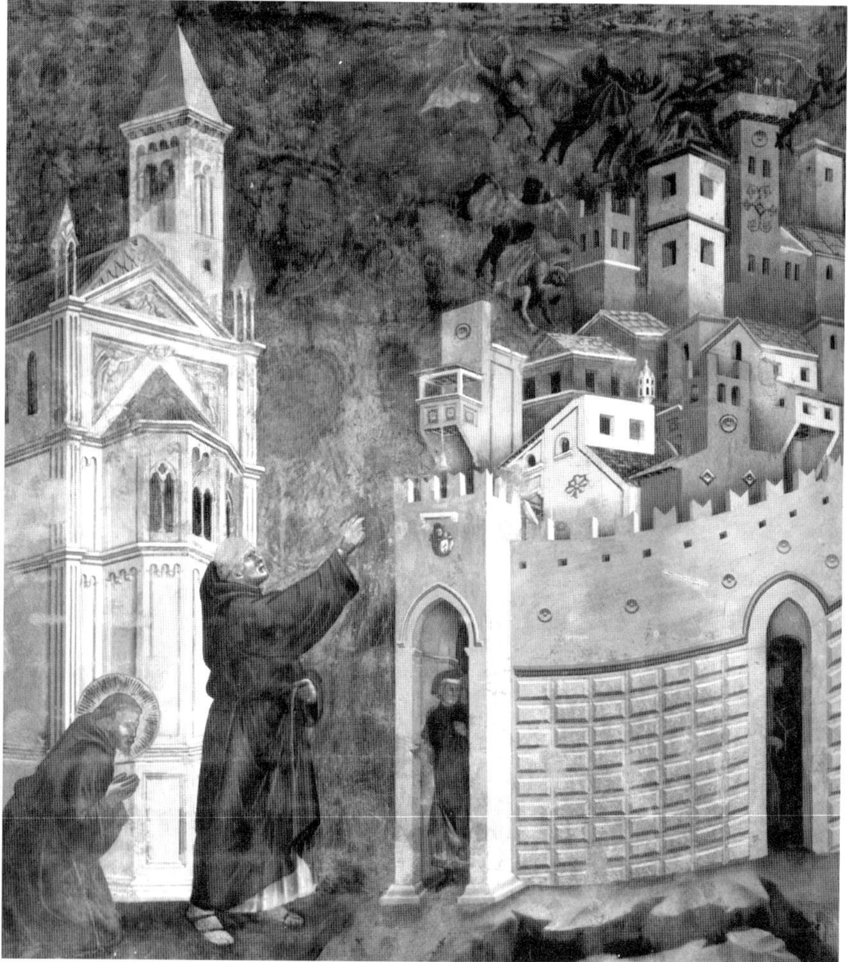

Attributed to Giotto di Bondone (1266–1336), The Saint Chases the Demons from Arezzo. S. Francesco, Assisi, Italy. (Alinari/Art Resource, N.Y.)

Bloomer referred us to proto-Renaissance painters for models to pursue.

value of perspective for its limitation to one direction of view and one standpoint. Instead, he referred us to proto-Renaissance painters such as Simone Martini, Ambrogio Lorenzetti, and Giotto for models to pursue. He pointed out that their paintings incorporated multiple directions of view and multiple standpoints. Sometimes they looked up, he said, and sometimes down. They might show a duke conferring inside his castle with his ministers and, in the same painting, a battle raging outside the walls.

Bloomer's constant criticism of perspective had a singular resonance for me, and it took me back to a fight I'd gotten into in a second grade classroom with my then best friend, Toby McCarthy. Each of us had made a picture of a military plane—this was during the Korean War—and I thought mine was better. Mine was drawn in perspective, from the side, with the near wing foreshortened and the far wing partly obscured. His was drawn from above, like a plan. He showed each wing, all four engines, and their propellers. He had drawn guns and bullets everywhere. He even had gun turrets on the wings.

I thought my drawing had authority behind it. The Christmas before, my Aunt Mary had given me two gifts, a subscription to a monthly magazine about trains and several recent Pennsylvania Railroad calendars. The magazine was filled with photographs of trains from every direction. The calendars, illustrated by Grif Teller, had large color images of trains that seemed to fairly leap off the page. It was this leaping-out-of-the-page effect that I wanted to capture, but that was not easy.

There was a round table in the corner of the family room where my oldest sister, Carolyn, used to do her homework while I drew. One day, I was trying to draw a train, and I wanted it to seem as if it were arriving in a station: first a faint light in the distance, then a whistle, and finally the engine growing out of the night. But I couldn't make the lines create the effect I wanted, and I got angry. A throwing-crayons-and-tearing-paper tantrum ended with my yanking at my shirt so violently that all the buttons flew off. Several rolled across my startled sister's homework, and one landed across the room.

My sister offered to help, and she told me about perspective. After a few suggestions about convergence and foreshortening, I began to understand how to make the picture work. Soon I could make trains appear to approach and planes appear to fly out of the page. I was ready for the art wars with Toby McCarthy.

Toby's argument was about function. His plane had four engines—mine had one full engine and three half engines. His had two wings—mine had one and one-half and a similar number of propellers. His plane might not *look like* it was flying, but at least, Toby argued, it *could* fly (and shoot!) because only his had the requisite parts.

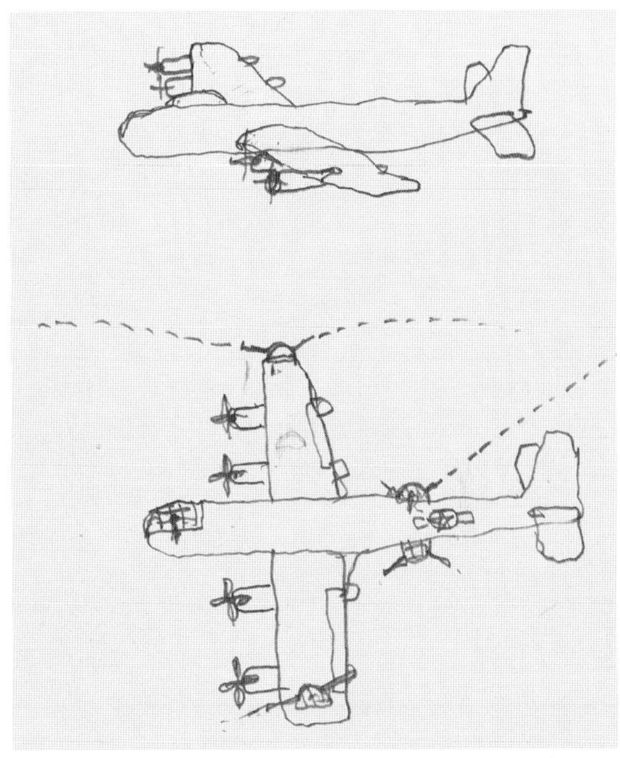

Recreations of drawings by myself (above) and Toby McCarthy (below).

Toby's plane might not look like it's flying, but at least, Toby argued, it could fly!

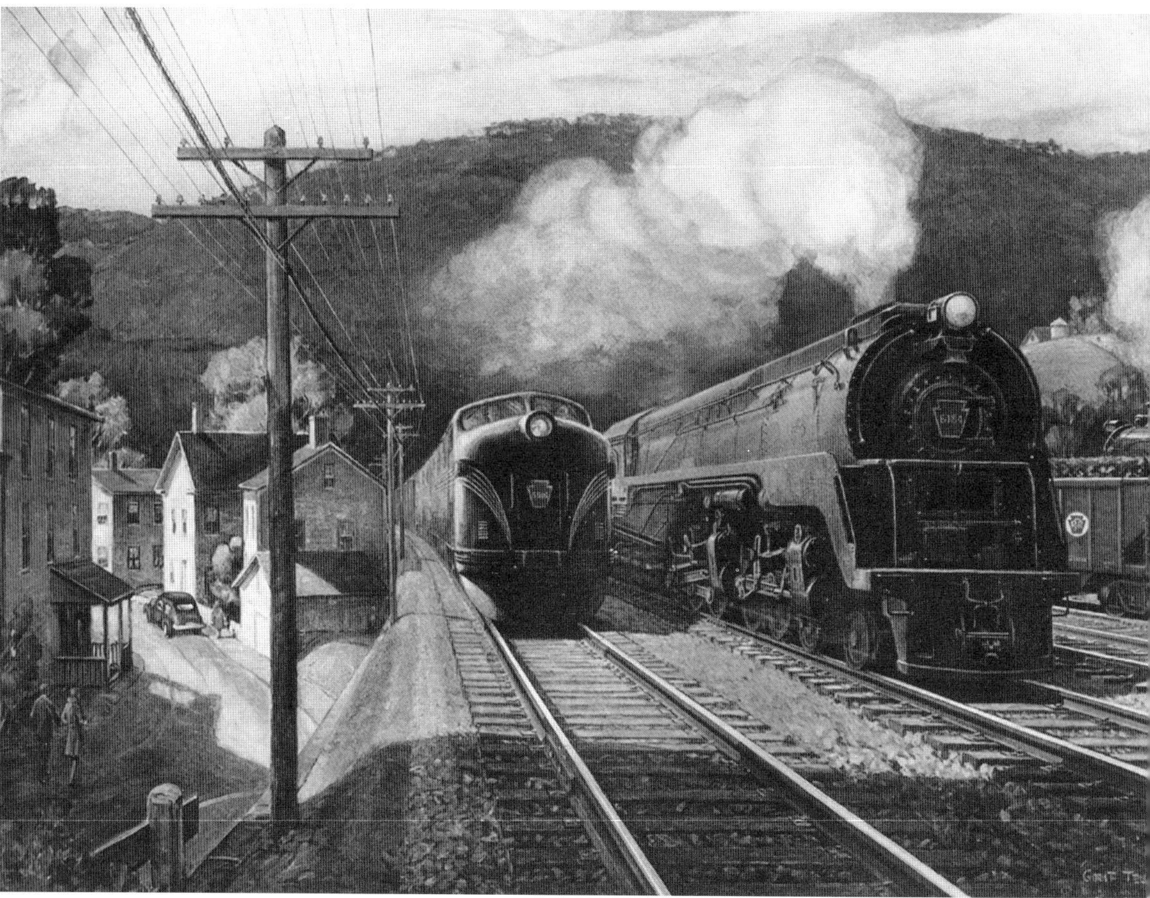

Grif Teller, Working Partners. 1949 Pennsylvania Railroad calendar.

It was this leaping out of the page effect that I wanted to capture.

The argument, which started at his desk at the left end of the front row near the blackboard, went on and on. My desk was at the other end of the row, and back and forth we went from his desk to my desk, from his drawing to my drawing. It was a dispute without resolution, and I subsequently remained infatuated with perspective. I drew planes, trains, ships, and ultimately buildings—in short, anything where making objects seem to leap out of the page mattered.

But this argument with Toby had remained strong in my memory, and Bloomer's criticism seemed to have the same functional ring as Toby's years before. Where Toby had argued that his plane was "flyable"—and mine was not—Bloomer was now asking us to make drawings we could use to walk

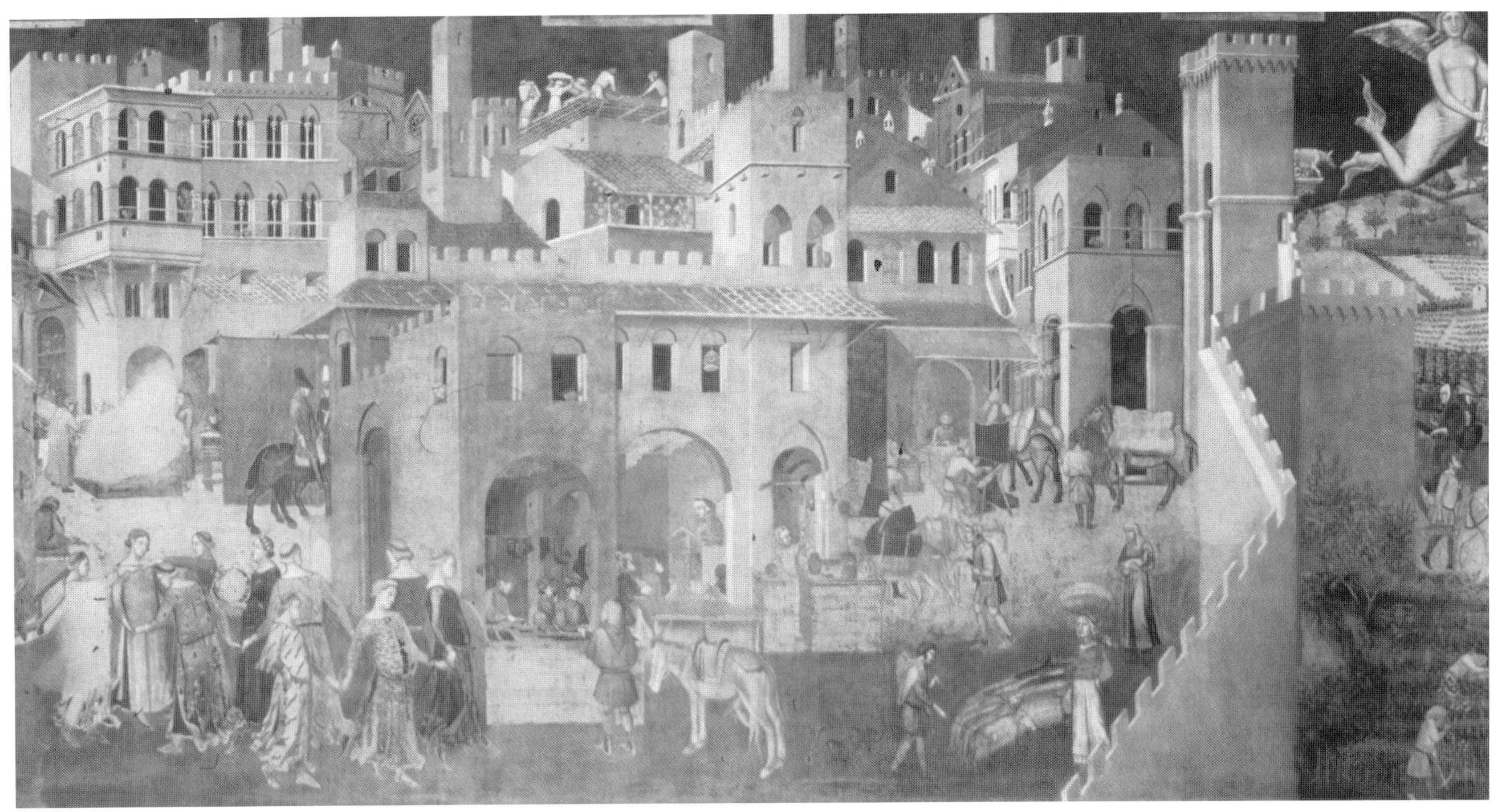

Ambrogio Lorenzetti (1319–1374), ***Allegory of Good Government: Effects of Good Government in the City,*** *1338–1339. Palazzo Pubblico, Siena, Italy.* (Scala/Art Resource, N.Y.)

In the Pittsburgh landscape, I found many of the visual characteristics Bloomer had pointed out in the paintings of Lorenzetti and others.

through, go into and out of, look up at and look down at. There is an almost godlike power that comes with perspective. It is the power to make things "appear to be" rather than merely "be." This is an alluring power. I believe it was the reason I continued to draw at all later on, during a period when most children, like Toby, cease drawing altogether. But Bloomer had questioned it all.

Bloomer's assignment eventually led me outside to draw Pittsburgh, far from his original classroom. In the Pittsburgh landscape I found many of the visual characteristics he had pointed out in the paintings of Lorenzetti and the others. It was a dynamic landscape, whose steep and twisting slopes presented multiple viewing directions. It made me look upward, made me look downward, and made me turn as I looked.

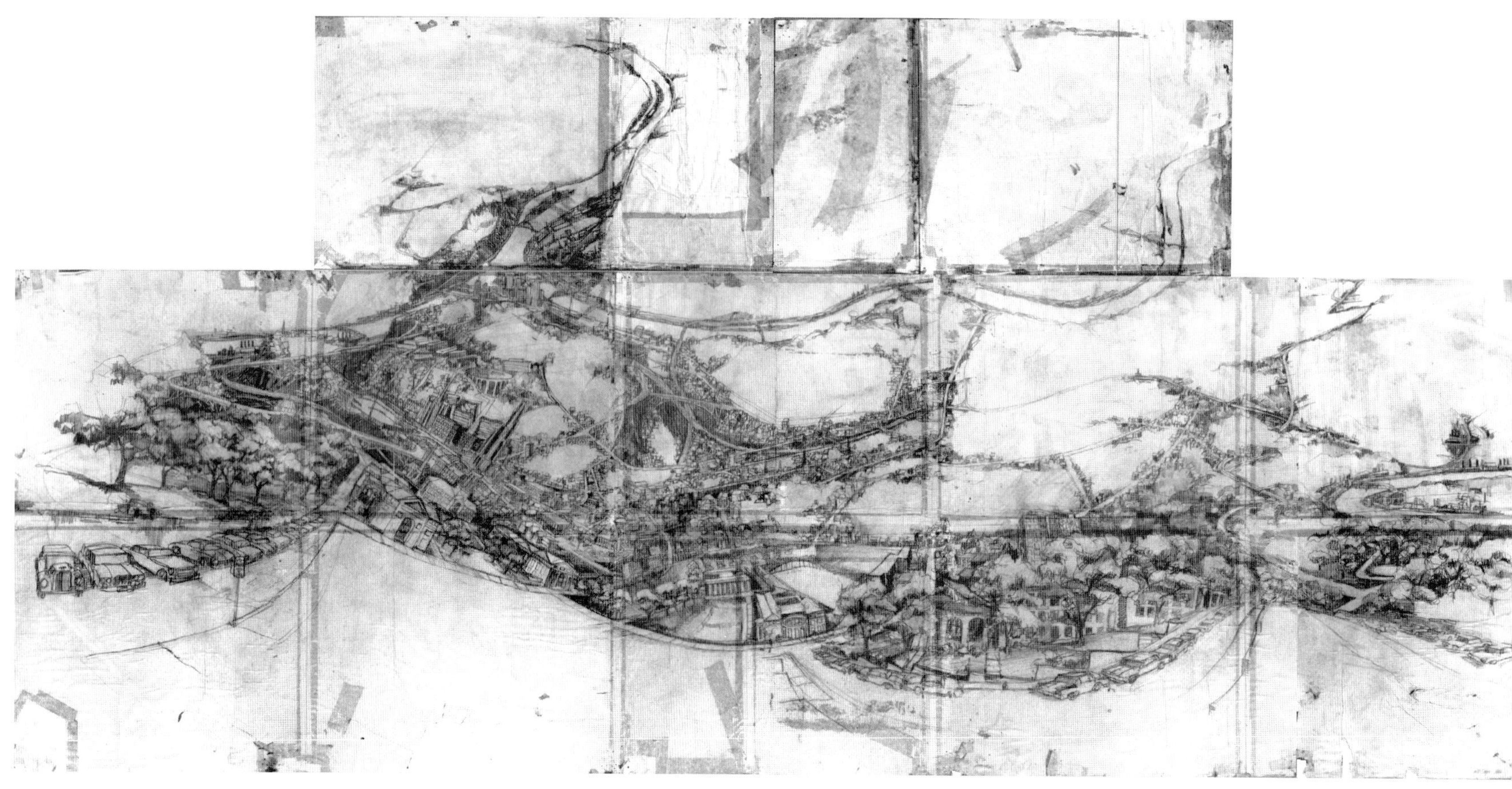

Drawing of Pittsburgh done for Kent Bloomer's class, 1965–1966.

I simply taped additional sheets of paper above and to the sides of the original sheets.

In the Pittsburgh landscape I also discovered a technique that proved useful for describing two places in one drawing—what Bloomer had so vividly described in the paintings of castles. This leap forward came about by accident. I had nearly filled two adjacent sheets of bond paper with a wide-field drawing of the Carnegie Tech campus and was wondering how I might also include the surrounding area. There was no room left. So I simply taped additional sheets of paper above and to the sides of the original sheets. Seeing the campus drawing in this new, enlarged context gave me an idea: Why not view this new area from a different direction than from the campus? And so the drawing proceeded as two drawings in one: the campus in the foreground, viewed horizontally, and the city in the background, viewed from above.

One day, Bloomer brought his good friend David Lewis (who was also teaching at Carnegie Tech) in for a look at what I was doing. David is an urban designer, but he spent several years in the 1950s in the St. Ives region of England where he was friends with a number of now well-known artists, including the sculptor Barbara Hepworth, the painter Ben Nicholson, and the potter Bernard Leach. He considered my drawing through the experience of those years and saw similarities with the work of the painter Alfred Wallis. Wallis had been a seaman all his life and lived around the harbor. He began painting at the age of seventy-five, using bits of old cardboard and ship's paint.

David described one of Wallis's paintings that showed a harbor and its surrounding village. David usually talks in a very animated way, and on this occasion, he was particularly dramatic. He described the painting in the local Cornwall dialect as if he were the artist and the painting were there in front of him.

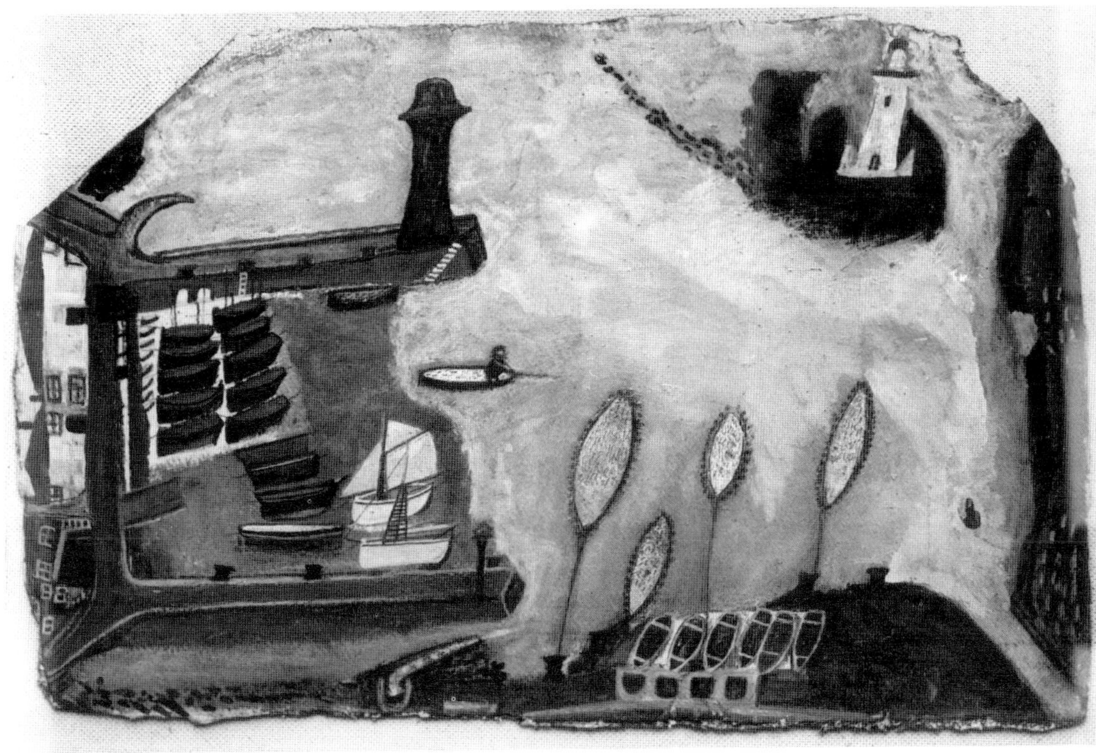

Alfred Wallis, This Is Sain Fishery That Use to Be, circa 1935. (Private collection.)

David described one of Wallis's paintings that showed a harbor and its surrounding village.

As he spoke, he pointed at things in the phantom painting. "This 'ere is William Cocking's boat. The sea's rough, and the harbor do keep'n boats safe from they big waves. This 'ere is Wally Stevens' house. The hill do climb up 'ere an' go over top an' come down 'ere to lighthouse. Under the sea is fishing nets, full o' pilchards."

I am grateful that David did not show me a photograph of this painting at the time. Instead he showed me "what" the painting was, a question of its essence, rather than "how" it appeared, a question of its technique. His gestures demonstrated the presence that a painting or drawing might achieve. David's phantom painting of the harbor was as real to him as Toby's assembled plane was to Toby. It was real because he could use it as if it were really there. He could point at it. This painting was no mere picture of a harbor; it *was* a harbor. David could sail his boat into it and dock.

Letting Drawings out of the Corner

M*eg and I married in 1967,* while I was still studying architecture at Carnegie Tech, and we moved into an apartment on South Bouquet Street across from Forbes Field. It was up a steep set of steps opposite the players' entrance. We weren't high enough to see over the grandstand, but our upstairs neighbors had a good view of Bill Mazeroski and Gene Alley turning double plays at second base. Summers we sat on our porch and listened to Bob Prince report the game on the radio while we heard the to-and-fro of the real thing from across the street.

In August 1969 we left on a trip to Europe. I had won a stipend for this trip to study architecture, but I left with a determination to pursue once again the ideas of Bloomer's drawing assignment, something I had put aside for several years, and with an intention to look at ordinary places rather than "high" architecture. Bars and train stations, I thought. We started in that nation with the least "high" architecture and the most bars—Ireland. Then we spent a week in London, where I found that, by taking the Circle Line on the Underground, I could visit most of London's late nineteenth-century iron and glass stations. What fascinated me about these stations was their breadth of field. In every direction space seemed to unfold endlessly.

I intended to begin where I had left off with Bloomer's assignment, with the multiple views of the taped-together drawings. At first working in the small format of my travel sketchbook was difficult. But eventually in Paddington Station, Louis Brunel's London masterpiece, I found an obvious solution—drawing small in one corner at the outset.

I was on a walkway that overlooked the tracks. I began by looking down the length of the station and drawing a small and fairly static perspective view in the upper left-hand corner of my sketchbook. Keeping it tightly constructed, I let this view reach some completion. Then as I had done with the taped-together drawings back in Pittsburgh, I let the drawing expand more impulsively.

As the drawing blossomed from the corner, the boundary of the page exerted an unavoidable force. Unlike the taped drawings of Pittsburgh, which always left the option for further expansion, my sketchbook had a fixed boundary I could not exceed. Whatever I initiated after letting the drawing out of the corner, I had to complete by the page's edge. The drawing became a race for

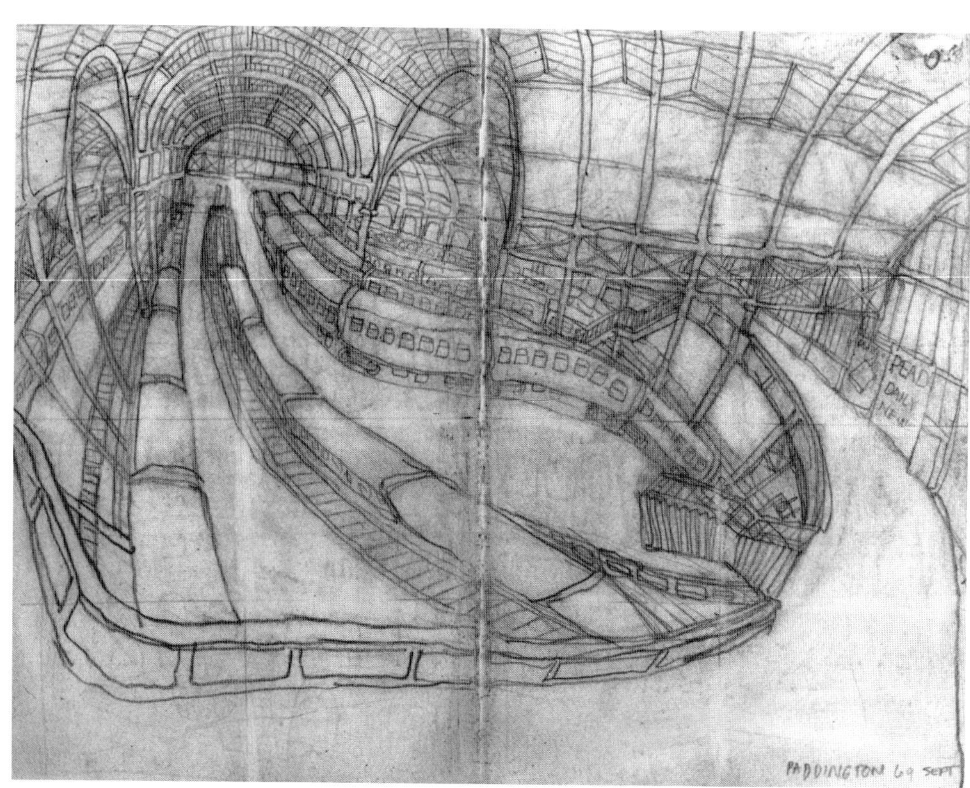

***Paddington Station*, *1969*.** *7″ x 10″.*

I started small in one corner at the outset. Then I let the drawing expand more impulsively.

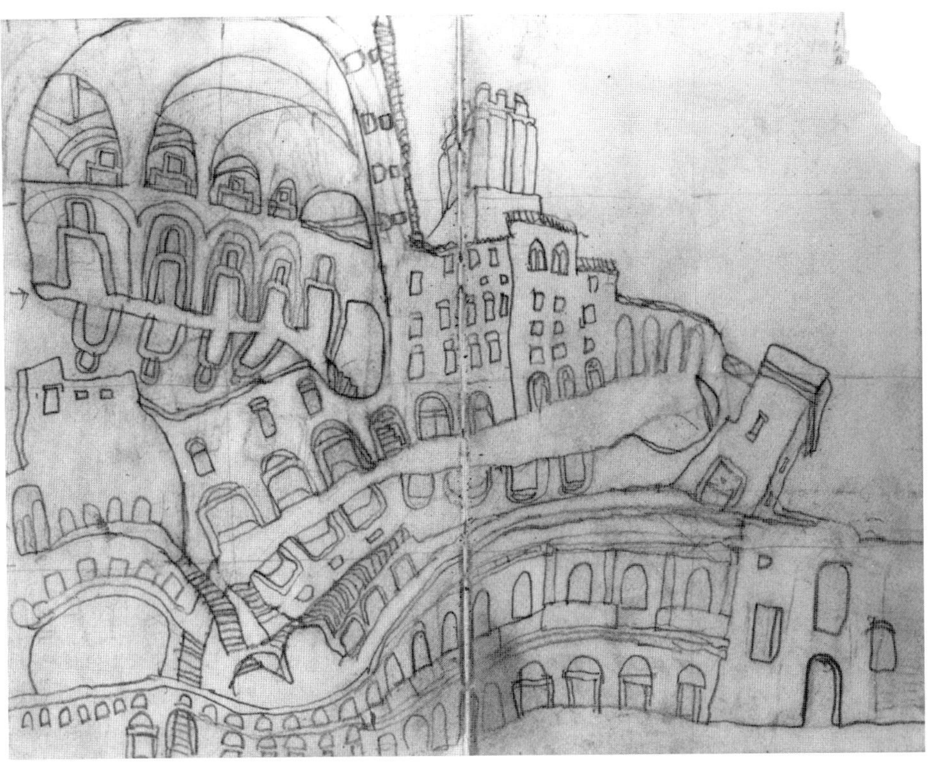

***Trajan's Market*, 1969.** 7″ x 10″.

The scenario of this drawing, half life drawing, half memory drawing, fascinated me.

available space: turning, squeezing, and distorting things in order to fit them in before the drawing reached the edge.

Other drawings took interesting turns because of a lack of available time. On our last day in Rome, Meg and I arrived late at Trajan's Market. The guard was tired and drunk and determined to leave by closing time, some fifteen minutes away. A small bribe secured us half an hour. As we walked in, I asked Meg to go one way while I went another. Meg went up and down every stair and along every arcade. I began in the upper left-hand corner of my sketchbook with a drawing of the market hall. As agreed, we met half an hour later at the gate so the relieved guard could let us out. Then, while I sat and drew, Meg told me where she had gone and what she had seen, and I fit her descriptions into the drawing next to what I had already begun.

The scenario of this drawing at Trajan's Market, half life drawing, half memory drawing, fascinated me. So it was this kind of a drawing that I immediately pursued when we returned to Pittsburgh. In one image, I wanted to string together the many sketches I'd done at the London stations in order to reconstruct a memory of my trips on the Circle Line.

It was early October 1969, and I began the drawing as the New York Mets, in the culmination of their "miracle season," opened the World Series with the Baltimore Orioles. I drew as I listened on the radio. I drew from sketches. I drew from memory. Starting in the middle from a sketch I had done on site in the Circle Line Station at Paddington, I pieced the drawing together, picture by picture, memory by memory. Rarely in my experience does a drawing proceed with an energy all its own as this one did. Just like the Mets, it seemed, this drawing had an irresistible, internal force. I just tried to stay out of the way and let it happen.

While I succeeded in keeping out of the way of this drawing, it would not keep out of mine. All that fall, the remembered pleasure of doing this drawing slowly undermined my resolve to go into architecture, my chosen field, in which I would soon earn a degree. The next spring several events and steps deepened my doubts.

Urged on by my thesis advisor, James Goldman, I followed my heart (not my reason) and made drawings of Pittsburgh in place of a traditional architectural thesis. This decision was a problem for many on the architectural faculty. But since it was 1970 and the Kent State shootings happened that spring, my level of rebelliousness was tolerated.

As part of this thesis, I was asked to lead an advocacy group of citizens and students under the direction of CMU professor Troy West in producing a map/mural of the Hill District. We worked maplike on the floor. What we produced was primitive and informally composed. One area was left blank when a participant arrived with a six-pack, drank the six-pack, and passed out in the middle of the drawing. But this work had an undeniable energy and ended up winning a design award that year from *Progressive Architecture*. The award needs no explanation. It was still 1970.

The wife of CMU professor Chin Pai worked in the office of Leon Arkus, director of the Carnegie Museum. Chin had taken a real interest in my thesis,

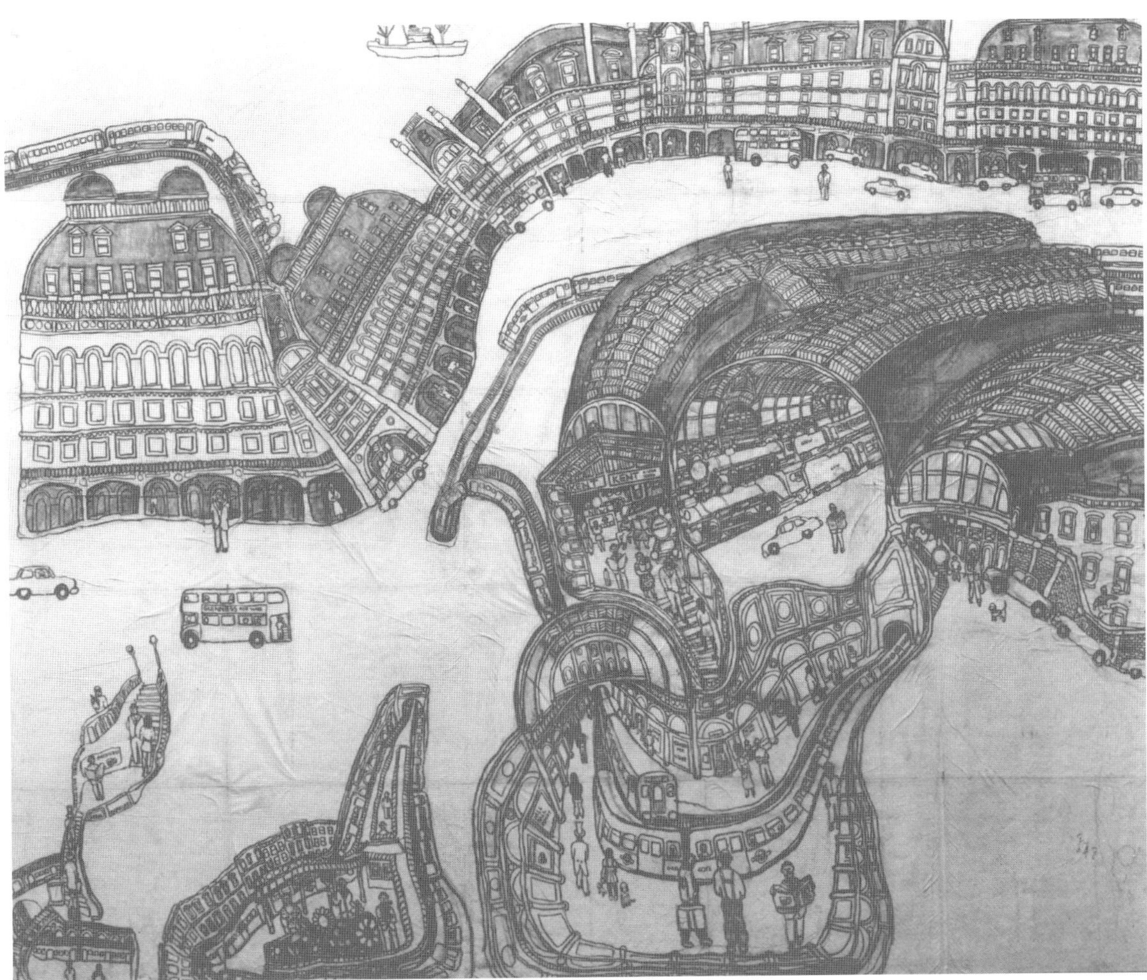

From Paddington to Victoria, 1969. 90″ x 110″. (Collection of the Carnegie Museum of Art, Pittsburgh, Pa.)

This drawing had an irresistible internal force. I just tried to stay out of the way and let it happen.

and his wife "worked" on Leon. Eventually she and Chin got Leon to come over to CMU to see my "thesis" drawings. Leon bought several for the museum right there on the spot. Later that spring, architect Ray Gindroz (who had also been a teacher of mine) bought several drawings as well.

But as tempting as all this was, I decided to stay in architecture for the time being. After a five-month stay in Siena, Italy, where Meg and I lived after I had won another travel stipend, we settled in Frankfurt, Germany. In 1971, I took a job with architect/designer Herbert Ohl.

The Day I Decided to Become an Artist

I *remember every detail* of the day in 1974 when I decided to quit architecture and concentrate on art. Meg and I were still living in Frankfurt, Germany. I was still working with Herbert Ohl. Ohl had been the director of the well-known design school, the Hochschule für Gestaltung, at Ulm, and he is the most impulsively creative person I have ever known. But my heart was just not in architecture.

My decision came together all at once—no long discussions, no long walks. I simply called up the Galerie Der Spiegel in Cologne, a contact I'd gotten from Leon Arkus back in Pittsburgh. I spoke to the gallerist's wife, Frau Stünke. I lied to her. I told her I was about to leave to go back to the United States forever and asked to meet with her that very day. She agreed, and I left for Cologne.

The train trip itself was memorable. I bought a beer in the Frankfurt station and, once on the train, quickly found an empty compartment, where I put my tube of drawings in the rack above and sat next to the window. The train was nearly empty. It had originated in Athens several days before, traveled through Yugoslavia and Italy, and was now on its final leg. From the various newspapers and discarded cigarette packs on the floor and seats, it was obvious this train had a "history."

Just as the conductor sounded his whistle, a very proper elderly woman entered the compartment with a flurry of *"Entschuldigen Sie mich mal bitte"* and hat boxes. She sat nearly opposite me, one seat from the window. She was dressed completely in black, and she wore a raked hat with a feather on one side. She eyed me from the start, and the start was bumpy.

This was no smooth German clockwork start. The train began to move in spasms: first one, then another, and then, gaining speed, a third. With each lurch, the train's history began to unfold. With the first lurch, an empty bottle of Retsina rolled out from under my seat. With the next came a bottle of Yugoslavian Red. As each new bottle rolled into view, the lady-in-black moved further down her seat toward the compartment door. She moved with great judgmental leaps—my bottle of beer was evidence enough. Finally, when a bottle of Chianti appeared, she could stomach no more. She gathered her hatboxes and coat, left the compartment, and left me to arrive alone in Cologne with the bottles and my drawings to meet with another elderly lady.

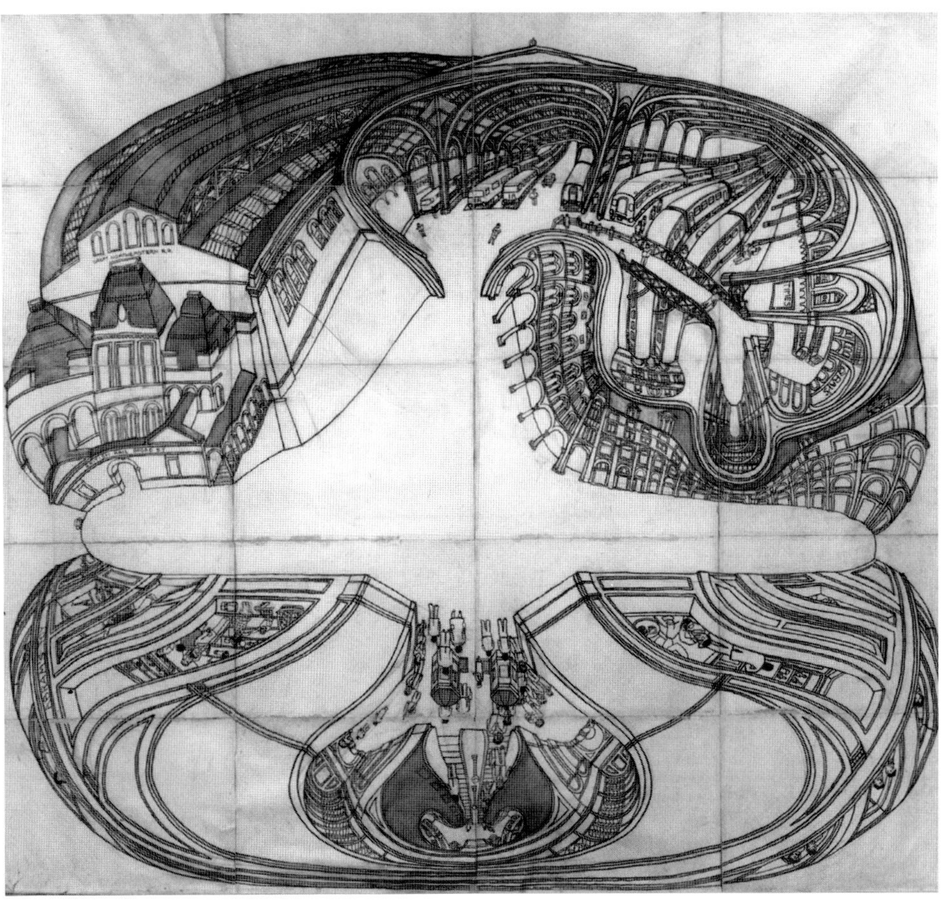

Liverpool Station, 1972. 130 cm x 160 cm.

I rolled out drawings of London stations. . . .

But Frau Stünke was no lady-in-black. She was a lovely grandmotherly woman who drank cognac. I liked her, and I liked her cognac. With all the drama I could muster, I rolled drawings out across the floor of the gallery. I rolled out drawings of London stations and a huge drawing in sections that showed the entire town of Siena. It was a kind of demountable wallpaper mural that I had taped together and drawn in our apartment in Frankfurt soon after we left Siena. It extended around the room and over the ceiling. It was a crude drawing, with holes where pipes came through the wall and cutouts to accommodate doors and windows. In a reprise of the Hill District map, it also had oddly composed empty areas. Because I often worked on the floor, I let our daughter, Laura, play on the drawing with her toy cars while I drew. The areas where she played were left blank.

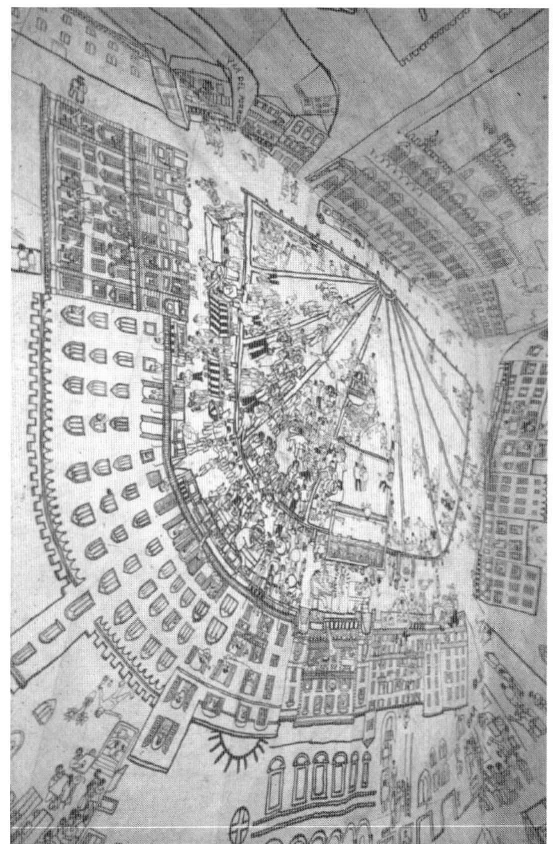

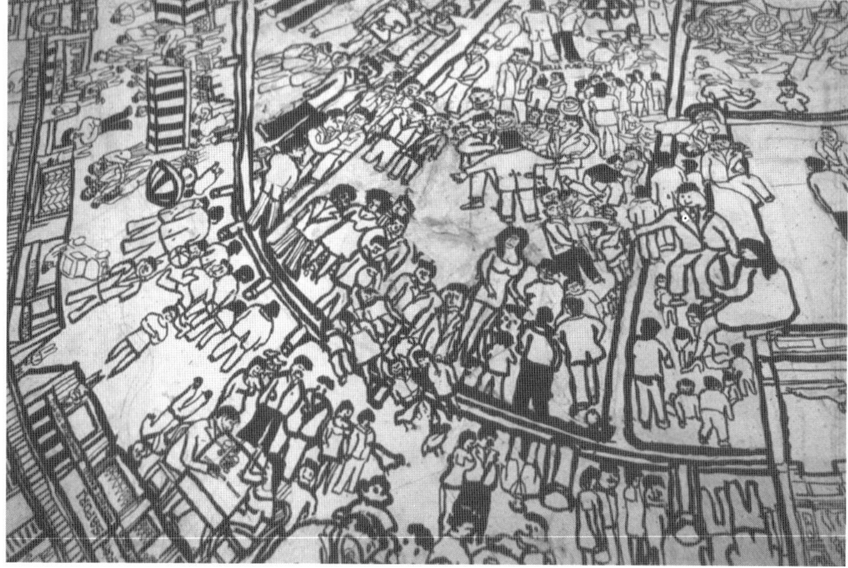

Mural of Siena. Painted on paper on wall in Frankfurt, 1971–1972. (Photos: Herbert Ohl.)

She liked the empty spaces. She liked the spaces that were filled.

Frau Stünke liked the drawings. She liked the empty spaces; she liked the spaces that were filled. She called in her husband, who also liked the drawings. And just like that it was set. I would have a show with them.

Then things moved rapidly. In the summer of 1974, our second daughter, Sarah, was born. The next spring I had the show at the Galerie Der Spiegel. When most of the drawings were sold, I quit my job with Herbert Ohl to start working on the next show. Soon Meg and I were nearly broke. It was clear we would have to leave Germany. When we left for the United States, where I had taken a job teaching drawing in the Department of Architecture at Carnegie Mellon University, we had fifty marks left in our account.

A Decade with a Sneeze and a Dead End

Over the next decade or so, I made highly detailed drawings based on architectural fantasies. At first these drawings advanced the ideas that had originated with Bloomer's assignment. One series was based on a sketch I had done in Siena of two symmetrical portals located opposite one of the main entrances to the Campo, Siena's much-admired shell-shaped central piazza. The portal to the right leads up to a small square, Piazza S. Christoforis, where all of Siena's powerful banks are located. The other, on the left, descends a long valley to the city cemetery. I found this juxtaposition wonderfully ironic, and so I followed this sketch with a set of large-scale drawings—initially built on the theme of juxtaposed *up* versus *down.*

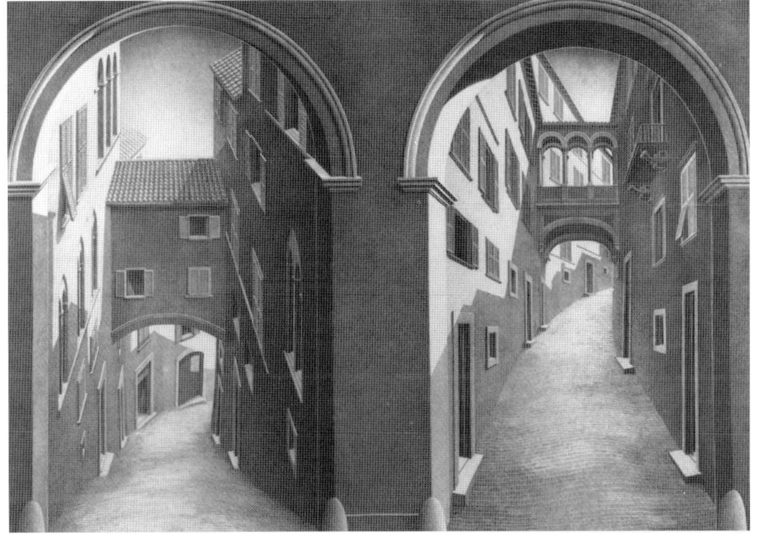

Two Portals, 1985. 80″ x 112″. Carbon pencil on paper. (Photo: David Aschkenas.)

At first the drawings still had a strong impulse that was based on real visual experience.

I also set about finding the elusive *New York Gallery.* Often I showed up cold, right off the street. As naive as these attempts were, some even got close to success. One day, without any advance call, I showed up at the Leo Castelli Gallery in New York. I just walked in and showed the man in front samples of my work. He loved them. He announced that Leo would immediately be finished with a meeting and that we would show the work to him directly! We headed toward Leo's office at the rear: the man with my portfolio under his arm, and I with a sense that my star was about to rise.

Just at that moment, Leo emerged from his office accompanied by a horribly pale client dressed all in black. Leo, kingmaker and discoverer of Andy Warhol, was resplendent in blue. My "guy" called out to Leo something to the effect of, "Leo, you've simply got to see this man's stuff!"

What happened next seemed to take place in slow motion. As Leo reached out to receive my portfolio, the image from the ceiling of the Sistine Chapel, of God about to touch the finger of Adam, flashed through my mind. But suddenly, with my portfolio only an inch from his outstretched hand, Leo's nose wrinkled, and he withdrew his hand and began sucking in air to sneeze. Great gulps of air he took in.

This was no ordinary sneeze. This was a sneeze brought on by an entire pepper. It was projectile vomiting. It was hemorrhaging. It was a great gust of wind. It was all of these at once, and Leo's perfectly tailored "power" blue suit was slimed with snot.

Leo flung his arm in disgust. An inch from my anointing, I was dismissed from the gallery. I remember thinking of this as a devastatingly bad break.

Independent of Leo's sneeze, over time my work moved further and further away from real visual experience and dealt more and more with a fantasy world solely of my own creation. I do not know why this happened. For some, turning inward does lead somewhere. But in my case, while I gained much technical facility, the work of these years proved a self-absorbed and repetitive dead end. When I think back, I remember too much time spent looking for galleries to exhibit my work—in the end I actually found one—and too little time evaluating the purpose and direction of the work. One thing is certain. The art I was making was utterly disconnected from my daily life and experience of the world around me.

Once, in the midst of this time, my good friend Joerk Habermann from Frankfurt, came by for a visit. He was about to undertake a year-long trip on his own around the United States. Over the years, Joerk had done many drawings for himself that I admired. I think my favorite has always been a drawing of a room in a house in Switzerland that both of us had visited. Some-

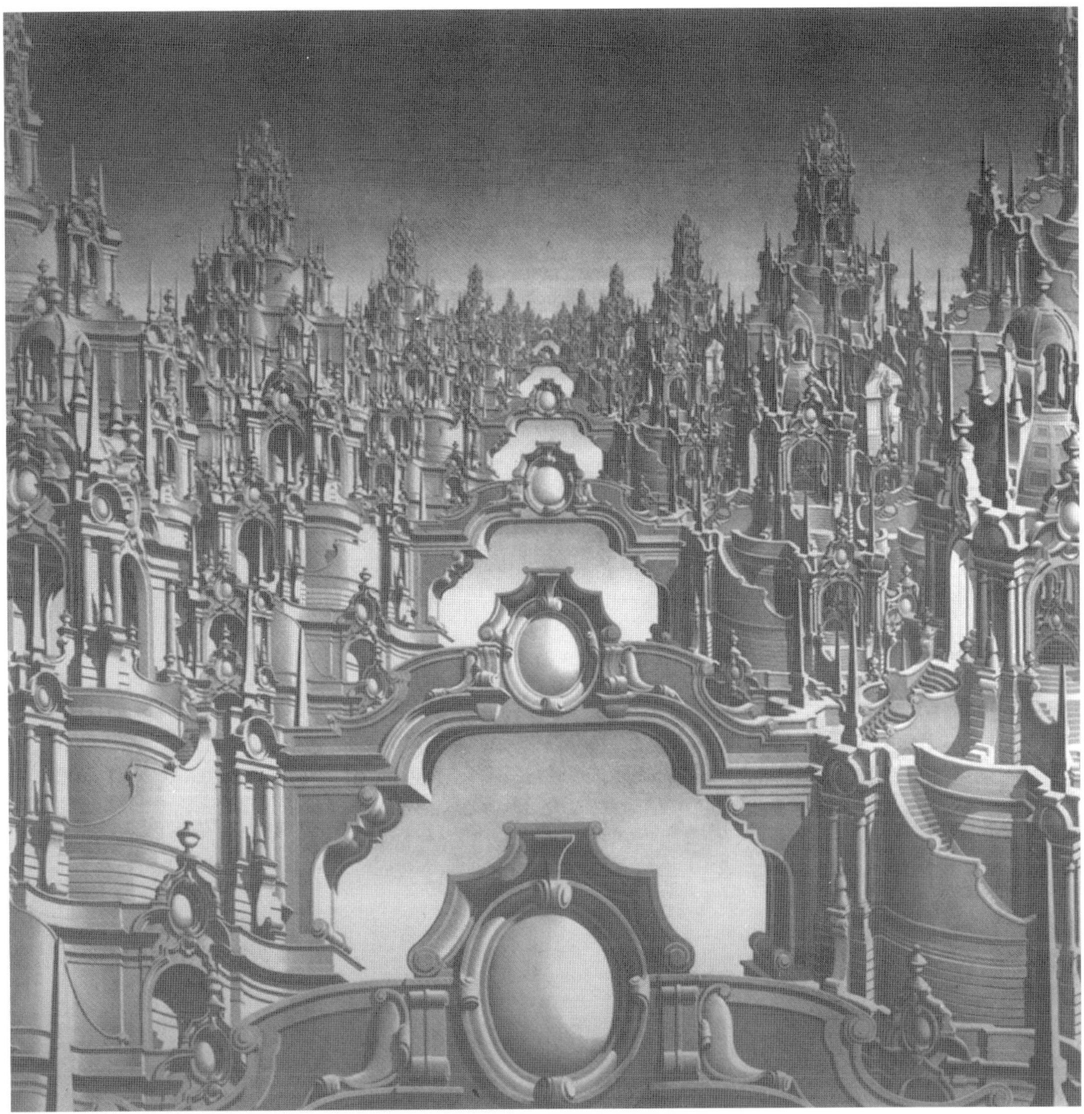

***The Approach*, 1979.** 96″ x 96″. Carbon pencil on paper. (Photo: David Aschkenas.)

Over time the drawings dealt more and more with a fantasy world solely of my own creation.

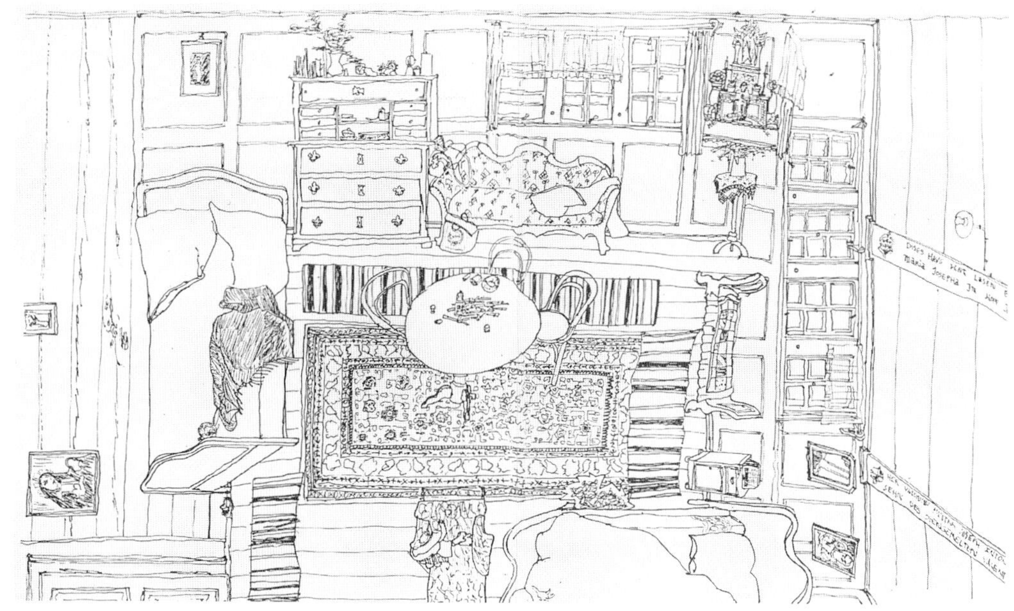

Joerk Habermann, A Room in Niederwald. (Photo: David Aschkenas.)

But somehow I did not make the connection.

what in the spirit of Toby McCarthy's drawing, in a room that would be impossible to photograph, Joerk's drawing assembles everything that was there to see.

For his own entertainment on this trip, he did many drawings of our house and our neighborhood. Then, as I showed him around Pittsburgh and as we looked for a car for him to buy for his trip, we talked about the importance to an artist of a locale and the long memories associated with it.

But somehow, I did not make the connection. I was too busy squeezing the very last measure of joy out of my technically proficient work.

Returning to Pittsburgh via Bryce Canyon, Utah

Looking back, it was the low point of my career. It was spring 1989, and I was in the process of assembling works for a retrospective at the national headquarters of the American Institute of Architects in Washington, D.C. Collectors in the vicinity of Washington had bought many of my drawings, and I was busy picking them up for the show. One collector had bought a large drawing called *The Bar,* which had taken six months to complete. Paul Desind, a gallery friend of mine in D.C., had named this collector the "King of the Malls," because he had made his fortune building shopping centers along the Beltway around Washington during the 1980s. I went to his office to pick up the work. He was not there, but a secretary showed me to the "art room," where his collection was kept.

It was a kind of windowless storage room, and the works were all stacked out from the walls. There, in the corner, was *The Bar.* It was rolled up unopened in the same tube in which I had packed it some four years

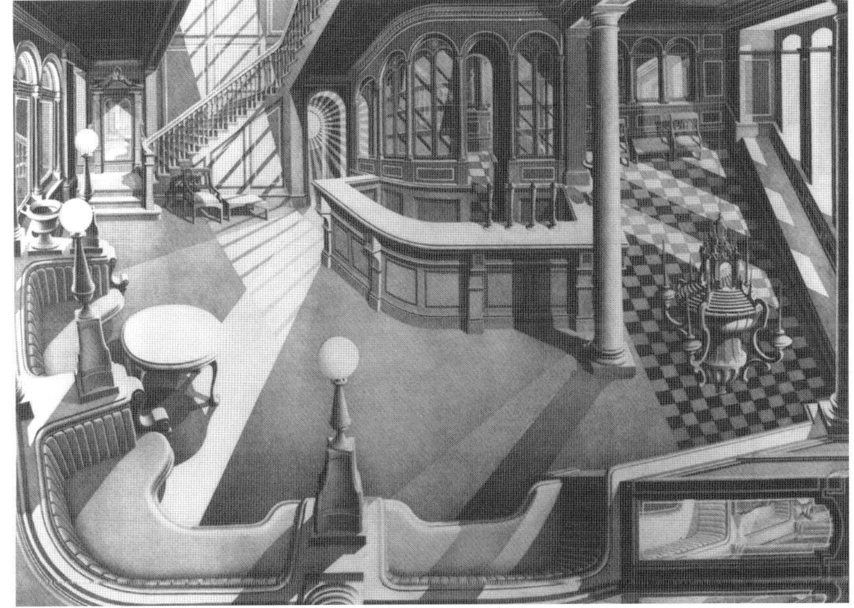

London Bar, 1985. 80″ x 112″. Carbon pencil on paper. (Photo: David Aschkenas. Private collection.)

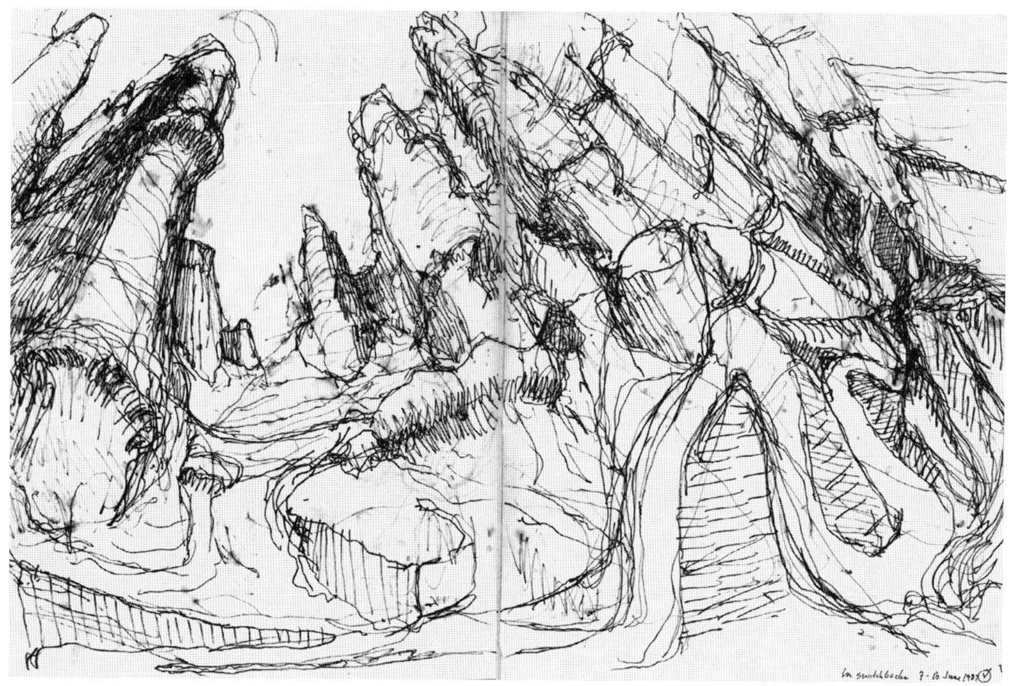

Bryce Canyon, 1989. 10″ x 14″.

I went to Bryce Canyon and drew rock formations.

earlier, when he had bought it from my New York gallery. The King of the Malls had never even so much as looked at it.

At first, I was simply angry with him. Then I was angry at the gallery system of producing and selling art. But gradually, with time, I began to recognize that there might be something wrong with what I was doing as an artist. It troubled me that I was engaged in working long hours producing works that were valued so little by those who owned them. It troubled me even more deeply when I began to admit to myself that I did not value them either.

Because it was under my own control, I addressed the work itself first. A month later, I went to Bryce Canyon in Utah, where I camped out for a week and drew rock formations. By drawing on site in that very three-dimensional

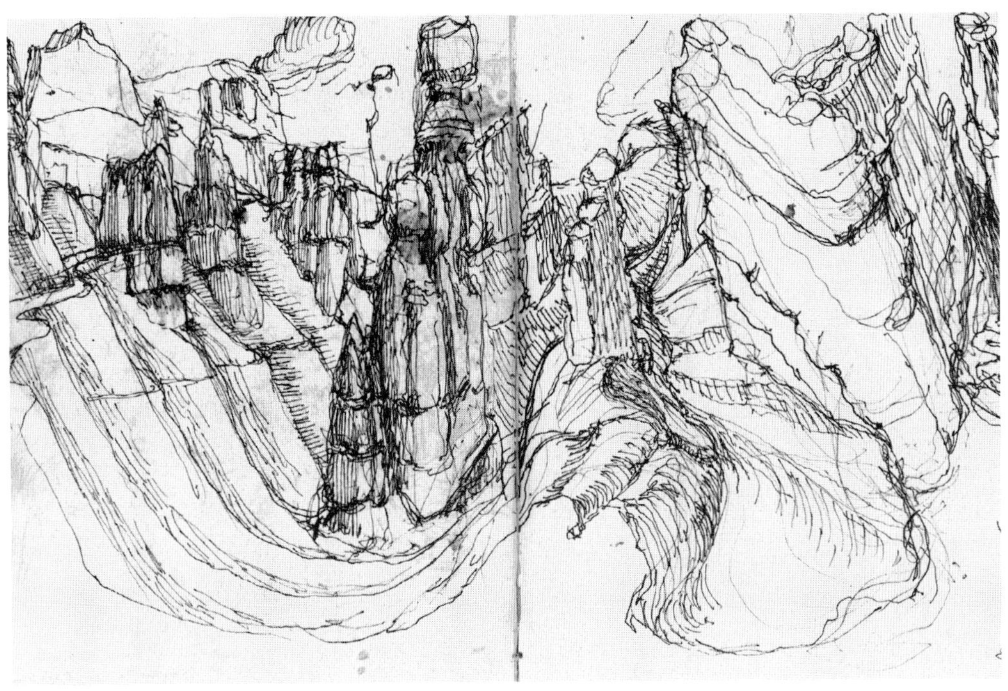

***Bryce Canyon*, 1989.** 10″ x 14″.

It took a while, but gradually my drawing came to life.

landscape, I hoped my drawing would assume once again the kind of immediacy and directness it had lost. It took a while, but during this week, drawing came to life for me once again.

I flew back home to Pittsburgh elated with what I had accomplished and fully expecting to do a series of drawings about Bryce Canyon. But something unexpected happened. I got off the plane, and I saw my hometown, Pittsburgh, with new eyes. The city I had ignored for so many years seemed suddenly alive. The trigger for this work may have arisen in Bryce Canyon, but what I set about to draw were the twisting steep slopes and gritty industry of Pittsburgh.

I saw the Pittsburgh landscape as I never had before. Sites I had never noticed now interested me. Drawings came swiftly throughout the summer of

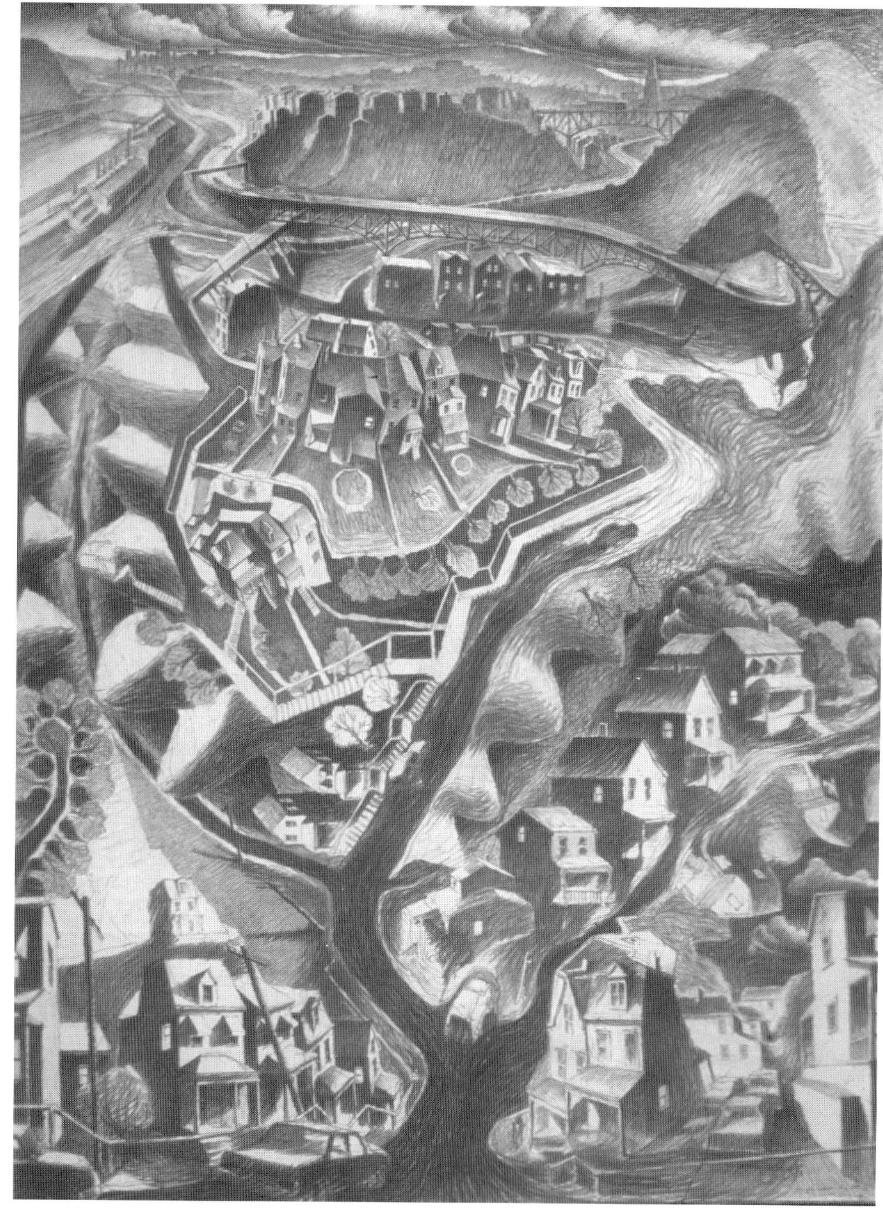

***Down Greenfield Hill*, 1989.** 80″ x 56″. (Photo: David Aschkenas. Collection of Robert Bosch GmbH, Stuttgart, Germany.)

What I set about to draw were the twisting slopes and gritty industry of my hometown.

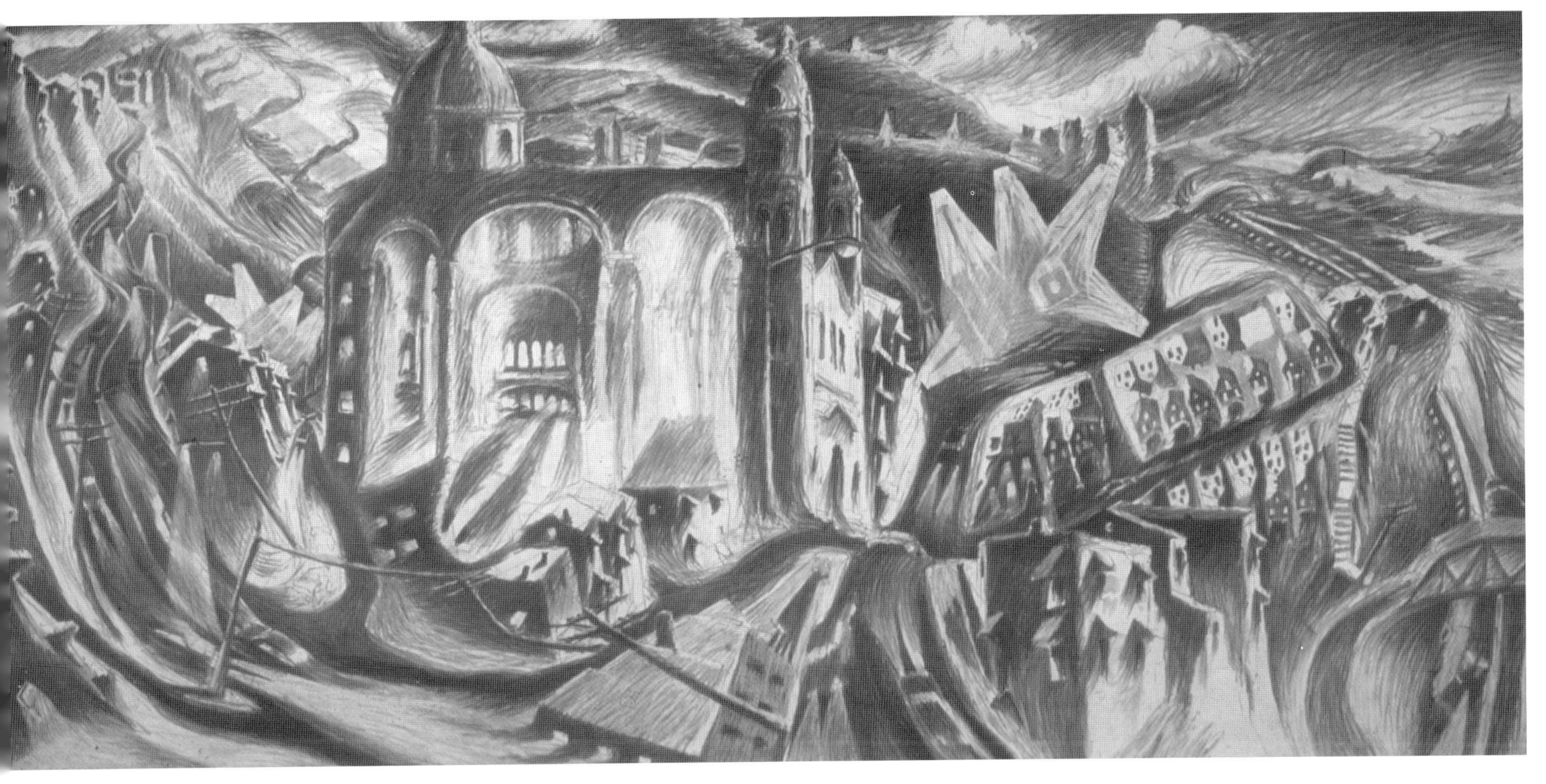

Polish Hill, 1989. 56″ x 112″. (Photo: David Aschkenas. Collection of the Carnegie Museum of Art.)

Drawings came swiftly throughout the summer of 1989.

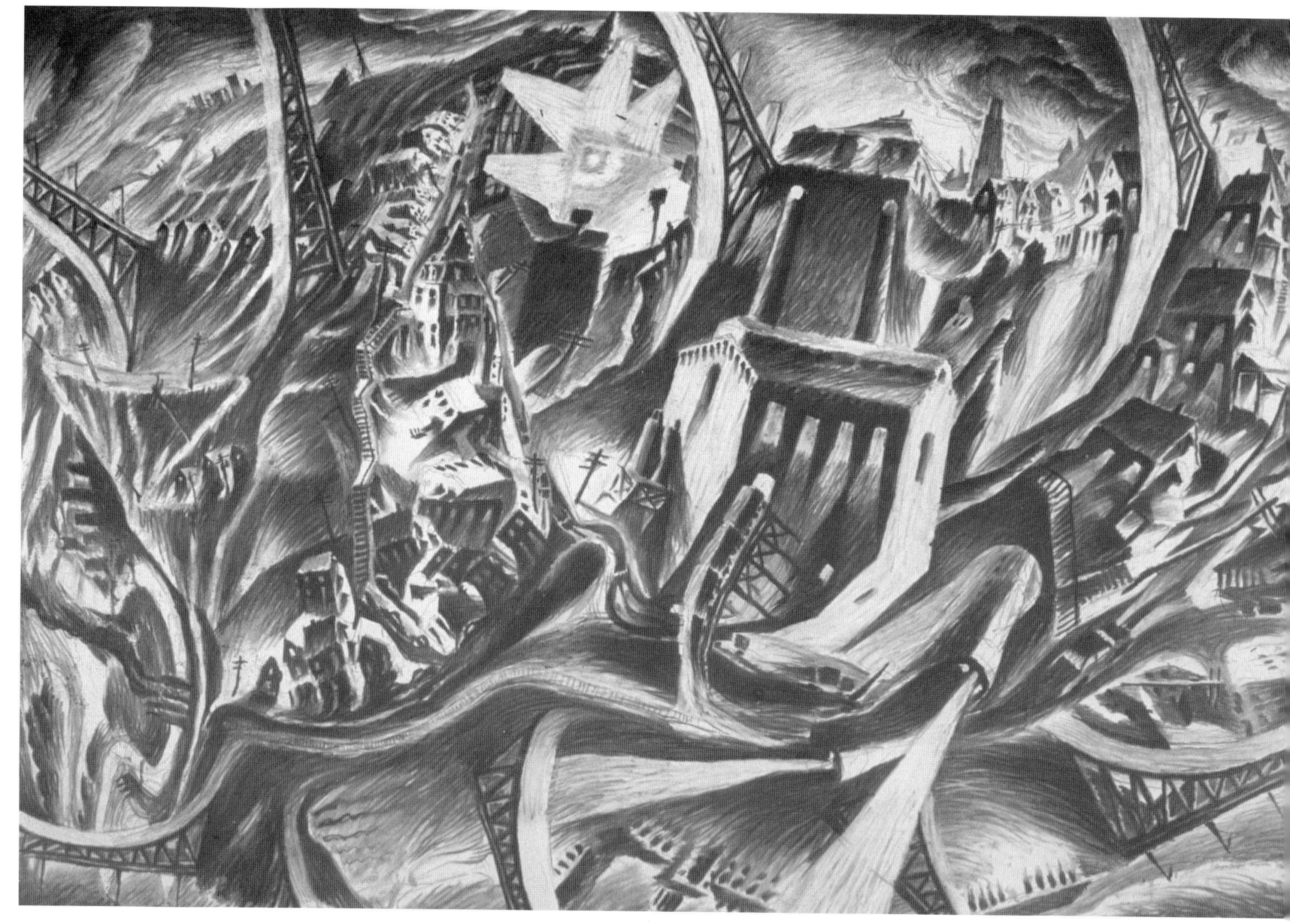

***Panther Hollow*, 1989.** 56″ x 80″. (Photo: David Aschkenas. Private collection.)

In their exaggeration of the hilliness of Pittsburgh, these works took on an expressionist feel.

1989, one after another. In their exaggerated registration of the hilliness of Pittsburgh, these works took on an expressionist feel. As I prepared this body of work for a show the next spring at the Galerie Der Spiegel in Cologne, I began considering the possibility of doing a large public mural of the city of Pittsburgh. In a size that might allow viewers to think they could almost walk into the work, I wanted to present the steep three-dimensionality of the Pittsburgh landscape that I now so keenly felt.

I proposed this mural for the Forum Gallery at the Carnegie Museum. What I presented would go all the way around the four walls of that room and show the city from multiple viewpoints. I had no idea how I could fund this work. At the time, I could not have afforded even the materials for a work this ambitious—it was to be 120 feet long. The museum showed some interest in the project, but nothing definite was emerging, and it was clear that whatever might develop I would have to fund myself.

Little Old Ladies and Me

W*hile I was searching for ways to fund the mural,* help suddenly came out of the past. I have a gift with little old ladies. Usually people don't expect to hear fascinating talk from me, and they don't. I feel shy and awkward in most social situations. But with little old ladies I am gregarious and even witty. The more blue rinse the better! And the payoff is that little old ladies like to tell me interesting stories.

I first recognized this gift one summer when Meg and I were visiting her two maiden aunts, Blanche and Alma. They were sisters and lived in Cornwall, Connecticut, in an old farmhouse. By the time of this visit, Alma was almost ninety and Blanche was in her mid-eighties. Their father had been in General Sheridan's army in the 1870s and 1880s during the years of fighting the Sioux, and Blanche and Alma had spent the first years of their lives at Fort Custer in Montana. Years later it was still a family mystery why Alma, every evening, immediately at sundown, went to each window one by one and pulled the curtains tight shut.

That evening Meg and Blanche wanted to go to the movies, and I agreed to baby-sit Alma. She was becoming senile by this time. She was almost childlike and often humorous. Among other things, she thought the characters on TV were visitors in their house.

Alma and I were watching the Mets on TV—Alma loved baseball—and I had just convinced her she didn't have to worry about being hit by a batted ball. Sitting in her favorite chair, she gradually began rocking rhythmically while humming and whistling to herself. It was a kind of sucking whistling that produced sound whether she exhaled or inhaled. This was her habit at the time, and it seemed to comfort her. But on this night it went on longer than usual and was more insistent. It seemed to cast an almost hypnotic spell over her, and when she achieved a metered pace of rocking and whistling, she suddenly began to speak. She spoke in an unusual voice, as if events were taking place before her eyes as she reported them. It was as if she were taking dictation from the past.

She was in their house at Fort Custer.

It was a room with small windows on three sides.

Her father was away.

It was dusk.

She was sitting at the table, and her mother was serving dinner. When Alma looked up from the table, she saw Indian faces peering in every window. They were just curious to watch the white people eat, but their faces were lit ghoulishly by the interior light. Terrified, Alma leapt up and raced from window to window pulling the curtains tight shut.

In Cornwall, eighty years later, Alma again went from window to window making sure they still were.

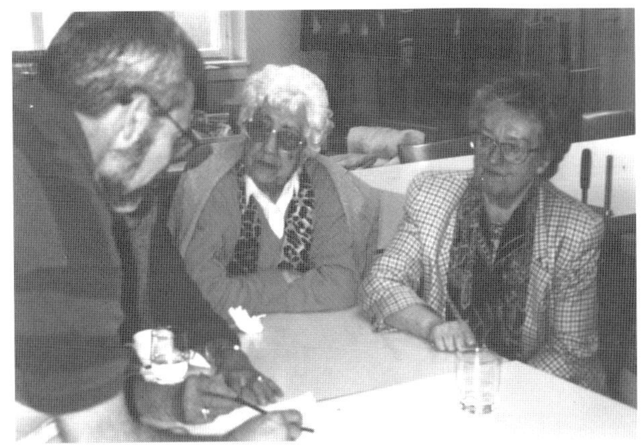

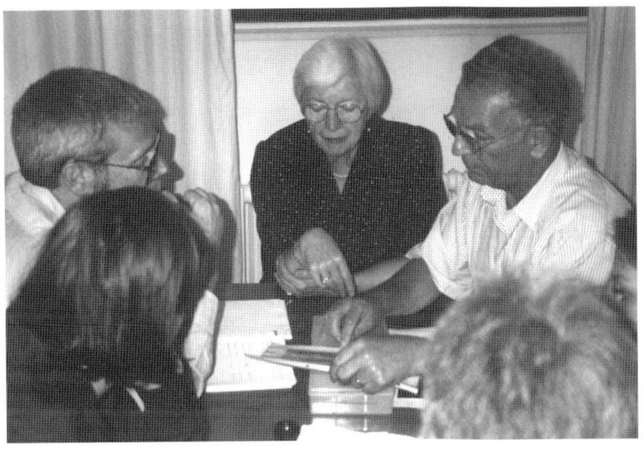

Working on a mural in Frankfurt am Main, 1996. (Photos: Joerk Habermann.)

I have a gift with little old ladies. They like to tell me interesting stories.

Ten years after that incident, when I was thinking of ways to fund the mural of Pittsburgh, this experience of solving the mystery of Alma's curious habit suddenly came to mind. The solution to the funding was at hand; I should work with elderly! I would be good at it, Alma had proven that, and there would surely be funding available to work with that large and influential voting bloc.

The more I considered this idea, the more I realized its power. I remembered the afternoons under the green awnings with my grandmother and our evenings of baseball. I thought of the train trip to Pittsburgh with my father and the views of the mills. These were among the first memories of childhood that had touched my heart, and the prospect of revisiting them thrilled me.

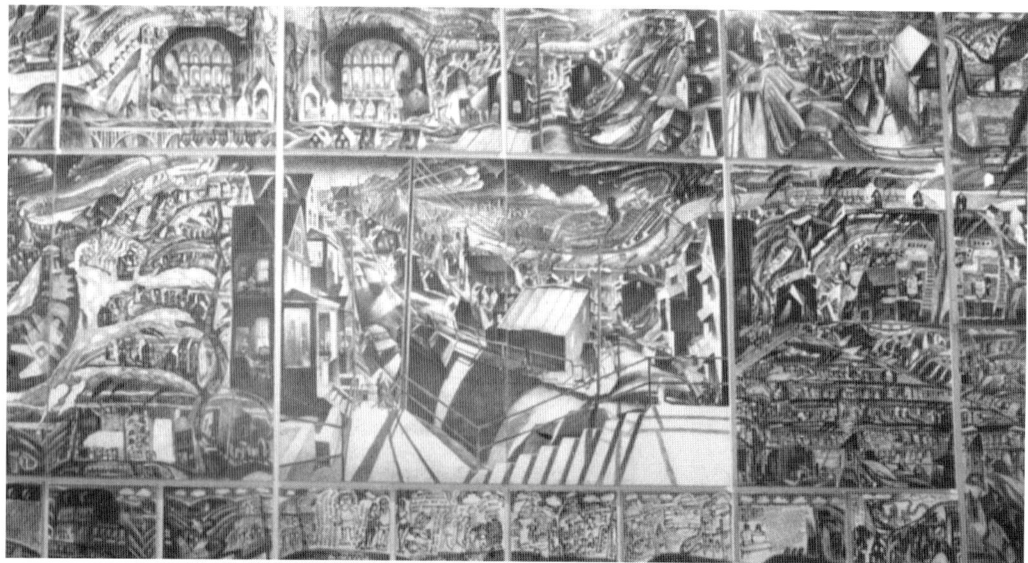

Senator John Heinz Pittsburgh Regional History Center Mural, 1992–1993.

I envisioned the mural as a composite made of many drawings of various sizes.

Working with elderly would not only be something I would enjoy; it would bring something unpredictable, something uncontrollable, into my work. I saw myself becoming really engaged by this work, and I knew that working with others would make the work valuable to someone other than myself, valuable in a way that would not leave it rolled up in a tube and left stored in a closet, unseen.

To get started, I met with Arlene Snyder, then the director of Vintage, an activities center for seniors located in the East Liberty district of the city. I got from her exactly what I needed, an enthusiastic commitment to work with me if and when I got the funding. With parallel commitments from Vicki Clark, Mark Francis, Bay Hallowell, and subsequently Richard Armstrong at the Carnegie Museum of Art to show the project as a work-in-progress, I was able to get funding through the Pennsylvania Council of the Arts and the National Endowment for the Arts. The work would be 120 feet long and, when finished, would go all the way around the museum's Forum Gallery. It would be exhibited twice as it progressed, during the summer of 1992 and summer of 1993.

I envisioned the mural as a composite made of many drawings of various sizes. I was wary of doing a continuous mural with a length of 120 feet—where would I put it when the show was over? If I did the mural as a composite, I could sell the parts after the show—like selling lots in a city.

Some of the images would be large vistas. Others would be more naively constructed, and in these I would enter the drawings of the elderly. Sometimes the image would be continuous from one panel to another, sometimes not.

Structured in this way, the mural could accommodate multiple time periods. I had come to think this capacity would be helpful in representing the way cities are actually understood by their inhabitants. Sites can mean different things to different people. I had been driving one day along the new street in Oakland that cuts through what had once been the outfield of Forbes Field. When I came to the T intersection it makes with South Bouquet Street—exactly opposite the vacant site where Meg and I had once lived—it was suddenly clear to me that this site meant something different to me from what it would to someone else. Where I saw our old house, and the steps leading up to it, and the porch where we had listened to Bob Prince, others would only see the barren parking lot that faced them. I wanted the mural to capture this same overlay of multiple meanings.

Working with the Elderly on the Mural

Leading up to the exhibitions, and with the organizational help of Marilyn Kraitchman, my work began with some forty senior citizens at Vintage. In groups of three or four at a time, and usually organized around neighborhoods, our work had the character of a kaffeeklatsch. We sat around a large table for an hour or two and talked about past experiences. The drawings we made were letter size. Sometimes we focused on the experiences of particular neighborhoods. Drawings of the Hurricane Bar in the Hill District, of Panther Hollow and the Schenley Theater in Oakland, emerged in this way. Other times we discussed broader themes. Memories of the 1936 St. Patrick's Day flood and the steel mills were, to a large degree, shared by all.

Wherever possible, I tried to get the elderly to produce drawings themselves. To get them started, I demonstrated a simplified way of drawing. I showed them how they could first draw the front of a house and then, as if they were making a plan, the inside as well. After they got used to this technique, they were amazed by how much detail they recalled. Through drawing her childhood home in South Oakland, Josephine Zielinski remembered a long-forgotten oval-frame picture of her father and the exact shape of the brackets that supported the kitchen sink. Josephine had lived a delightful childhood (she was still a very beautiful woman) and seemed to remember every movie theater in Oakland.

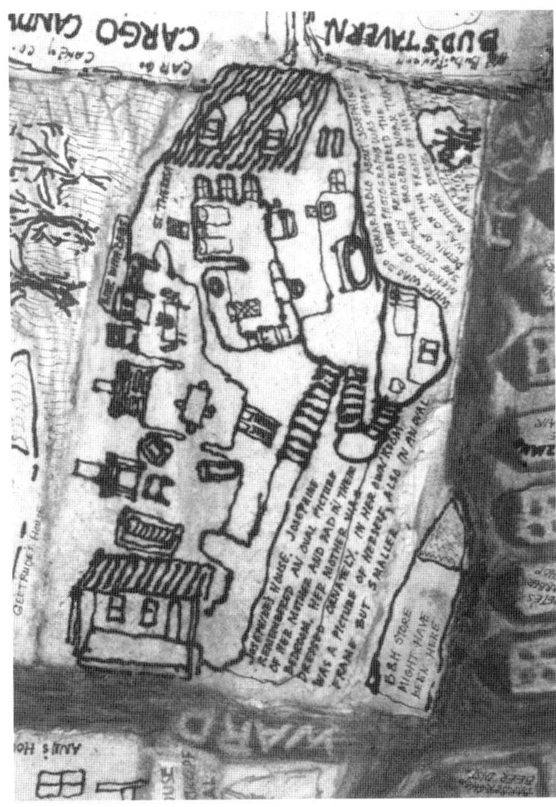

Josephine's House (by Josephine Zielinski). Heinz History Center Mural.

Josephine remembered an oval frame picture and the exact shape of the brackets on the kitchen sink.

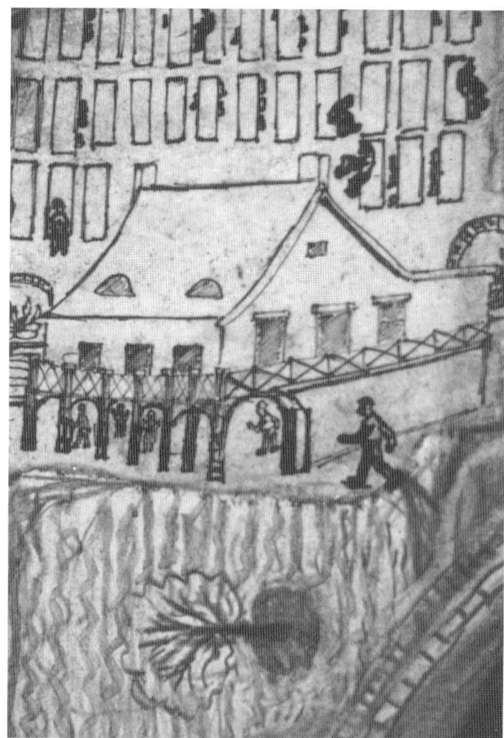

The Boathouse (by Gertrude Diskin). Heinz History Center Mural.

There was a little island with one tree that they would skate to.

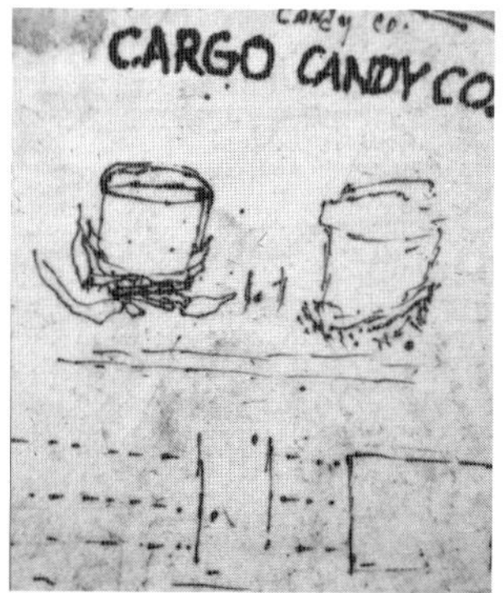

The Cargo Candy Company.

The dots and dashes were shorthand.

Gertrude Diskin drew the boathouse by the lake in Panther Hollow. In the winter she and her friends used to descend the long steps by the Adams Bridge (where the Boulevard of the Allies Bridge is now) to go skating. They always carried potatoes to roast in the great stone fireplaces at each end of the boathouse. Both Gertrude and Josephine spoke often about a little island with a single tree that was out in the middle of the lake. It had been important to them because it was something to skate to. I guess I had forgotten about this detail—Panther Hollow Lake now has no island. Several weeks later, when I saw an old photograph of the lake, there was the little island with its lone tree.

As it turned out, many of the elderly were willing to draw, and when they were not, I simply acted as scribe. The key aim of the drawing was that it be rich enough to evoke memory but not so cumbersome as to slow it down. In other words, it had to work better than words alone.

Anna

One woman, Anna M. Edmondson, developed an unusually abstract technique, which I came to call "Morse code drawing" because of its many dots and dashes. She usually worked alone with silent intensity. When I sat next to her and had her explain her drawings, their abstraction became clear. The dots and the dashes were shorthand. When she drew the Cargo Candy Company (a factory/store in South Oakland that no longer exists), she used dots and dashes to represent the candy she remembered seeing in the cases at the front of the store at Easter time.

Because it tells an entire story, her drawing of the 1936 St. Patrick's Day flood stands out. She lived in Lawrenceville at the time. On the seventeenth of March, she came home from her job as an elevator operator at the Fort Pitt Hotel just as the water was reaching the curb. During that night, the water continued to rise, and she had to be rescued the next day from her second-story window.

I sat next to her as she drew and talked. First she drew a kind of house shape. When I asked her how high up the water had risen, she drew the water rising to her second-story window. Then she drew events. She remembered

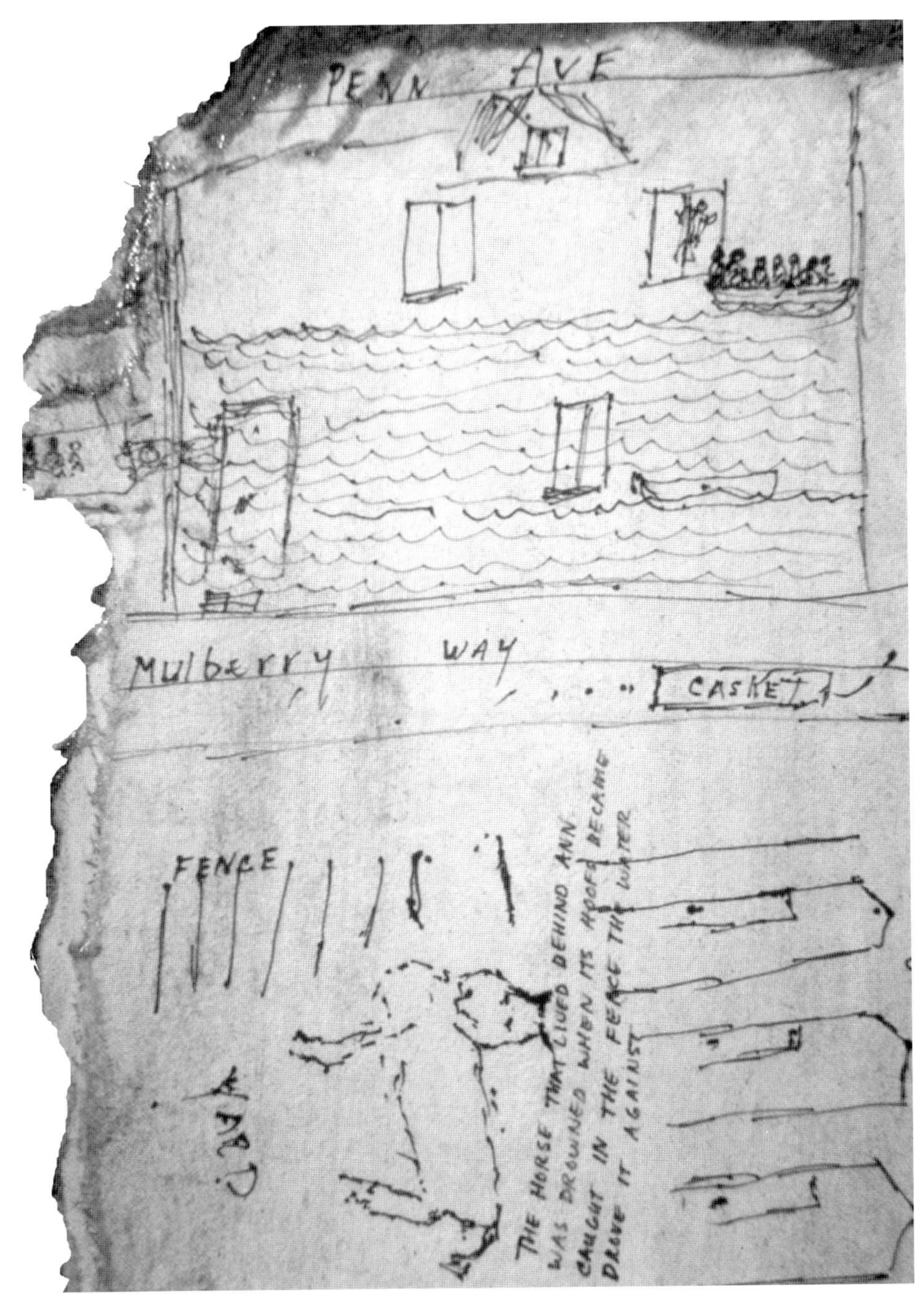

Anna's House (by Anna Edmondson). Heinz History Center Mural.

She drew the water rising to her second story window.

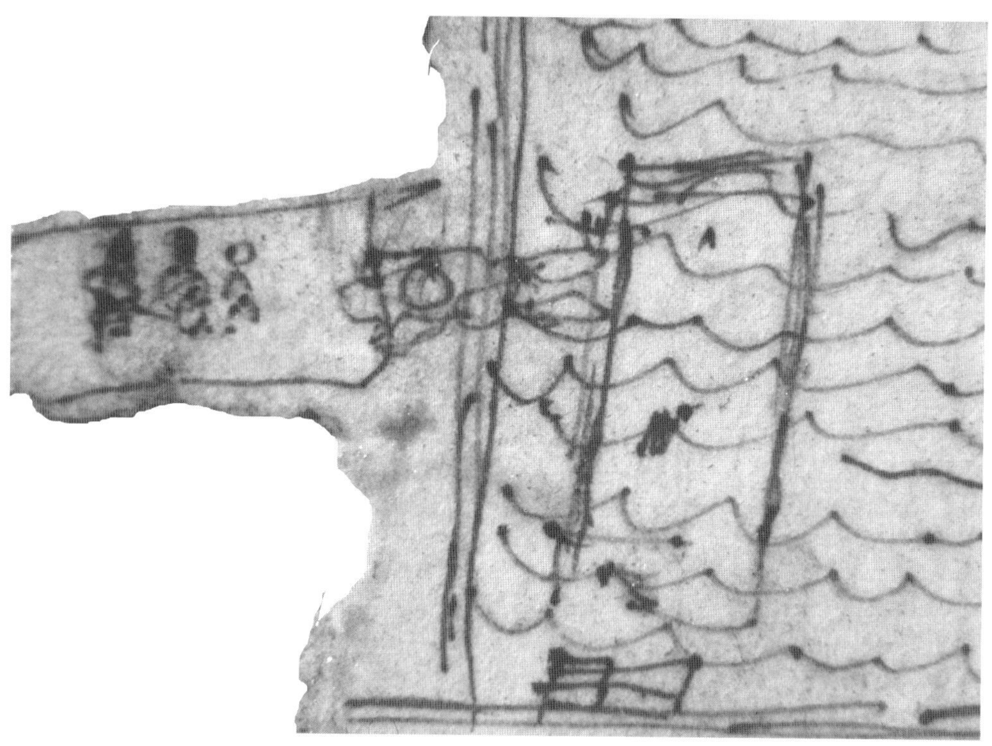

Sometime in the night, her neighbor tore the door off the house and floated his family to safety.

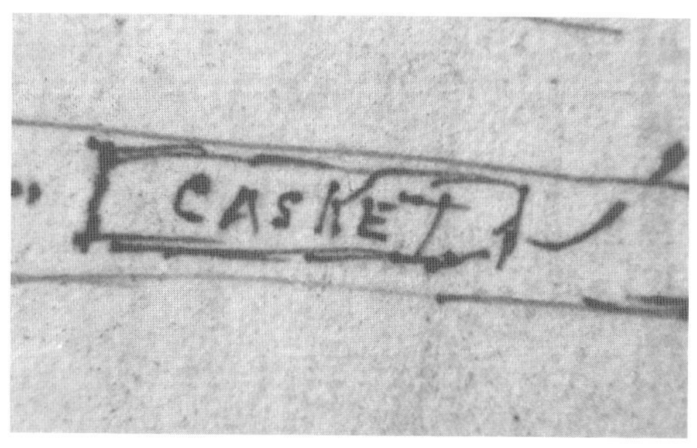

Later a casket floated by.

that as the waters rose through the night, her downstairs neighbor had torn the door off its hinges, put his family on the door, and then, using the door as a kind of kickboard, floated his family to safety. This event she drew in the lower left-hand corner. Later, a casket from a nearby casket factory had floated by. In the early morning she had seen terrified cattle from the nearby stockyards being swept through the backyard. Driven against the picket fence, where their hooves caught, they drowned in the rising water. By later that day, the flood had reached the second floor, and Anna, terrified, ran from window to window looking for help. In the distance, she saw boats looking for trapped residents. Prisoners had been let out of jail to man these boats. She called one over to her and was rescued. Anna could not swim.

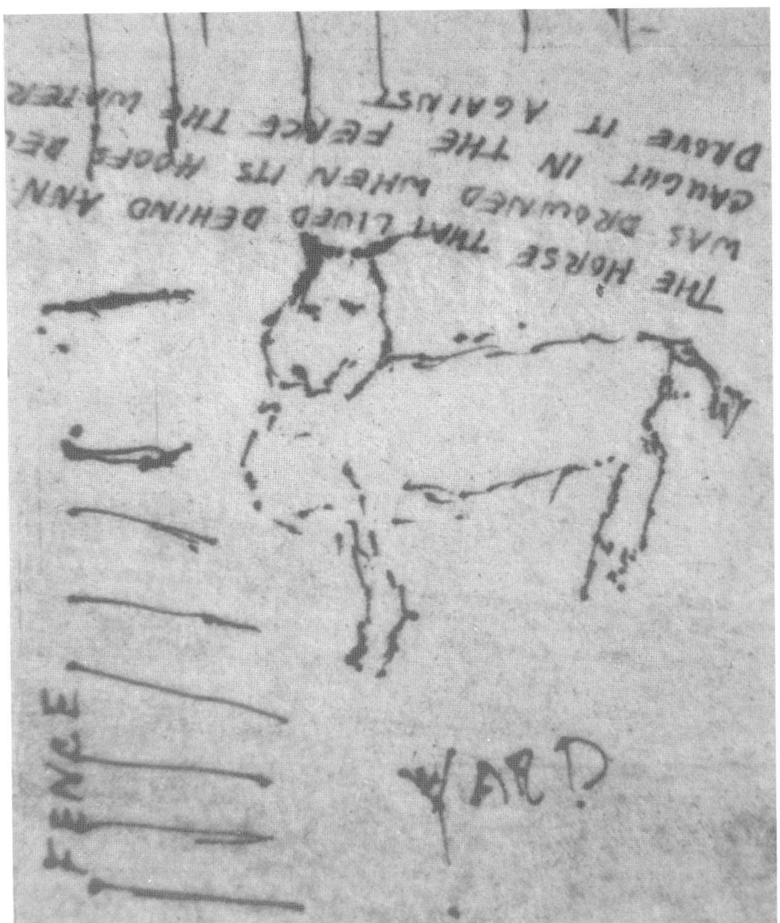

The cattle were driven against the fence, where their hooves caught, and they drowned in the rising water.

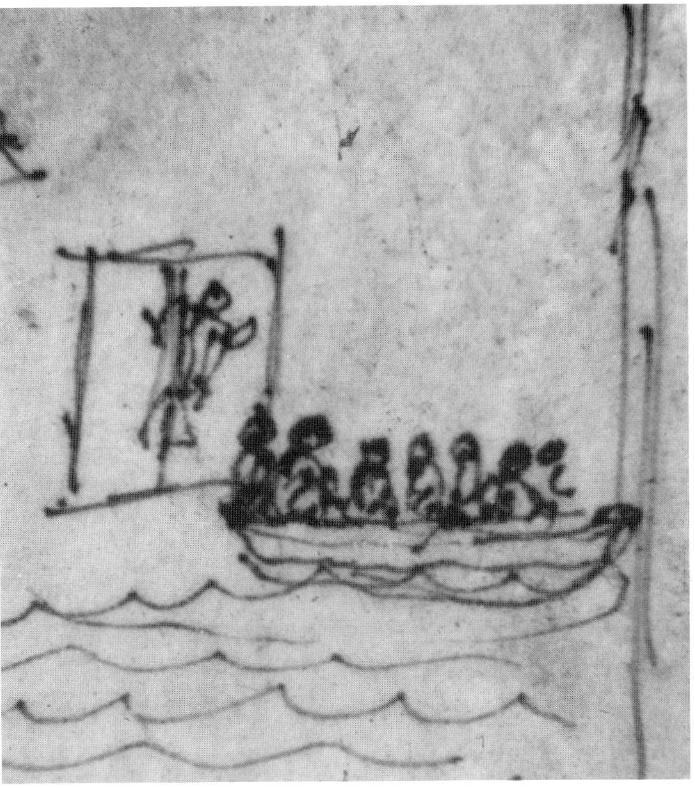

Anna called the boat over to her and was rescued.

Reverend Tinker

One day at Vintage, I met the former center fielder of the Pittsburgh Crawfords, one of the legendary teams of the Negro Baseball League. Though he was by this time almost ninety years old, Reverend Harold Tinker had an impressive presence. He was wearing a clerical collar and had a narrow face with prominent cheekbones. When he stood up to greet me as I entered the room, I noticed how bowed his legs were. But above all I noticed his hands.

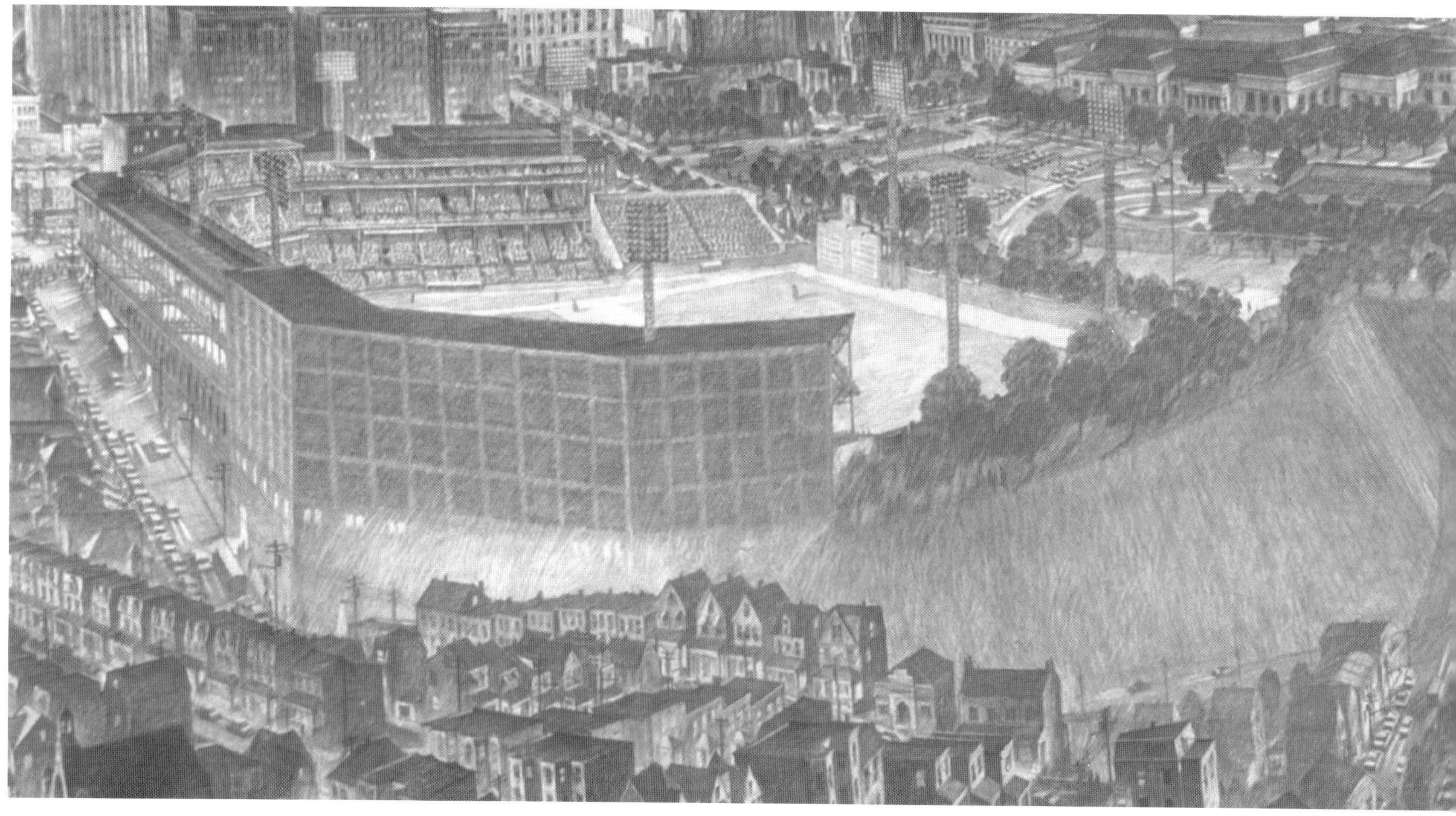

***Past Summers*, 1997.** (Private collection.)

Harold Tinker never thought he would play in Forbes Field.

They were huge. And in the center of his left hand was a baseball-size pocket worn into his palm by thirty years of catching fly balls.

Reverend Tinker's father had originally brought his family to Pittsburgh from Birmingham, Alabama, in 1916, during the World War I production boom. 1917 was the last year Honus Wagner played for the Pirates, and Harold Tinker remembered sneaking into Forbes Field several times through the board fence behind the bleachers to see him play. Being black, Reverend Tinker had never expected to play there himself.

Reverend Tinker first joined the Pittsburgh Crawfords in the mid-1920s, when they were still a sandlot, semi-pro team. The Crawfords were then just one of several teams he played for on top of his regular job with RKO films. But in the late 1920s, with the addition of players such as Josh Gibson, the team grew stronger. Gibson would go on to a legendary career with the Crawfords and subsequently the Homestead Grays and be called the "Black Babe Ruth" because of his home-run power. But it was Harold Tinker who had originally discovered him hitting monstrous home runs at a ballfield on Spring Hill and brought him to the Crawfords.

By the summer of 1930 the Crawfords were ready to challenge the Homestead Grays, Pittsburgh's outstanding and nationally known black team. The game was played on August 25 in Forbes Field, where Tinker had assumed he would never play.

Tinker told me about the game while I acted as scribe. Though the Crawfords were not favored—Gibson had jumped to the Grays several days before—the game remained close. Gray's pitcher Oscar Owens held the Crawfords hitless through five innings, until Tinker hit safely in the sixth. Though the Crawfords scored two runs that inning, they still entered the ninth inning down by a run. They finally lost by a 3–2 margin when Bill Harris made a running catch of Charlie Hughes's line drive with two outs and two runners on base.

After Reverend Tinker finished describing the game, I drew a baseball diamond on a sheet of paper and asked him to list the players at each position. He named all but one. On the field that day were three future Hall of Fame players: Judy Johnson, Oscar Charleston, and Josh Gibson.

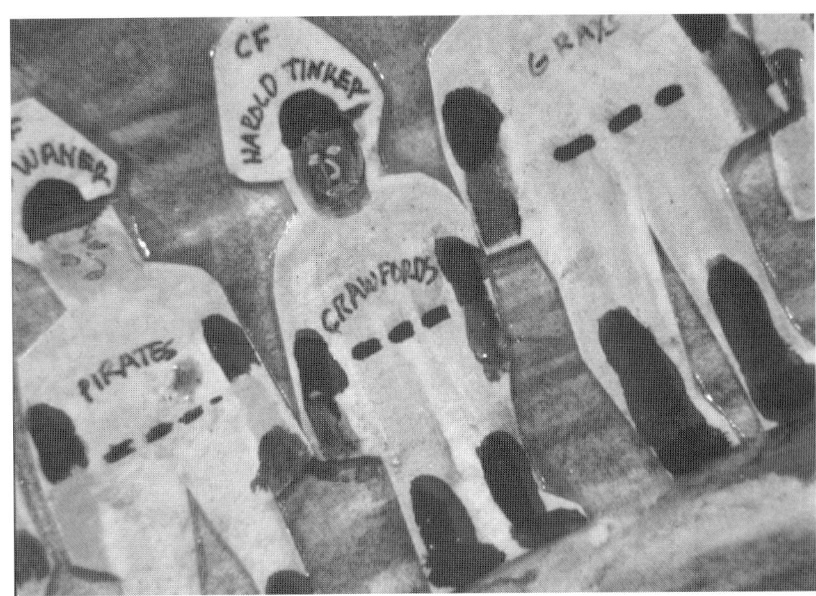

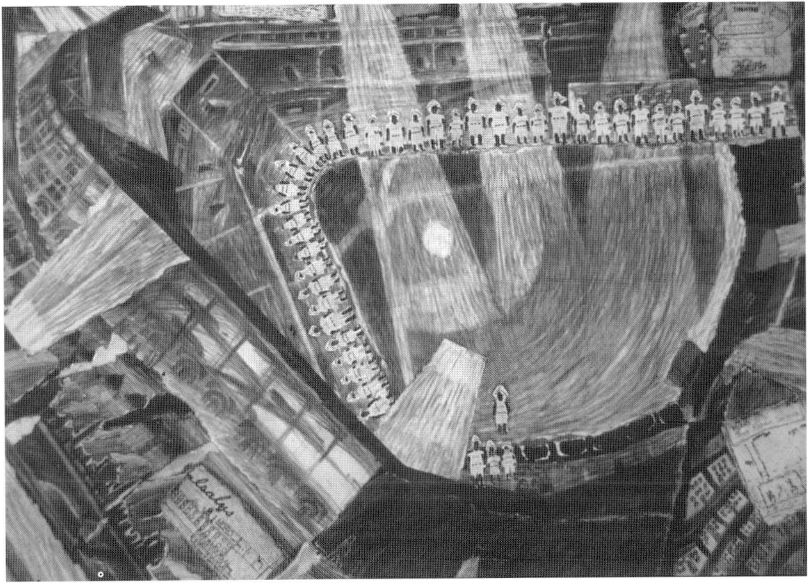

Forbes Field and Reverend Tinker. Heinz History Center Mural.

Later in 1930, Gus Greenlee, the Hill District's well-known numbers racketeer, bought the team. Greenlee also owned the Crawford Grill, the center of Pittsburgh's jazz scene. Greenlee put the players on full salaries and pointed the team in a direction that would make it the premier black team in the United States by 1935. Reverend Tinker knew he would eventually have to quit the team because, with a large family to support, he would have to maintain his regular job. But he did not quit until the Crawfords finally beat the Grays in the summer 1931.

While I was driving Reverend Tinker back to his home, I asked him who was the best all-around player he ever saw—on the Crawfords, on the Grays, on any team. He said Roberto Clemente.

Tragic Memories

Not all of the memories were joyous. At the downtown Vintage on three consecutive Mondays in the winter of 1992–1993, I met with a group from Manchester and McKees Rocks. Ten minutes into the first meeting, a woman, I will call her Louise, entered the room still dressed in her coat from the snow outside. After sitting down, she abruptly said, "I'm not going to draw, but I have one story to tell, only one story, and I'll tell it now." She told us her story in the most matter of fact way.

She had been eight years old.

She was living on California Avenue in Manchester.

There was a heavy wet snow falling.

She was walking up California Avenue.

When she reached the corner at Metropolitan Street, she turned. Two city workmen were clearing snow from the street by swilling the slush into an open manhole. Just as she turned to look, a little girl suddenly slipped in the snow and fell into the open manhole. The little girl's body was found the next day in the Ohio River near the storm sewer outlet. She was nine years old. Louise knew her vaguely. There had been no barrier around the open manhole. A hearing was held, but no responsibility was established.

The next Monday, Louise told the same story again, but important details were added. Her family had known the little girl's family well. The little girl's family had grieved for years over her loss.

The last Monday, Louise told the story a final time, and its importance in the rest of her life became clear. The little girl had been her best friend. They had been playing tag together, and Louise had been chasing her at the moment she slipped into the open manhole. At the hearing, Louise was not allowed to speak because she was too young. The city workers who had left the manhole unprotected were not held accountable, but Louise had held herself responsible for the little girl's death all the days of her life.

The Impact of On-Site Sketching

During the fall and winter before each summer's exhibit at the museum, I walked the streets of Pittsburgh doing preparatory sketches for the more panoramic parts of the mural. I found it was helpful to draw outside at that time of year because of the temperature swings.

On really cold days, I had to carry schnapps. If I was doing an ink wash, I would put schnapps in the wash to keep it from freezing. I would put schnapps in me, too. But most important of all, the cold made me work quickly and helped me avoid getting trapped in detail.

I usually began with something small and static and then let the cold speed up the pace. It was a frigid day in late February of 1992 when I did a drawing of Rinne Way on Arlington Heights. I started in the upper right-hand corner of my sketchbook with a level view between two houses. But then I turned to the left and looked down the steep city steps toward Arlington Road below. Working quickly to keep warm, I exaggerated the downward convergence of the verticals. To me, overstating their inclination seemed to "capture" the steep and turning sense of vision that is so typical of the Pittsburgh landscape.

But on warmer days I took my time. I let the drawings remain more static and invested them with more detail. Like the drawing of View St., which I did on the last warm day in November 1991, these slower drawings were more like maps. They showed where all the houses were located along each street. Harking back to Toby McCarthy's airplane, this more maplike style maintained true

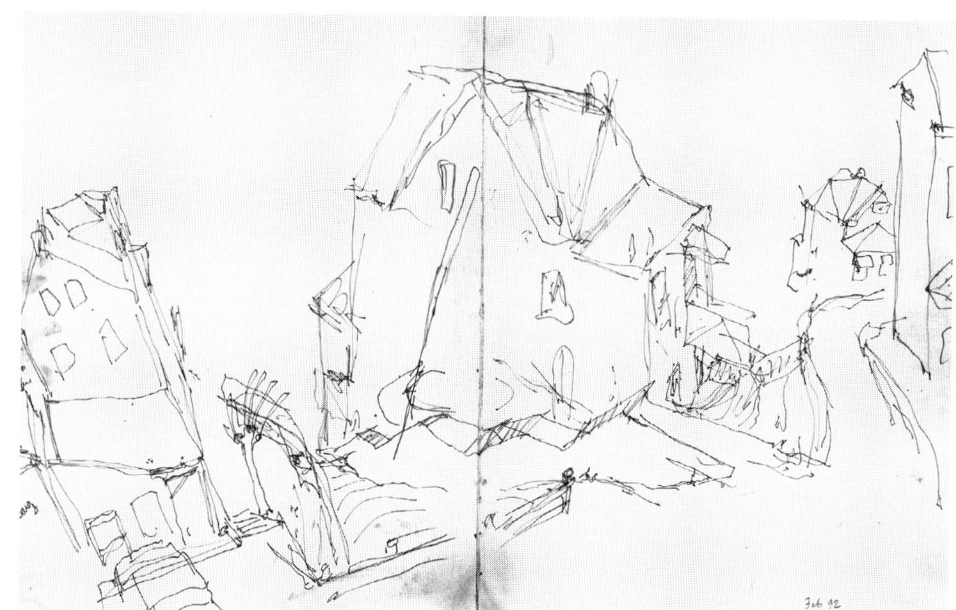

Sketch at Rinne Way, February 1992.

On colder days, I hurriedly exaggerated the convergence of the verticals.

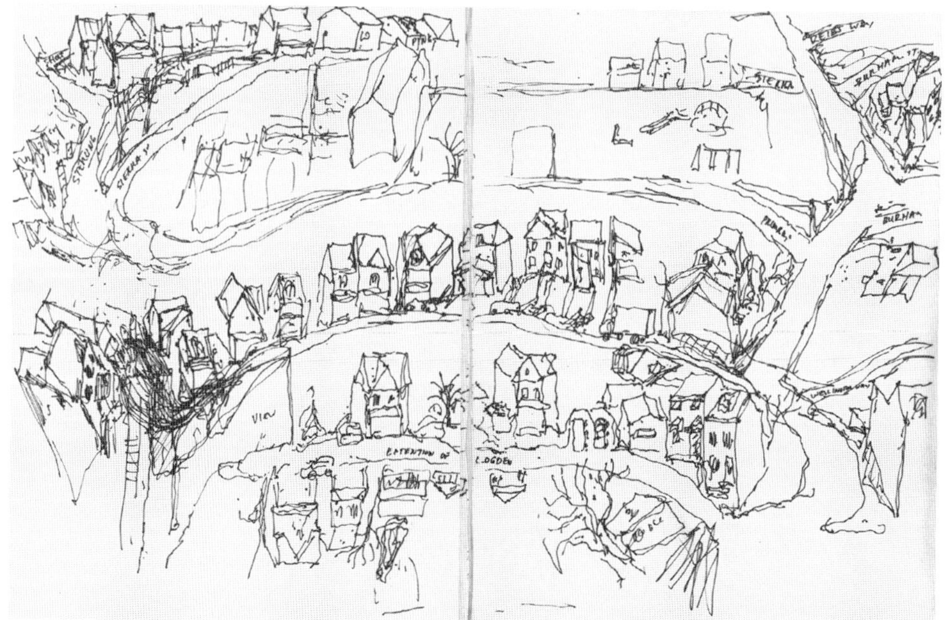

Sketch at View St., November 1991.

On warmer days, I took my time.

spatial relationships and road layouts. I anticipated that bringing these two contrasting kinds of views into one work would create variety of a most essential kind: the variety of mood and pace; the variety of weather.

Work at the Museum

As I drew the mural at the museum during the summers of 1992 and 1993, these two kinds of views provided the primary formal contrast in the work. Setting the issue at the fore, I positioned one of each type side-by-side opposite the entrance to the Forum Gallery.

But as I composed this contrasted pair, I needed to find some way to unify them as well. As shown on the following pages, eventually, I hit upon the idea of using some measure of both techniques in each image of the pair. The right-hand view shows a panorama from the corner of Holt and Barry Streets on the South Side slopes. Its dominant characteristic is that of a steeply inclined perspective. But in the upper right corner, this view tilts the Monongahela River upward in a planlike fashion resembling the spatial sense of the neighboring view of the 18th Street Valley. Likewise that neighboring view presents perspective vistas in its midst. As the mural developed, other images came to share similar reciprocal relationships with their neighbors.

Ultimately, the most important source of unity in the mural is the rivers. They are a fact of living in Pittsburgh. People locate themselves in the city in reference to them: they cross them; they look down on them; they are near to them; they are far from them. A constant in Pittsburgh, they form a constant line through the mural.

All this time in the museum, I was working right there in front of the public; I was part of the exhibit. People were not shy, and they came right up behind me to watch while I worked. At first I found this unnerving, feeling somewhat like an animal in a zoo. But after a while, I got used to it and saw the benefit for the work in my being there. People told me stories which I incorporated into the mural—sometimes while they watched. Among other things I learned:

• The mystery B-25 that crashed in the 1950s into the Monongahela River between the Homestead Hi-level and Glenwood Bridges and was never found

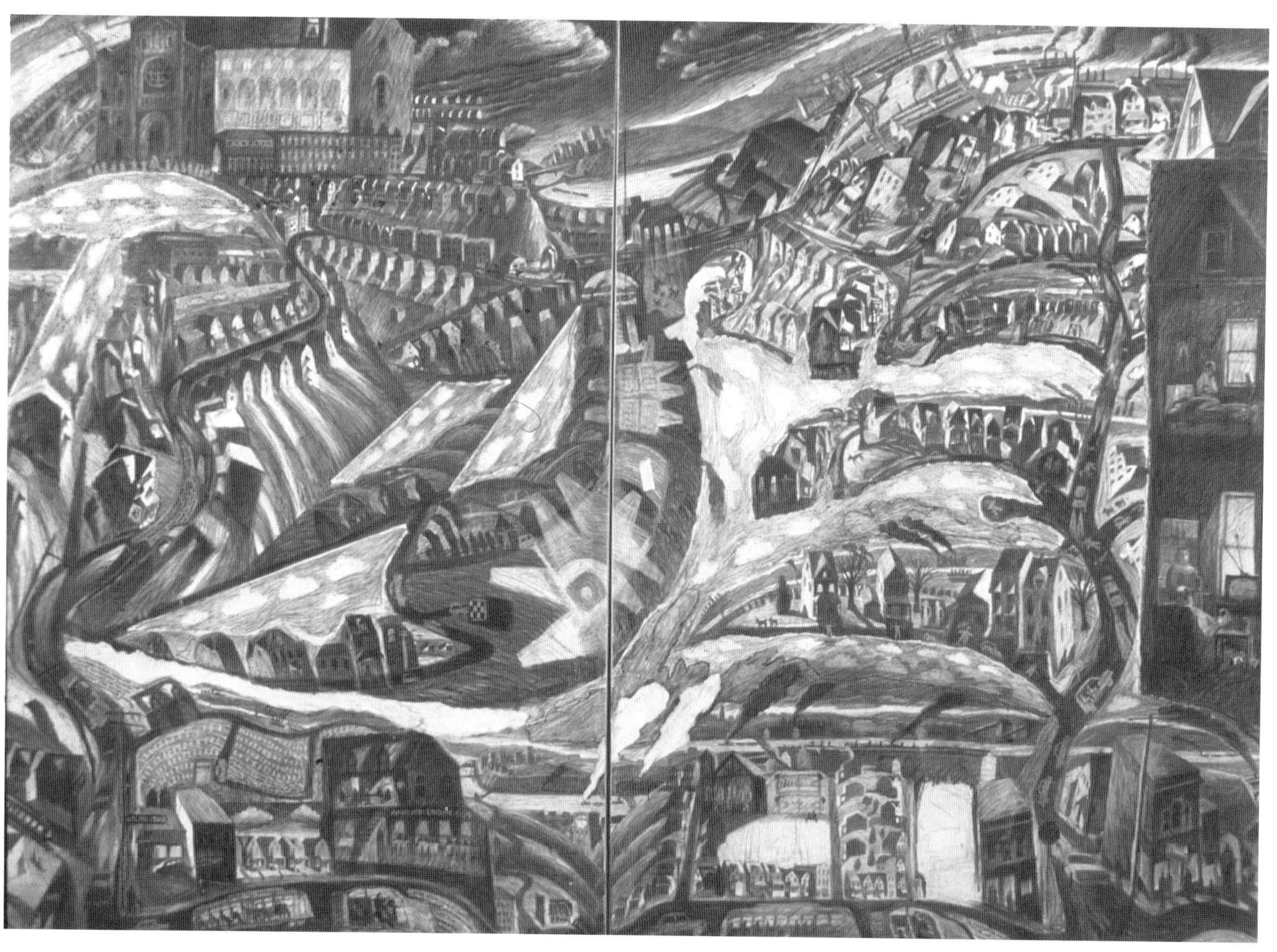

18th St. Valley.* 80″ x 112″. *Heinz History Center Mural.

One way of representing space was more maplike and maintained true spatial relationships and road layouts.

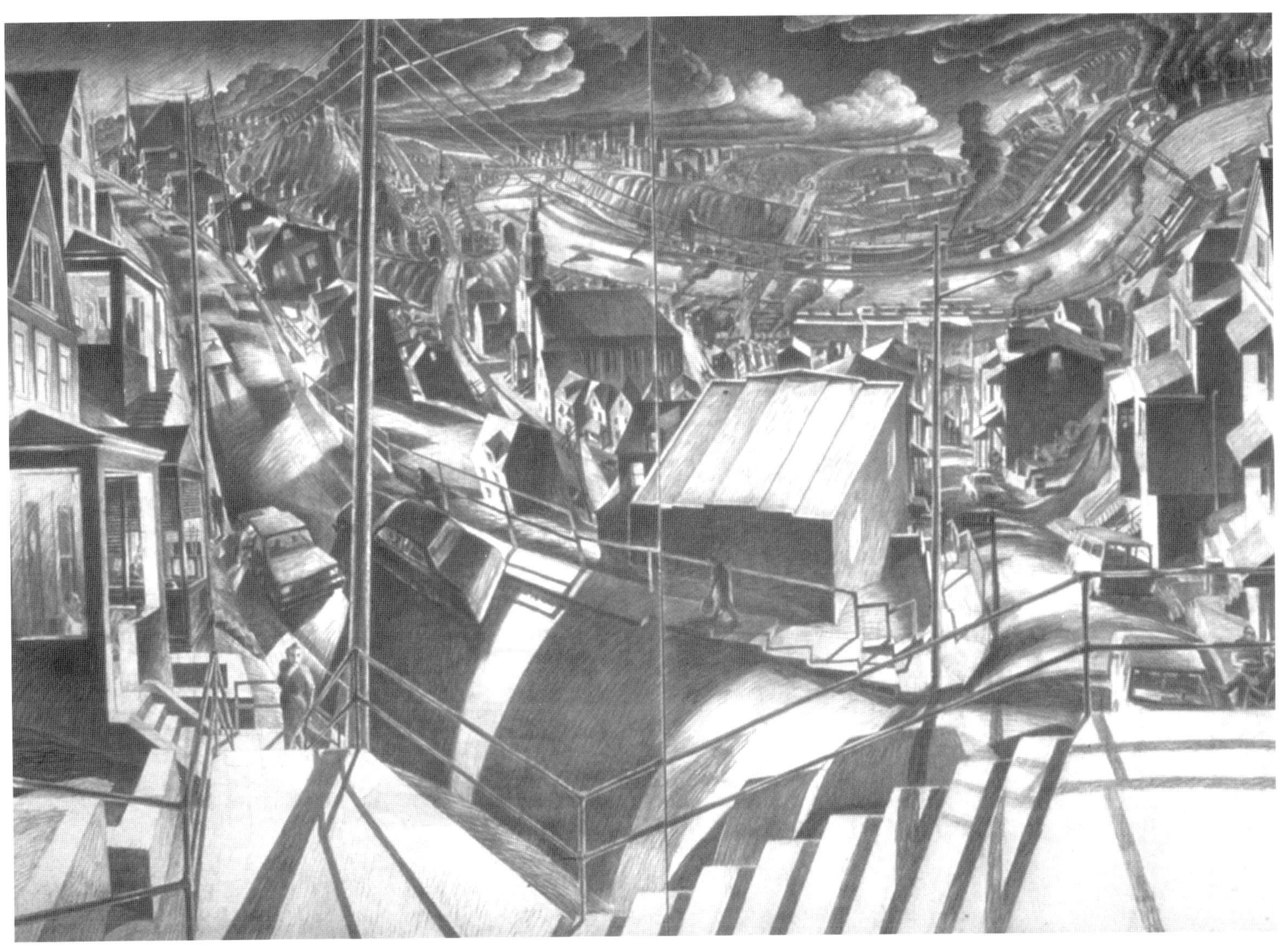

Holt and Barry Sts. 80″ x 112″. ***Heinz History Center Mural.***

Another way of representing space was rooted in perspective and presented the steep and turning vistas that are so typical of Pittsburgh.

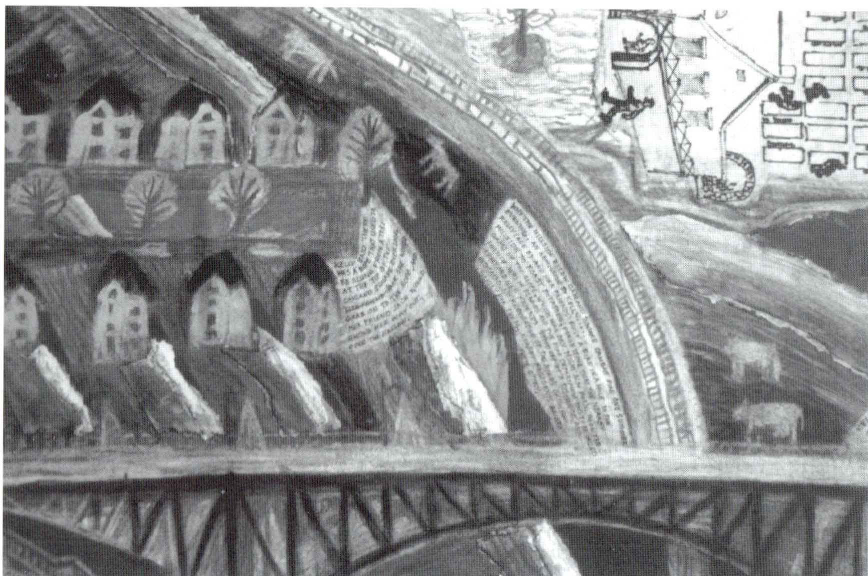

Kelly's Fire. Heinz History Center Mural.

The fire below Oakland Square in 1946—Kelley started it.

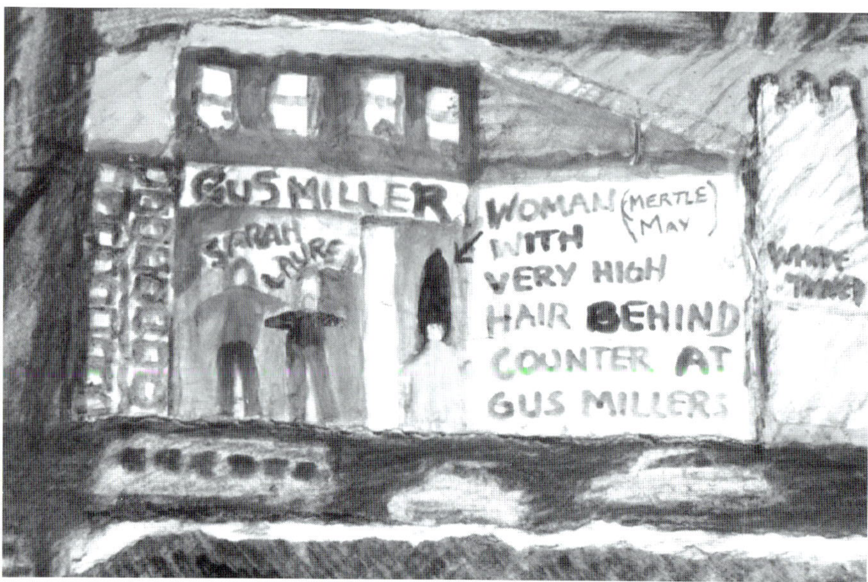

Gus Miller's Store. Heinz History Center Mural.

The woman behind the counter at Gus Miller's—her name was Myrtle-Maye.

when the river bottom was dredged? It had two engines, not the four I had drawn. (I changed it to two engines right away.) One of the museum guards told me this. He had worked at Mesta Machine Works directly opposite the crash site and said the plane was definitely removed the night of the crash. He saw people out on the river salvaging it.

• In the 1930s, relatives of a prisoner at the state penitentiary moved into a house next to the prison wall. They moved in a piano. At the same time each night, their child practiced the piano—loudly. While she practiced, their relative worked on his escape tunnel leading directly to their house. He successfully escaped. A neighbor told me.

• In 1946, there was a brush fire on the hillside below Oakland Square. Until that summer in the museum, no one had known how it started. Kelly had started it roasting potatoes. The brush was dry, and the fire took off up the hill. Kelly told me.

• The woman who worked the cash register at Gus Miller's newsstand, who had "high hair" and who, year after year, had shooed the boys from Central Catholic away from *Playboy* magazine? Her name was Myrtle-Maye.

• The painter John Kane was right. Cows did used to graze in Panther Hallow. Kelly told me this too.

In a way, the public was part of the exhibition those summers. Not only did their stories become part of the mural; their responses to it guided my drawing. Sight lines were the key problem for the mural's composition. Some areas of the mural, those

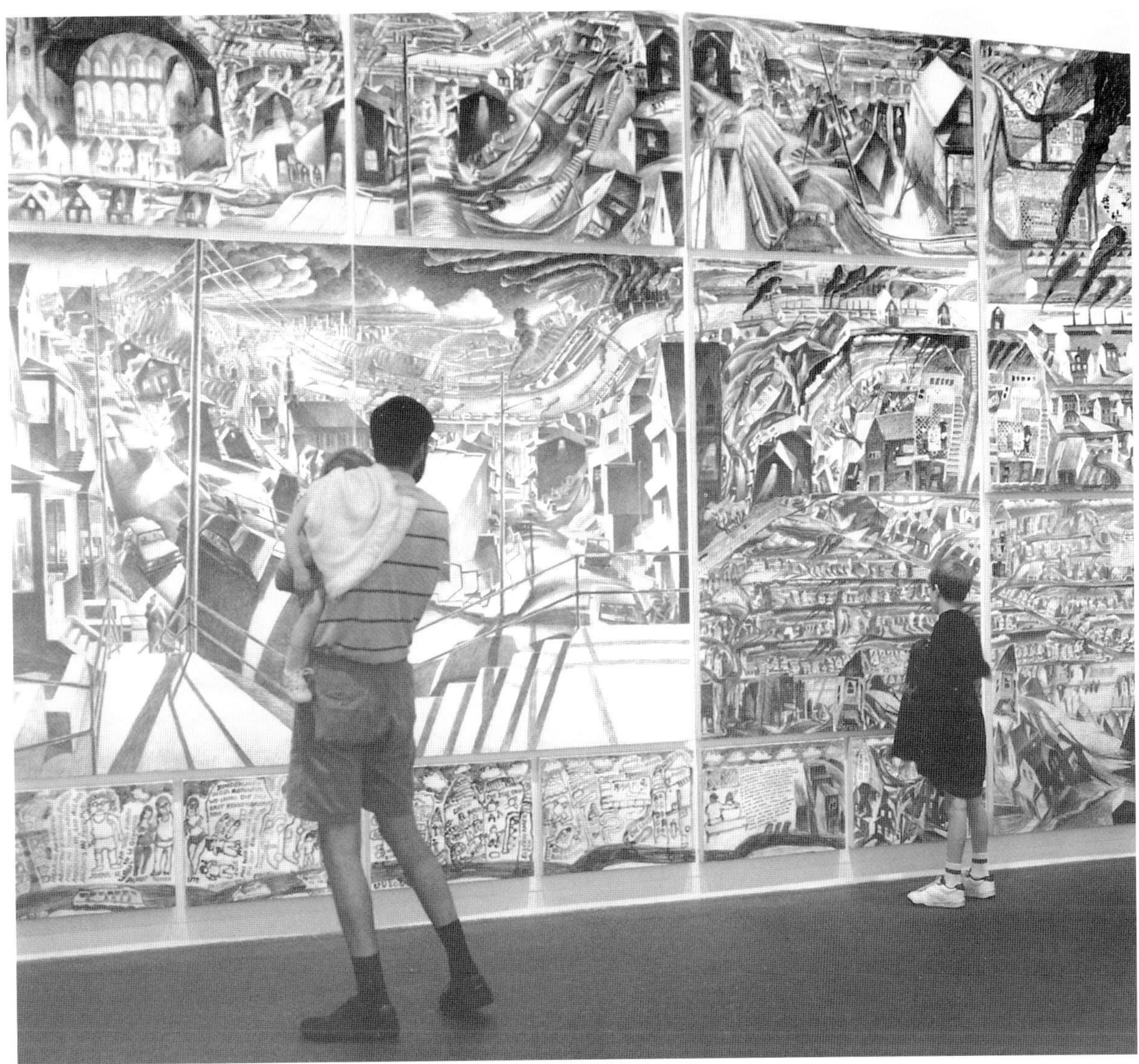

Installation at the Forum Gallery, Carnegie Museum of Art, summer 1993. Heinz History Center Mural.

(Photo: Richard A. Stoner.)

I found these large vistas acted as visual hooks.

opposite major directions of approach in the gallery, had to project effectively over great distances. I had to remain watchful that the level of detail in these areas did not make the mural confusing at a distance. With the public right there, I could try out various approaches to this problem and then observe how people responded.

In the end, what worked best was positioning large vistas opposite major lines of approach. I found these large vistas acted as visual hooks. Time after time I watched viewers walk right up to them and then move laterally to the small, more detailed drawings on either side, which they were then able to see clearly.

Having the mural broken up into images of various sizes also offered the wonderful chance for me to employ my younger daughter, Sarah, to help. Built out of multiple parts, the mural was enormously resilient and could incorporate a variety of styles. Sarah draws differently than I do, but I could set her work into the mural right next to mine and use her individual style of drawing as a foil to my own work. The mural was resilient for me personally as well. Whatever my mood on a given day, whether patient or frantic, I could always find a place appropriate for its expression.

All the while I was doing the mural, I was also looking to find a suitable permanent, public home for it. While I was unable to finish the mural while it was still at the museum, I was able to interest the Historical Society of Western Pennsylvania in its eventual purchase. It is now permanently installed at their new downtown facility, the Senator John Heinz Pittsburgh Regional History Center.

The CMU University Center Mural

In *1995, after completing the Heinz Center Mural* and a large mural with the elderly for Philadelphia's downtown justice center, I began a mural for Carnegie Mellon University's new student center. Although that work would become my most ambitious work to date, the idea for it was not mine. It originated with Martin Prekop, dean of the College of Fine Arts.

Martin asked if I might be interested in doing a mural for the new center, which was just under way and a year and a half from completion. He suggested I meet with architect Michael Dennis to find a suitable location. I think what Martin had in mind was something on the order of a fifteen-foot-wide mural for one of the center's meeting rooms. But when I saw the large entrance hall in the architect's plans, a two-story rotunda, I knew I wanted to do the mural for that space. I envisioned the mural extending three-quarters of the way around and measuring over 200 feet long.

What interested me about the rotunda was its central role in orienting visitors to the campus. It would be the first place they would arrive, and I thought I could use the cardinal orientations of its walls—north, east, and west—to locate visitors in the campus and city and show a bit of the history of both along the way.

The rotunda's many openings offered an opportunity I had always sought. People would be able to see the mural from across the rotunda through the openings between its piers. The mural would not be just a picture on a wall. It

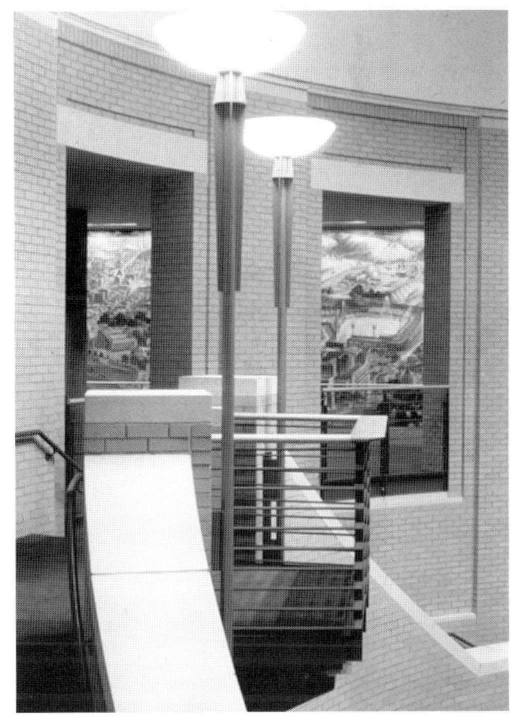

Carnegie Mellon University Center Mural, 1995–1996.

11′ x 200′. (Photo: Bill Riddick.)

I positioned key sites to be visible through the rotunda's openings.

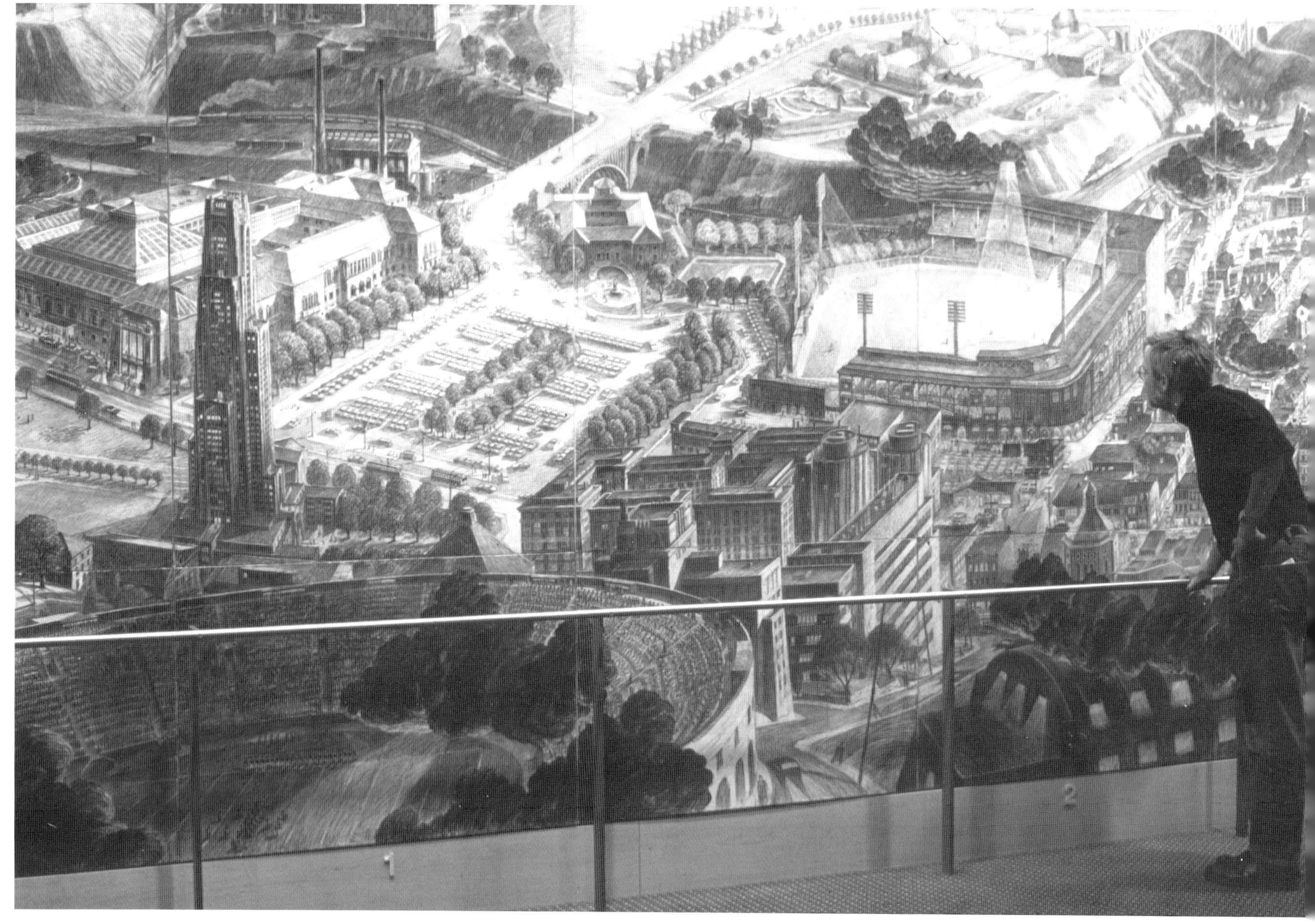

University Center Mural. (Photo: Bill Riddick.)

I used the wall's eleven-foot height to give viewers the sense they could walk into the mural.

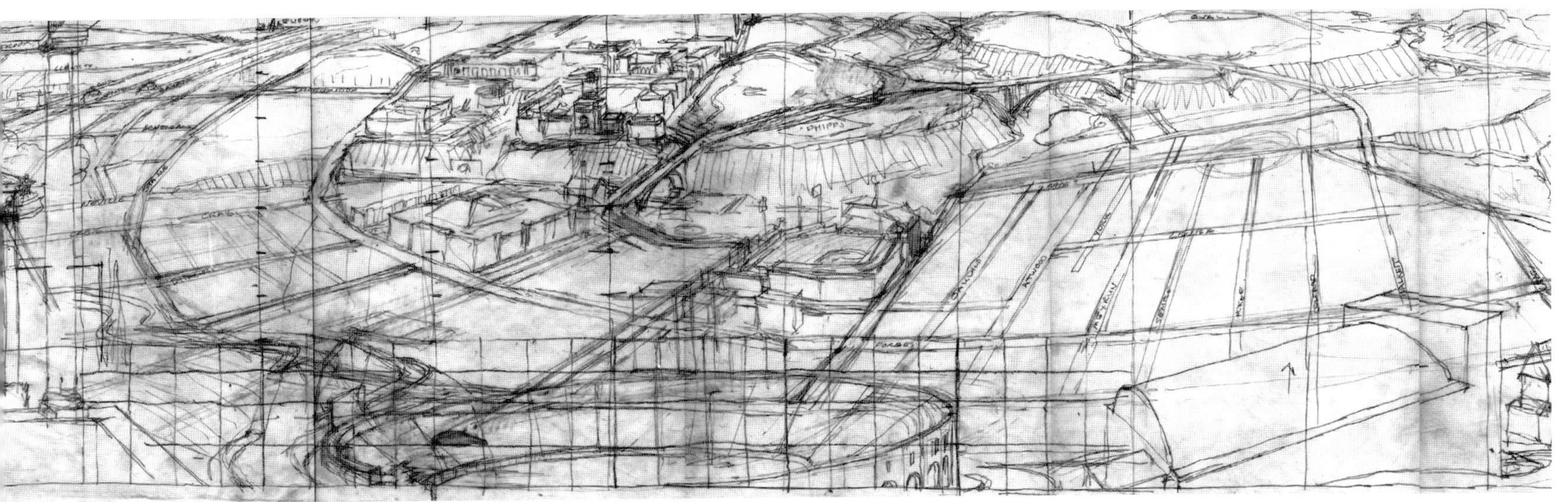

would be a real landscape in its own right, and like a real landscape, it would be seen through real openings.

In the same spirit, I wanted to use the walls' eleven-foot height to give viewers the sense they could walk right into the mural. By following all wall returns around corners and by extending the image full height, from baseboard to ceiling, the mural would present no visible edges. The sense I was seeking was that of a borderless view into a space beyond.

The key compositional problem was clear from the start. Just as at the Carnegie Museum, I would need to anticipate the sight lines and distances from which the mural would be seen. But because the center was still under construction, I would have to do this using only the center's construction plans. And the sight lines at the student center would be diagonal.

I laid out cones of vision over these plans along key sight lines, and with these in mind, I developed full-length cartoons of the mural at a scale of one inch to the foot. Working back and forth between the plans and the cartoons, I was able to anticipate exactly what would be seen through each opening and know the size at which the mural would project at various distances.

I began work on the mural in early June 1995. I employed two assistants with ties to Carnegie Mellon: Jonathan Kline, at that time a student in architecture,

University Center Mural.

I used a cartoon, together with the cones of vision, to plan the rotunda's sight lines.

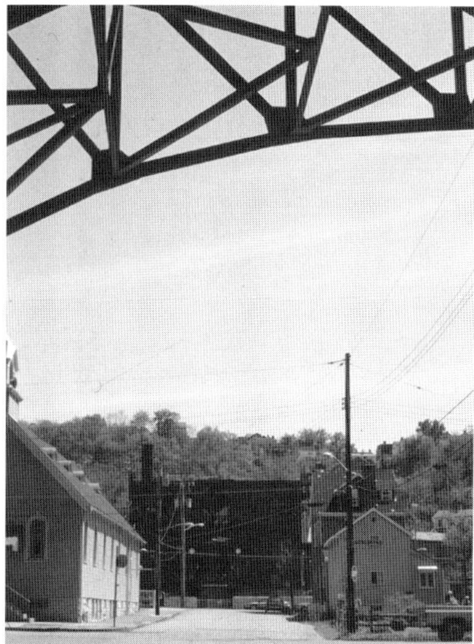

Greenfield Studio. (Photo: Sarah Cooper.)

We worked in a former schoolhouse under the parkway bridge.

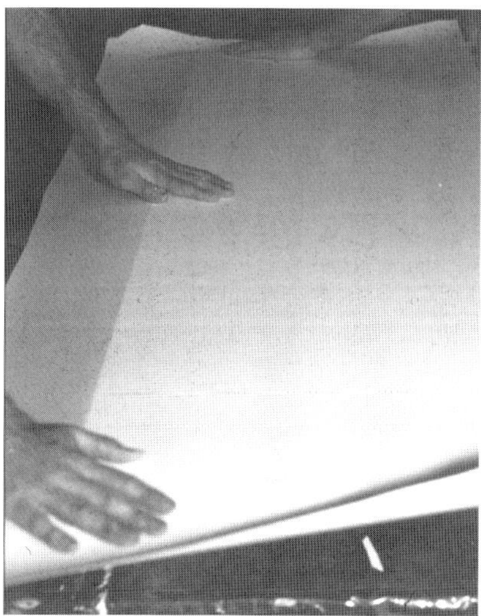

Rolling out the paper. (Photo: Sarah Cooper.)

The next day we formed our drawing surface by mounting the paper with acrylic glue.

and John Trivelli, a recent graduate of the art department. Because there were two Johns, I called John Trivelli "JT."

I anticipated completion and installation in early June of 1996, but there was one wild card. I had developed cataracts. The operation was still a ways off—the cataracts would have to "ripen" before they could be removed—but at my last checkup, it had been impossible to forecast when that would be.

We worked in a classroom in a former schoolhouse under the Parkway Bridge at the end of the Four Mile Run in Lower Greenfield. It's an imposing building, which is now owned by a union, the Local 95 Operating Engineers. It was once the elementary school of St. Joachim's Church, a Slavic Catholic church which served generations of families whose men worked in the nearby Jones and Laughlin ironworks at the end of the run.

The seventy-five-year-old schoolhouse seemed to have floors and walls that spoke. The water fountains and chalkboards were low to the floor, so we could easily visualize the children who had once attended. Here and there we found initials furtively scratched into the slate. The stairs leading up to the studio still showed the yellow lines on the treads that the nuns had once used to file pupils up and down the stairs in orderly rows at lunchtime and recess.

In many ways these same stairs became our biggest headache. Every stick of charcoal, every gallon of acrylic, every fiberboard panel (half of which weighed over 100 pounds) had to be carried up the fifty-one steps that lead from Saline Street up to the studio, and then back down those same steps when the mural was done.

On our first day we received delivery of thirty fiberboard panels. We sealed these outside the building in the school's former playground and then hauled them upstairs. The next day we formed our drawing surface by mounting paper with acrylic glue. We mounted the paper both front and back so the panels would not warp. These were the hottest days of that summer, as I remember, and lucky for us, Big Jim's restaurant served cool drinks just around the corner.

The East Wall Mural

We began with the east wall mural because my intention for that wall had been the clearest from the beginning. I wanted to show Oakland in the late 1960s, as I remembered it from my student days living across from Forbes Field with Meg. This had been an auspicious time for CMU as well. It was then that the Mellon Institute had been joined with Carnegie Tech to form the university as it is now constituted.

We built a scaffold along one wall of the studio to hold the upper and lower echelons of panels in place while we worked. With the cartoon in hand, we laid out the mural in pencil first, shuffling through its length from left to right. Given the length of the classroom wall, we were able to work with a width of twenty-eight feet (seven panels) at a time. The first thing we drew in charcoal was Rodef Shalom Synagogue.

After completing about half of the east wall, I decided the time was right to address a lingering political issue. When the student center had been originally designed and put out for bid, it had not included the kind of wall-washing lights and guardrail that the mural would need when installed. The anticipated cost of these was substantial—great enough so that Ed Schatz, the university officer in charge of the building's completion, was very much concerned. I knew I would need his full support, so when I thought we had a representative portion of the mural done, I invited him and some other university officials down for a look-see.

After one look at the twenty-eight-foot-wide section of the mural, Ed and the others were fully committed to it. There were some lucky coincidences. I had included steam engines in Junction Hollow. It turned out Ed's first memory of Carnegie Tech was a view from a train window looking up at Machinery Hall as he rode the B&O down the hollow into Pittsburgh on his way to start school. Ed became one of my biggest allies.

As the east wall mural progressed into South Oakland, I took time to do some on-site sketching at the top of Robinson Street where it crosses Aliquippa Street and overlooks Oakland. As I had often done with views for the Heinz

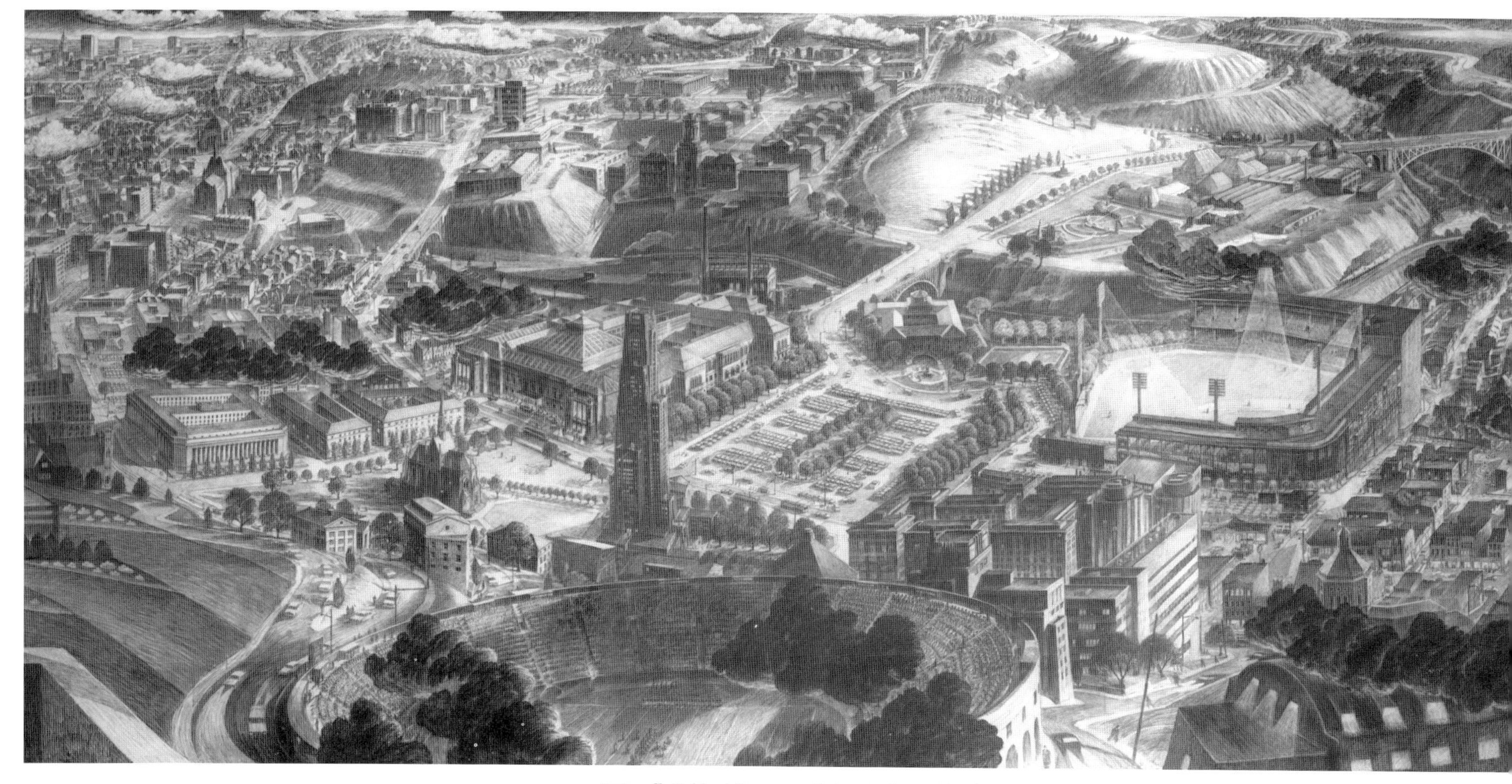

East wall, Oakland Panorama. University Center Mural. (Photo: Ken Andreyo.)

Center Mural, I gave this sketch a broad breadth of field and let the verticals converge sharply downward. I wanted to give viewers the sense that they were high up on this hill and looking down at Oakland—the prototypical Pittsburgh view. I also wanted to use the more active and disjointed character of this neighborhood scene as a foil for the more tightly controlled and maplike depiction of Oakland below.

As it approached the Monongahela River, the view of Oakland assumed a more active character on its own. Jonathan laid out the J&L mills on each side

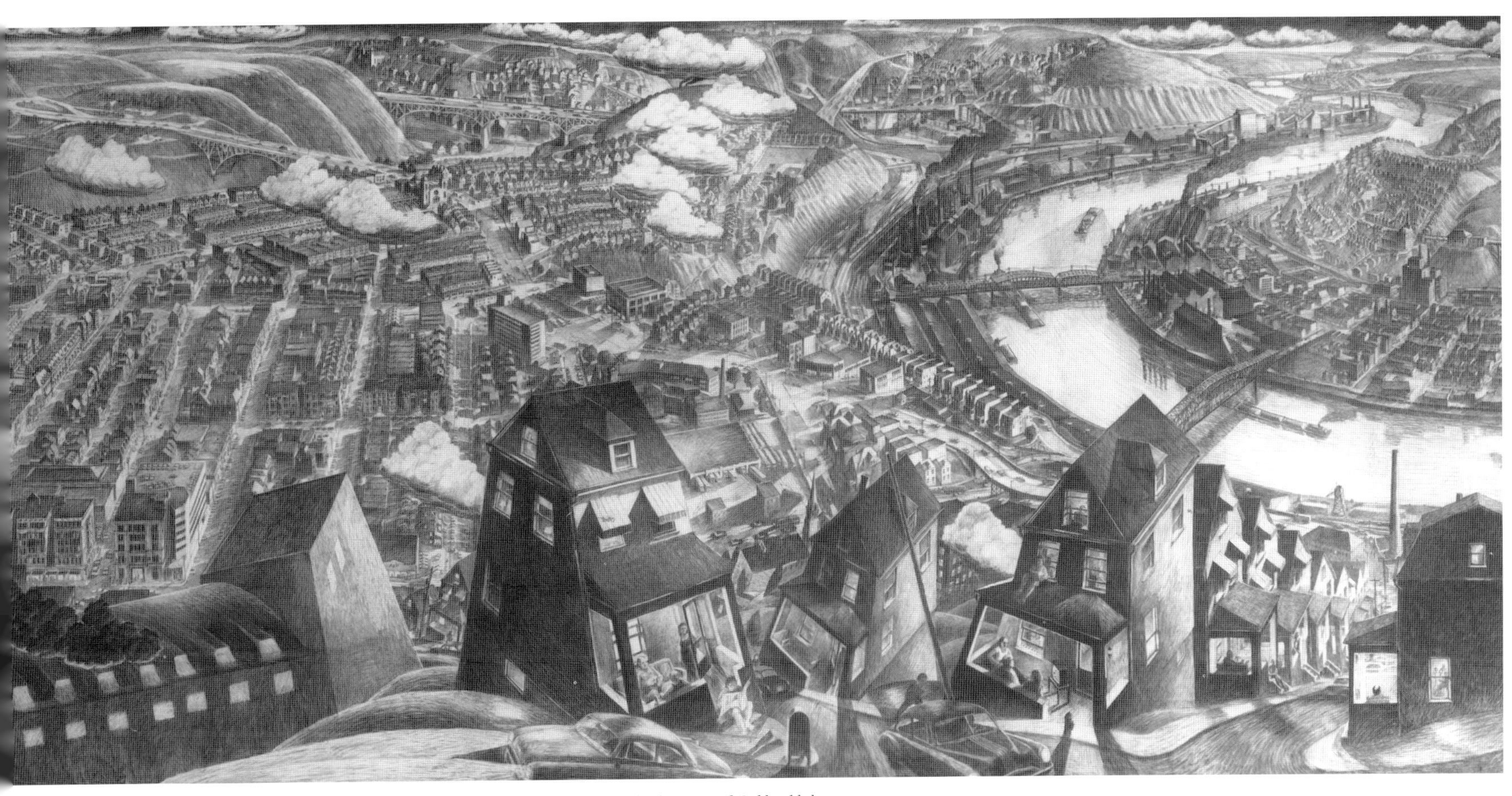

I used the neighborhood in the foreground as a foil for the more maplike depiction of Oakland below.

of the river, and I bent the river to construct a scene that offered a view both up the river toward Hazelwood and down the river toward downtown. This 180-degree panorama was positioned so it would neatly fit between a pair of columns when seen from the overlook at the south end of the rotunda.

West Wall Mural

By mid-August 1995, when Jonathan had to resume his studies, we had more or less completed the east wall. There were still some things that needed to be

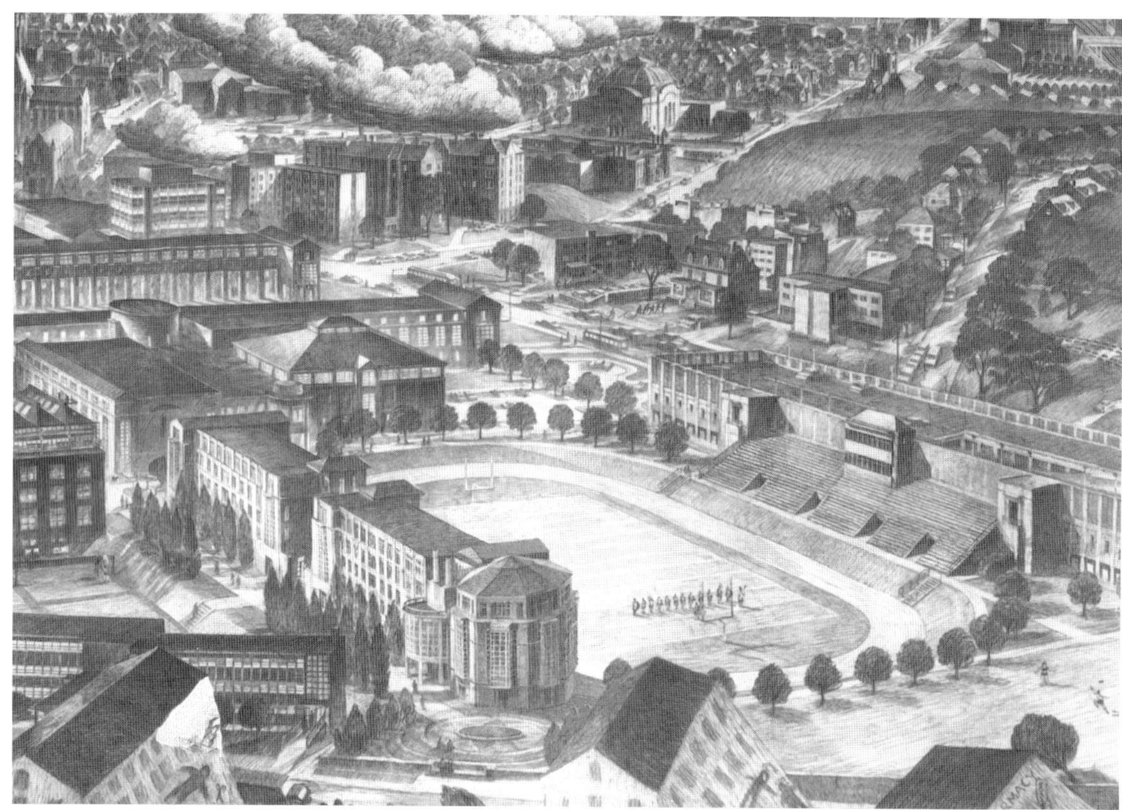

West wall. *University Center Mural*. (Photo: Ken Andreyo.)

When viewed frontally, the image seems flatter.

done—I hadn't completed the area of the mural around the entrance to the building's kitchens, and I had left the drawing of the Hill District for later—but I felt we were well enough along so that JT and I could start the west wall. I wanted this wall to be centered on the CMU campus and be set in the present day.

With the west wall, I took a different approach with the rotunda's sight lines. I borrowed a technique from Baroque painting called anamorphic perspective. That technique had first been used for painting ceiling frescoes on curved vaults high above the heads of viewers. With this technique, images are made to order for diagonal instead of frontal viewing, exactly the way viewers would approach our mural on their way from the top of the rotunda's stairs to the dining room.

With this in mind, when JT and I laid out the campus, we used an unusually

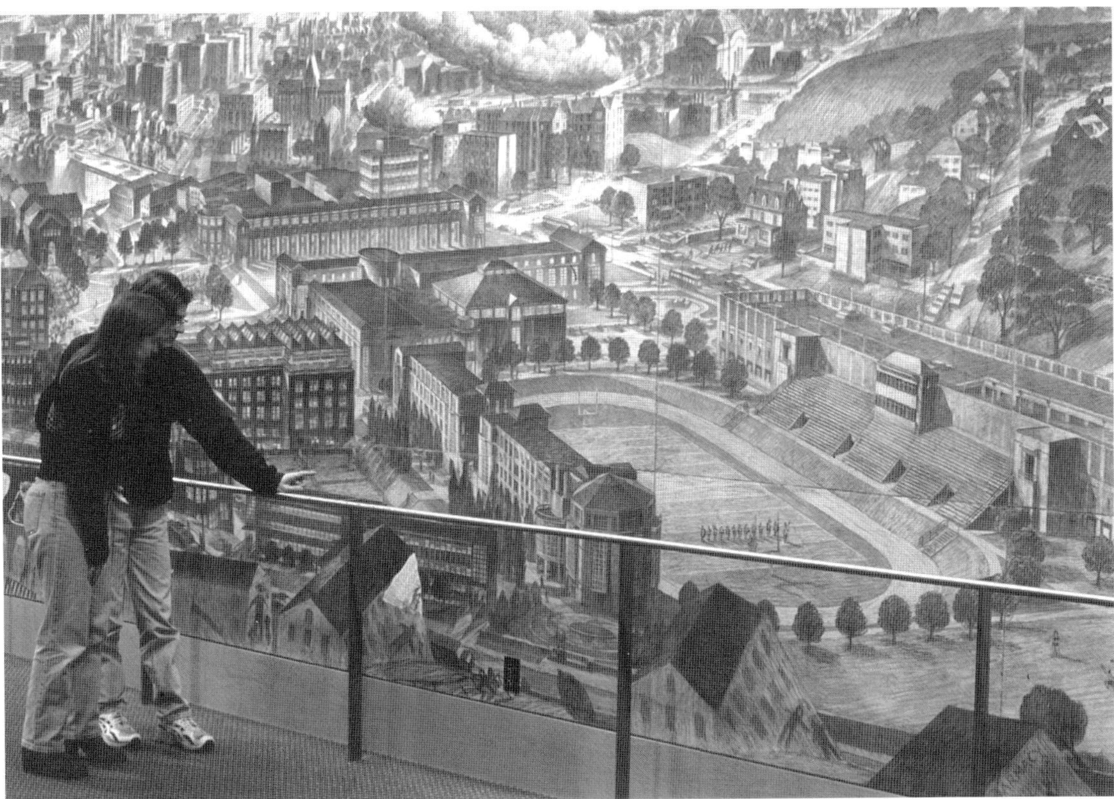

slow rate of convergence. We showed buildings frontally and constructed their sides with lines that barely converged at all. Seen frontally from close up, as much of this portion of the mural would be, this lack of convergence had the effect of making all the campus buildings seem equal to each other. I thought this approach would be "politic" given the rough and tumble territorial sense of any university community.

But when approached from the acute angle that viewers would likely take as they walked toward the dining room, this same area would project a deep and believable convergence. With the panels in place on the scaffold in my studio, I was able to test the rate of convergence and adjust it for this angular view. In the end, it presented exactly the kind of deep-space view which would lead viewers into the mural, even as they would be led toward the dining room by their stomachs.

West wall. University Center Mural. (Photo: Bill Riddick.)

When viewed from an angle, the image seems deeper.

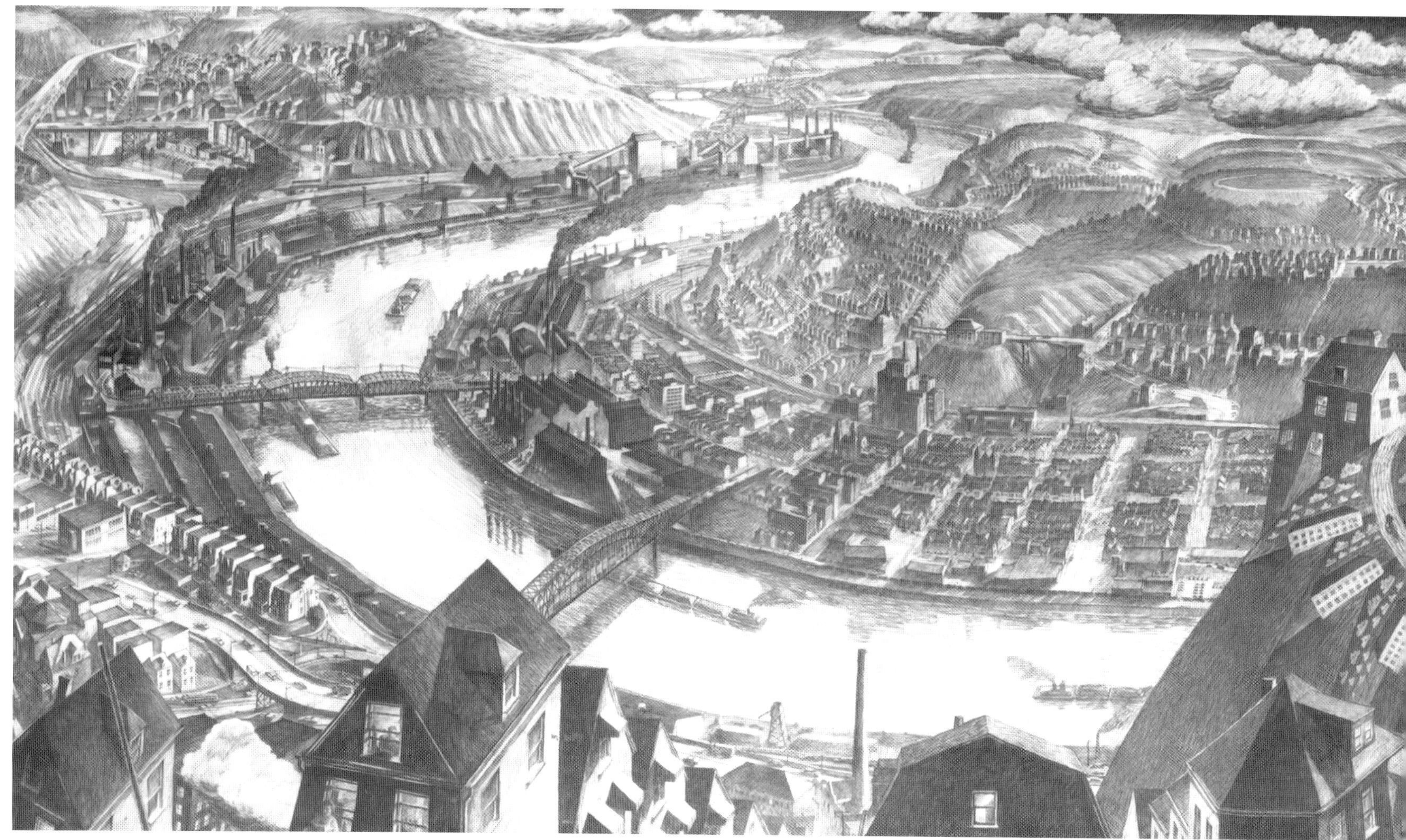

East wall, South Side panorama. University Center Mural.

(Photo: Ken Andreyo.)

I used the simpler, more naive areas as a foil for the mural's dense detail.

The Benefits of Time Pressure

Sometime in early October, I began to wonder if we had any hope of completing the mural on schedule. I was under considerable time pressure as it was. I was associate dean of the College, I was teaching a full load of classes, and I would need to co-chair a search for a new department head in the College. These tasks I could deal with, but by early fall, my vision had badly deteriorated. A visit to my doctor confirmed what I suspected. It was time for my cataracts to be removed.

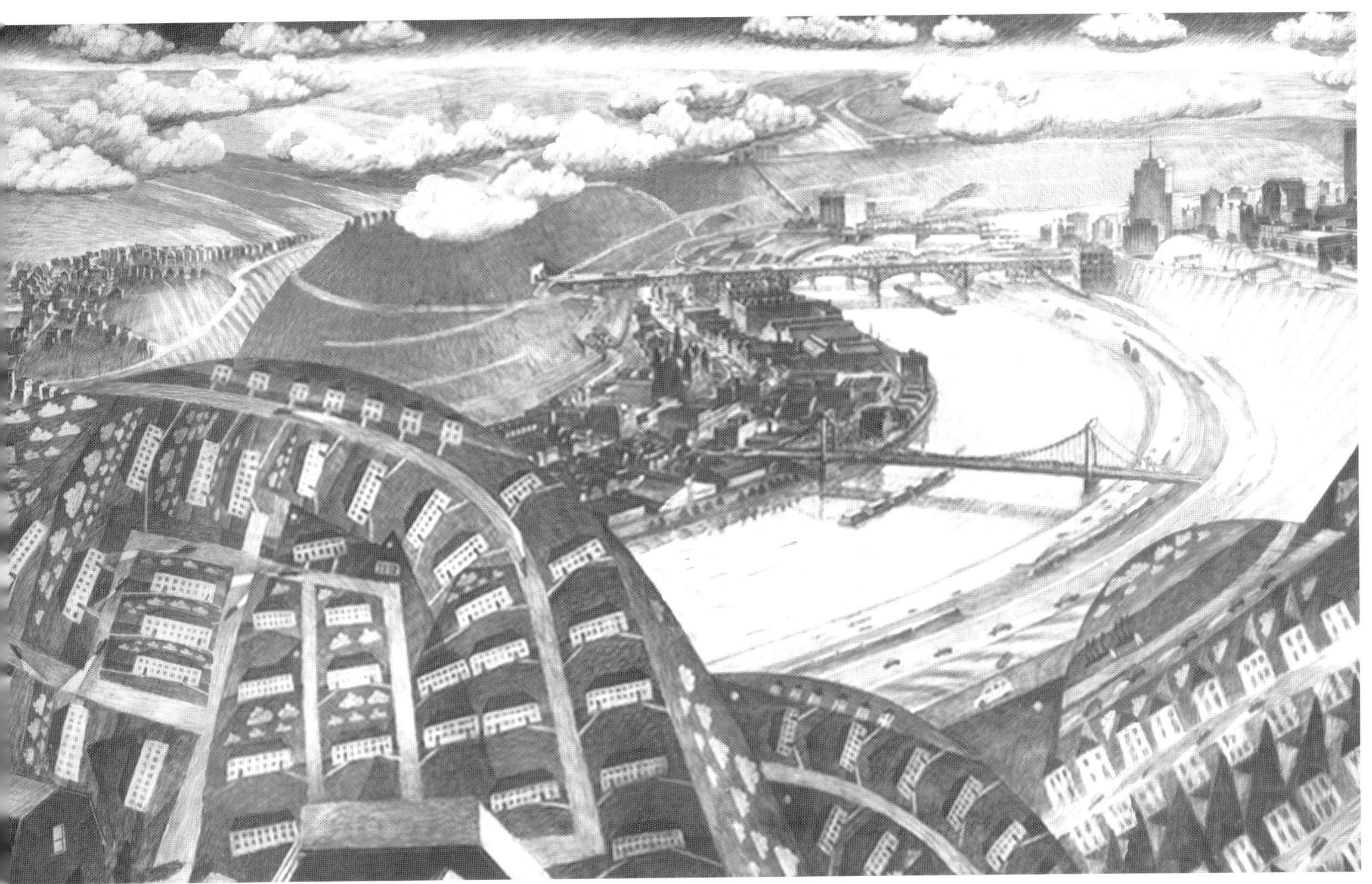

I had already set the schedule for my next project, a mural with students in Frankfurt that next summer. That project would start June 15 and need to be completed and fully installed by August 15. There was no wiggle room in my schedule at all. I called architect Michael Dennis's office and tried to get some agreement that, if time forced it, I could reduce the scope of the north wall mural.

They were not agreeable.

Looking back, I'm glad they were not.

I had already planned to handle the Hill District area of the mural in a looser, more naive style. But the time pressure now forced me to include more such areas. It turned out these areas not only let me work faster, but they also had the beneficial visual effect of breaking the continuity of the mural's dense detail. I do have a weakness for detail. It's like a drug of sorts for me, so alluring that I often have to find some external force to break its habitual charm. The time pressure served as that force.

The waitresses at Big Jim's also helped bring me out of my funk. In the weeks before Halloween, some of the waitresses started dressing up as cows with gigantic udders. No small details at Big Jim's! No small details in the mural!

Right after Halloween I had the cataract removed from my right eye. When the doctor removed the patch the next day, I could suddenly see with clarity that I had not experienced since third grade.

That first day without a cataract in my right eye was something of a revelation. Colors, particularly blues and violets, seemed unusually saturated. As Meg drove me home from the doctor's, I commented on the color of every sign, every car, and every house that had any trace of blue or violet. That night it snowed. The snow falling out of the night sky looked purple.

I had read somewhere that Monet had cataracts in his last years. That night as the purple snow fell, I was thinking I might have stumbled upon the reason for his extensive use of purple in that period. I was explaining the extraordinary explosiveness of the purples and blues in my own vision by speculating that in the preceding months I had been overcompensating in some way for the cataracts' effect of yellowing or graying out their complements in the blue/purple part of the spectrum. Might Monet have been doing the same thing? Had he oversaturated the blues and purples in his later years in an effort to make them appear normal through his eyes? Perhaps Monet had never actually seen the colors we now so appreciate in his later work.

My first day back at the studio brought another surprise. I noticed for the first time that several areas in the mural were somewhat yellow. Several years before, I had occasionally run into cans of fixative that developed a yellow cast.

I had been told that yellowing sometimes occurs when cans have frozen during shipment. Whatever the cause, with my vision now clear, I could plainly see that numerous cans used on the mural had been defective. These were from a manufacturer I had used without problem for twenty years. Though these areas were distracting, there was nothing I could do. I reconciled myself to it as part of the process. Maybe thinking of Monet gave some reassurance. Anyway, I had no choice.

North Wall Mural

Following surgery on my left eye and a break for the holidays, JT and I began the north wall mural. I had left this wall for last. With three niche entrances into an adjacent ballroom along its length, it would be the most complicated of the three to lay out. The key challenge for the north wall was its unity. The mural would split at each of the ballroom entrances, with part going over the top and part turning the corner into the niche. With large columns out from the wall flanking each entrance, it would be difficult to get a continuous read along this wall. I decided to use the Monongahela River to tie the mural together. I thought it would provide a strong enough graphic thread. As it turned out, it also developed the mural's content. Up until that point, I had been unsure what the north wall mural should show. But with the river there as a given, it occurred to me that I could use this mural to show the river's history.

At the left end, it would start in the present day. Looking north from Mt. Washington, it would show downtown as it now looks. Then it would follow the Monongahela River to the right. Each time the river would enter one of the entrance niches, it would go back in time: first to 1946, when Pittsburgh was at its industrial height, and then to 1900, when Carnegie Tech was founded.

Once I decided on that course, the mural's composition took care of itself. The most important question, as it turned out, was a technical one: how to handle the dimensional tolerances of the entrance niches. We were still working in the Greenfield studio. The student center was not yet complete and could not yet be precisely measured, but the mural had to fit all these niches exactly.

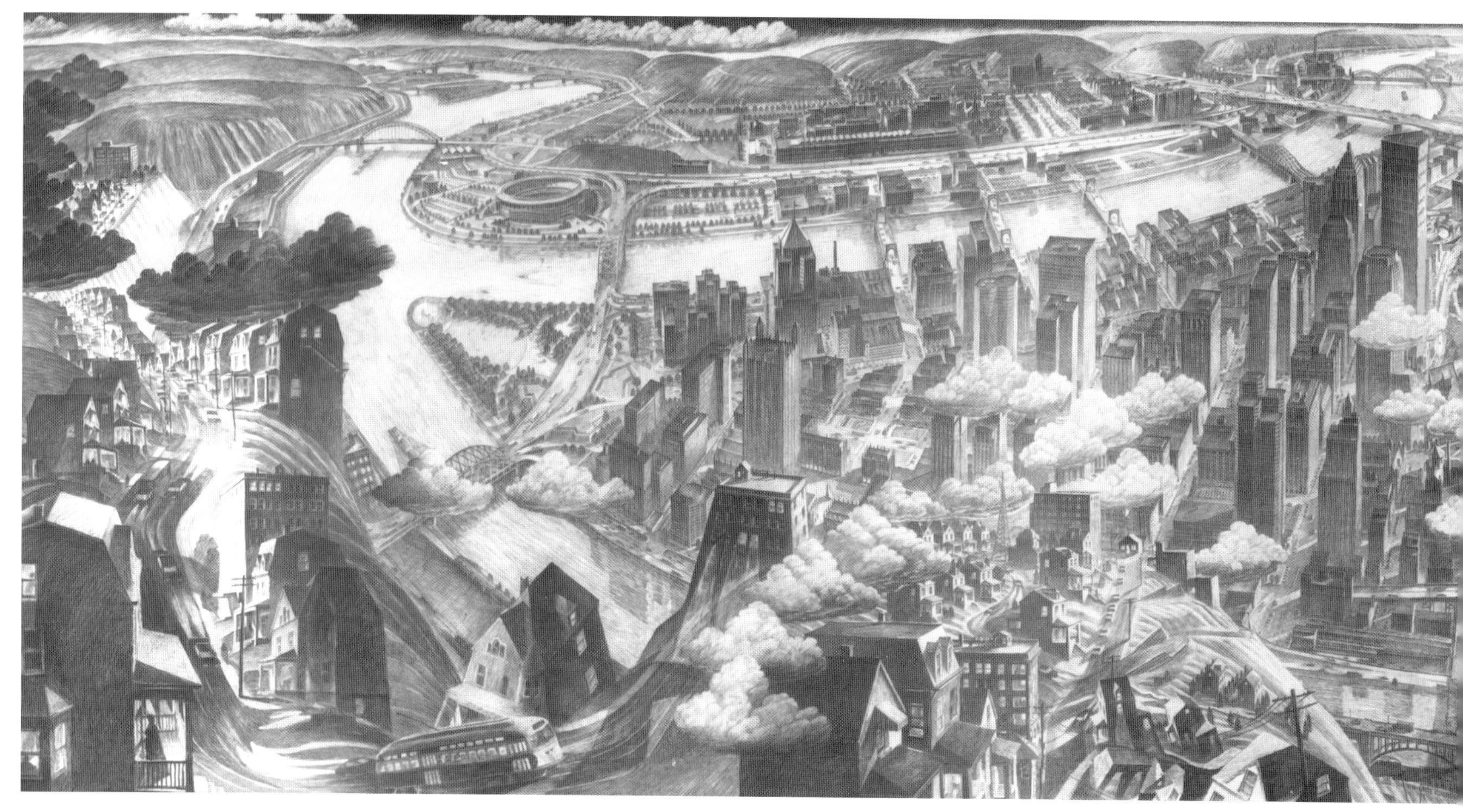

North wall, present-day downtown, from McCardle. University Center Mural. (Photo: Ken Andreyo.)

At the left end, it would start in the present day.

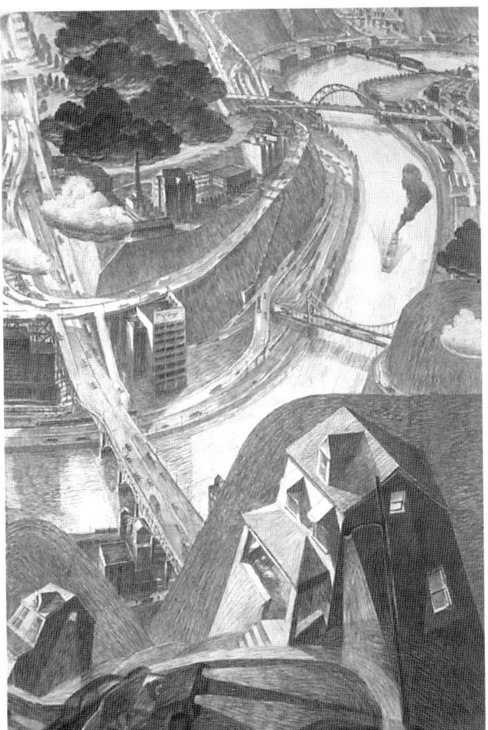

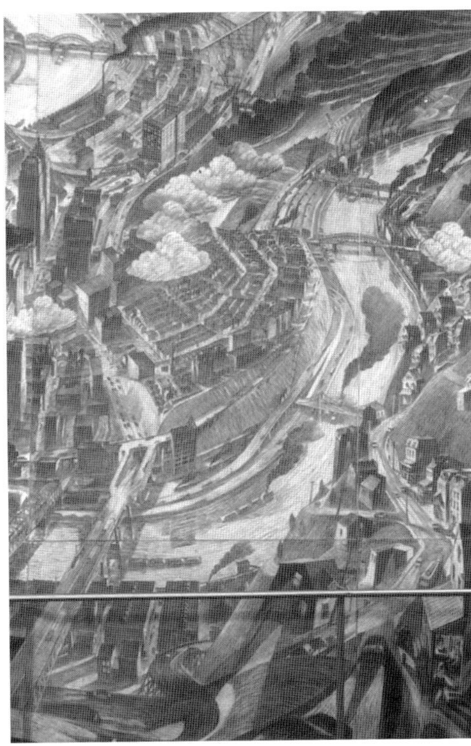

North wall. University Center Mural. (Photo: Ken Andreyo.)

Then it would follow the Monongahela River back in time.

First we built full-scale mock-ups of the two outboard niches. We pinned our panels in place and built into each mock-up a "keystone" piece centered over the entrance. These keystone pieces could be cut to size on site. We planned that when we would install the mural in early June, we would install these two outboard niches first, in effect working the ends toward the middle. With this method, the only panels we would have to cut to size and draw on site would be the two corner panels on each side of the central entrance niche.

Installing the Mural

We finished the drawing in late May 1996. After negotiating with the building trade unions on the job site, I had reached an agreement that I would hire one of their finish carpenters, Bill Nichols, to help with the installation. I would also hire my good friend Ross Kronenbitter, who had previously

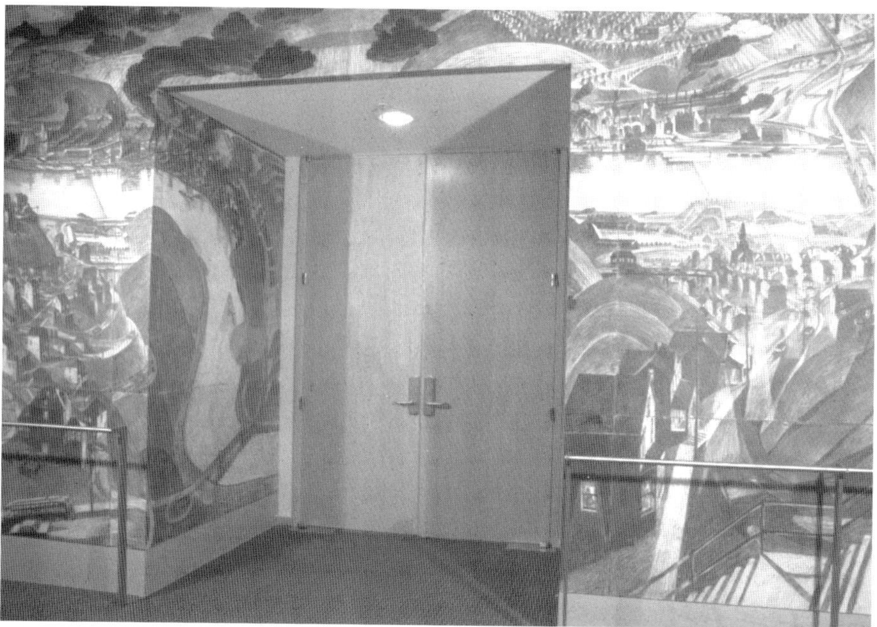

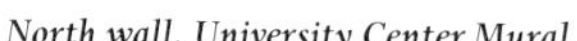

North wall. University Center Mural.

Fitting the panels to the entrance niches was the most difficult task.

installed murals with me at other sites. The two of them would do most of the installation. JT and I would serve as helpers.

We installed the mural over eight working days at the University Center. To connect the panels to the wall, we used aluminum mending plates affixed to the back of each panel. The plates on each panel slid into the slot provided by the thickness of the plates on the adjacent panel. In this way, sliding the hardware of each panel in behind its adjacent panel, we were able to install the mural with little visible hardware. We completed the installation on June 5. On June 9, I left for the next project in Germany.

Numbers

When I look back at this mural, which remains the longest, most time-consuming, heaviest, and most difficult I've ever done, raw numbers appear more and more to be part of the work's content. I am always asked questions such as "How long did it take?" and "How many panels are there?" It is therefore a fitting end to the story of this mural just to list the inventory.

There are 150 mural panels of varying sizes; the largest are 48″ x 90″.

The 48″ x 90″ upper panels weigh 100+ lbs. each.

The mural weighs approximately 7,000 lbs.

4,000 square feet of acid-free barrier paper are glued front and back to the ¾″ medium density fiberboard (MDF) panels.

30 gallons of acrylic Liquitex Gel Medium were used to glue the paper to the MDF panels.

3,120 sticks of vine charcoal were used to draw the image.

25 gallons of acrylic Liquitex Gloss Medium and varnish form a plastic undersurface to protect the paper.

10 gallons of Liquitex Soluvar picture varnish form the mural's outer surface. The mixture was 70 percent matte, 30 percent gloss.

The 150 panels are attached to the walls by 800 custom-made 1″ x ⅛″ x 6″ aluminum clips.

2,400 screws fasten the clips to the backs of the panels.

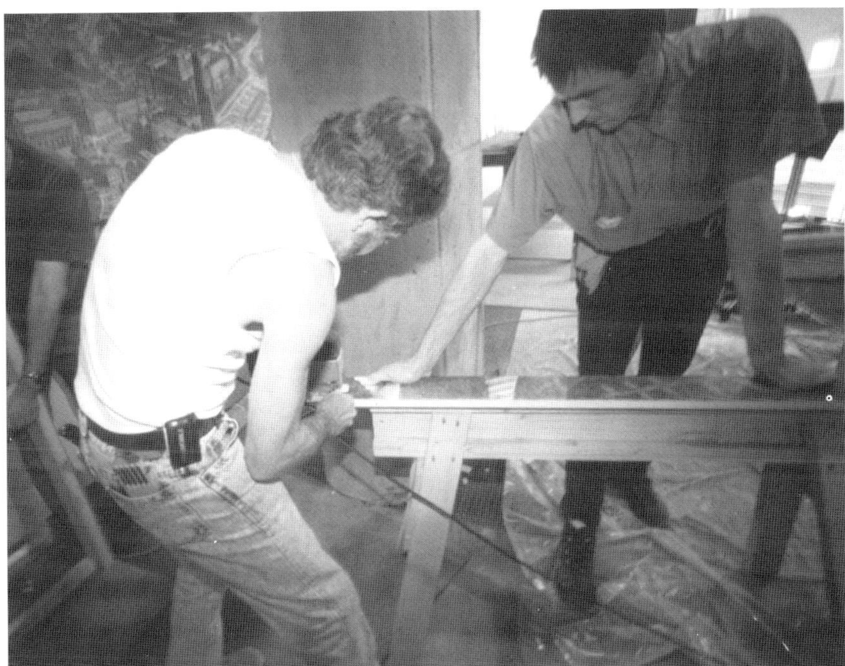

Installing the mural, June 1996. (Photo: Sarah Cooper.)

Bill Nichols (front) and Ross Kronenbitter (back) led the installation.

Local Works

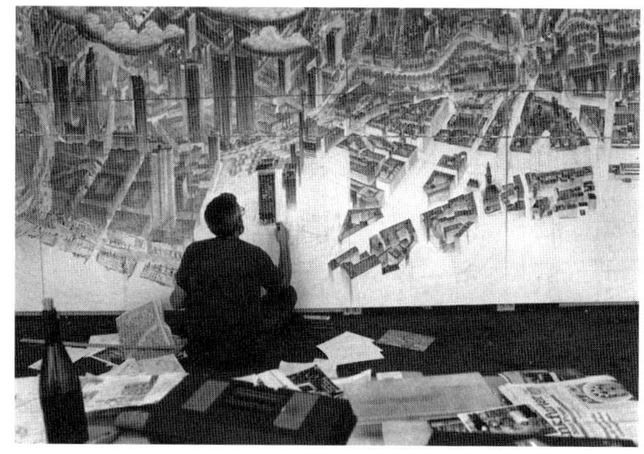

Working on the Kleinmarkthalle Mural, Frankfurt, 1996.

(Photo: Karl-Heinz Daniel.)

By late spring of 1997, I was burned out.

I *was exhausted.* By late spring of 1997, after completing two other large murals, one in Frankfurt and one in New York, I was burned out. Meg recognized it: the obsession with work, the lack of sleep. I did not.

But after a thirtieth anniversary trip to Hawaii, I went to Sam Berkovitz of Pittsburgh's Concept Gallery and arranged to do a show of smaller works on Pittsburgh's hillside neighborhoods. A second show about Pittsburgh's many bridges followed the next year.

I had been wary of working with a gallery. After my experiences with New York and Washington clients, I wanted no part of a high-profile gallery scene. But unlike those earlier experiences, working with Sam and the people at Concept has been rewarding.

Perhaps it has to do with the "local" and "regional" nature of the relationships involved. These are labels that in the art world are treated with disdain. In many quarters, to be characterized as a local or regional artist is to be dismissed as irrelevant. But to my way of thinking, there is integrity in the relationship between me and the people buying my works through Sam, and that integrity derives from its local nature. The works are bought out of genuine interest. They are bought out of love for the Pittsburgh landscape. I contrast this to what might have motivated the "King of the Malls" years ago. And on another level, I contrast this to what was said to me by a New York gallerist when I was just thirty-eight and about to have a show in New York. "You

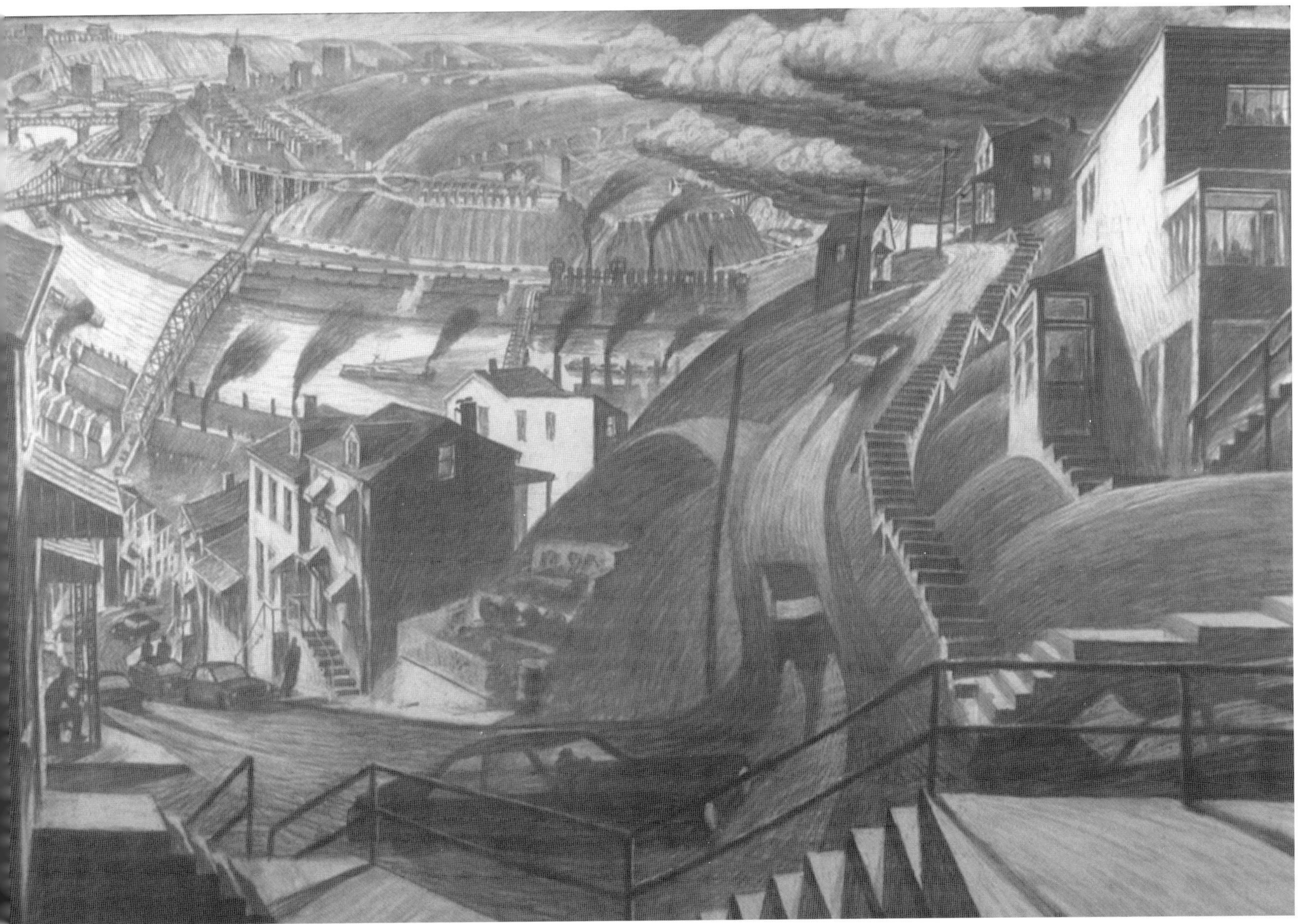

***West Wind*, 1997.** 36″ x 48″. (Private collection.)

I decided to do local works.

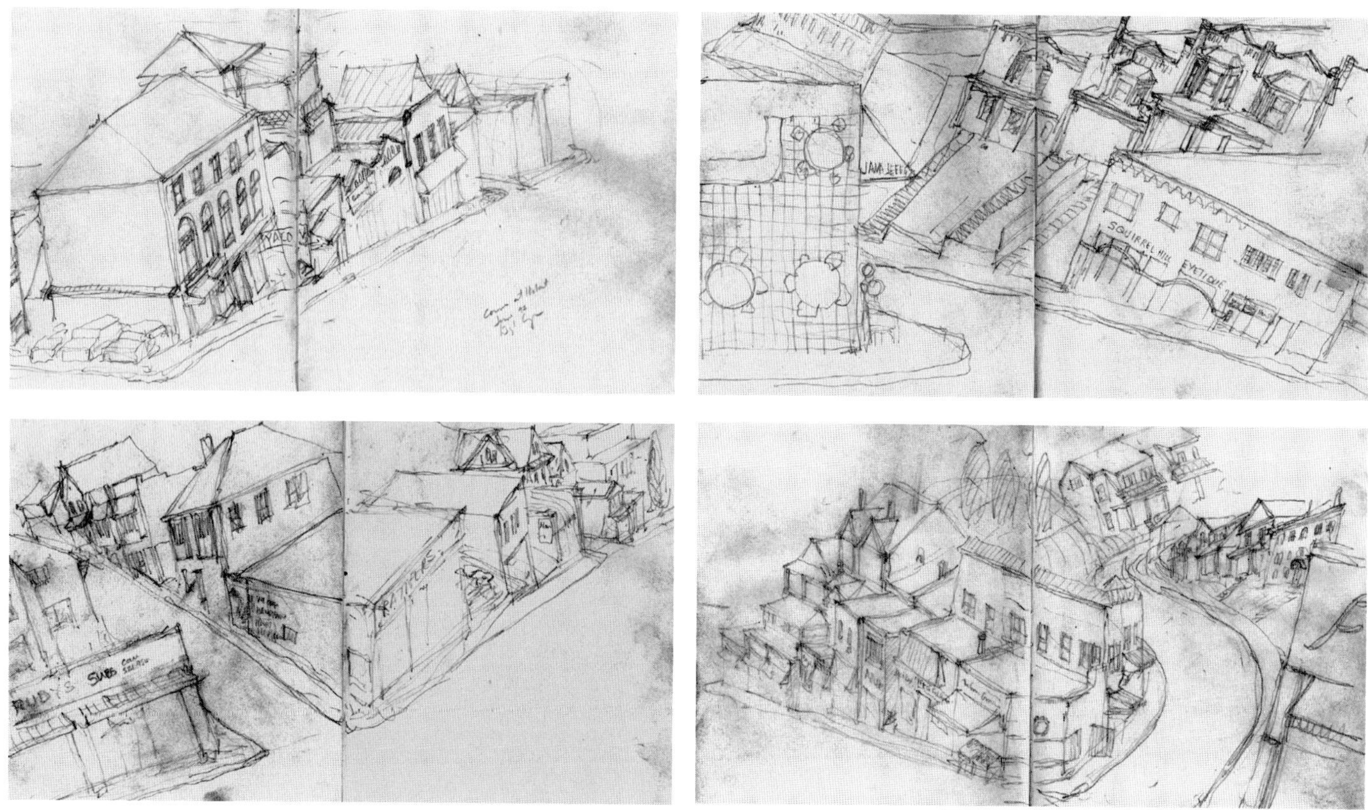

Sketches for Murray Hill Zig Zag.

know," he said, "You're probably too old. Most collectors will want to see a longer career so that the prices have sufficient time to rise."

And there have been other benefits. By doing smaller individual pieces, I have been able to draw sites in Pittsburgh which have long interested me but which could not fit into the context of whatever mural I was doing. For years, I have been fascinated by the part of Murray Avenue that leads steeply down the hill from Beacon to Forward. I've driven down it often enough—it's on the way to my studio. Driving down Murray, I've had several near misses; what has distracted me has been a desire to look up the many side streets that rise up to the left and right. I tried to capture this sense of distraction in one drawing. The

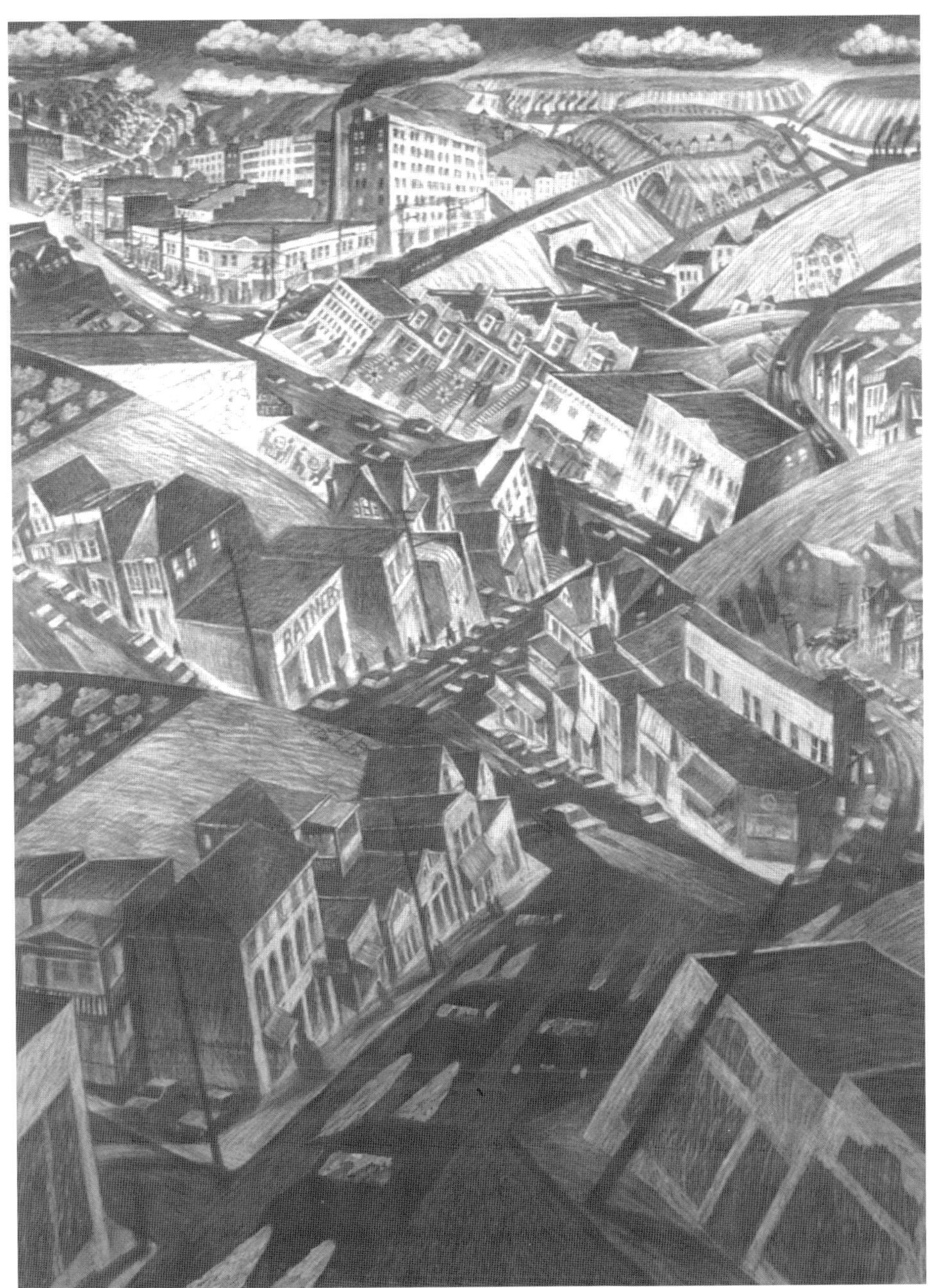

Murray Hill Zig Zag, *1997*. 64″ x 48″.

I walked down the hill, did the sketches as I went, and then pieced them together.

drawing is a composite of sorts, based on a series of sketches I did one day in June of 1997.

I started near the top of the hill opposite the gas station and looked across Murray at an interesting set of houses and stores. Then I walked down further, crossed the street, and drew Hobart Road sweeping up and away from the corner at the Green Grocer. Then I crossed the street again, and then I crossed the street again, and then I paused for a coffee. The zigzag structure of the work arose in setting these discrete views together.

Another "journey" drawing describes a steep section of Monteiro St. that Meg has often driven me down. I hate roller coasters. I don't have the stomach for them. When my cataracts were at their worst, Meg took on the task of driving me to my studio. That part was very nice, but the payback she required was the right to torment me with daily detours down this steep, narrow, down-then-up hill that she had discovered one day as we drove through Greenfield. And she took this hill at a speed with enough G-force to pool my breakfast in my feet. So steep was this hill that it had five salt boxes for winter ice along its curb.

Sam has also brought me clients for several mural commissions in the Pittsburgh area, one for the offices of Deloitte Consulting in the PPG Building and the other for Mascaro Construction Company in Manchester. Deloitte Consulting is a company that very much prides itself on its personal interaction with its clients. Thus the mural is centered in a Pittsburgh neighborhood—I chose Spring Hill because of its view over downtown from the north, a direction I had never drawn, and includes several of the buildings associated with Deloitte Consulting's many public sector clients.

With the Mascaro mural, the height of the entrance lobby in which the mural was to be installed became the first issue. The space is twenty-five-feet tall but only fifteen-feet deep. Near the ceiling, viewing angles are steep indeed. In our early discussions, Jack Mascaro, the company's owner, emphasized that he wanted the mural to communicate his company's business—that it is a construction company. Jack is wonderfully direct, and he put it this way: "When

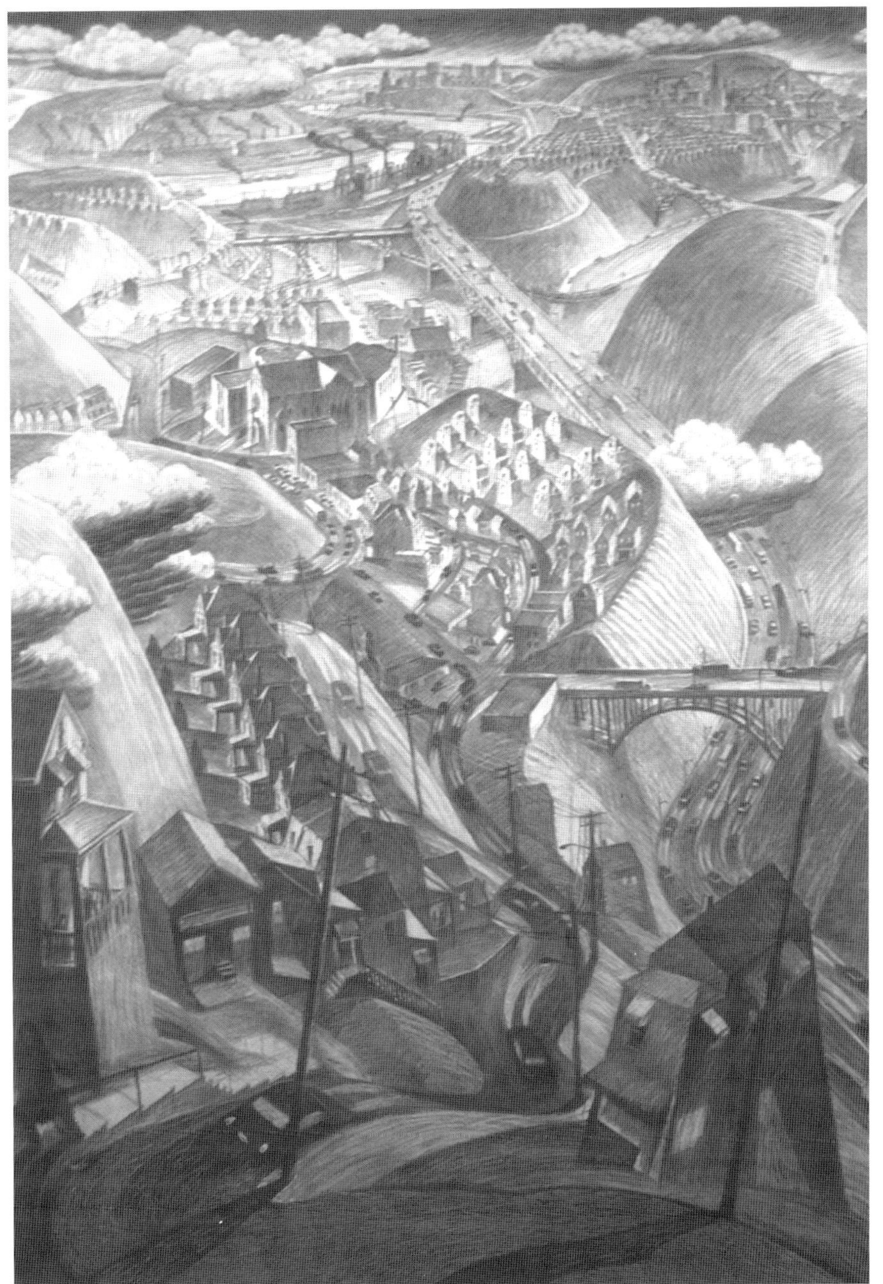

***Five Saltbox Hill*, *1997*.** 64″ x 48″. (Private collection.)

Meg always takes this hill with enough G-force to pool my breakfast in my feet.

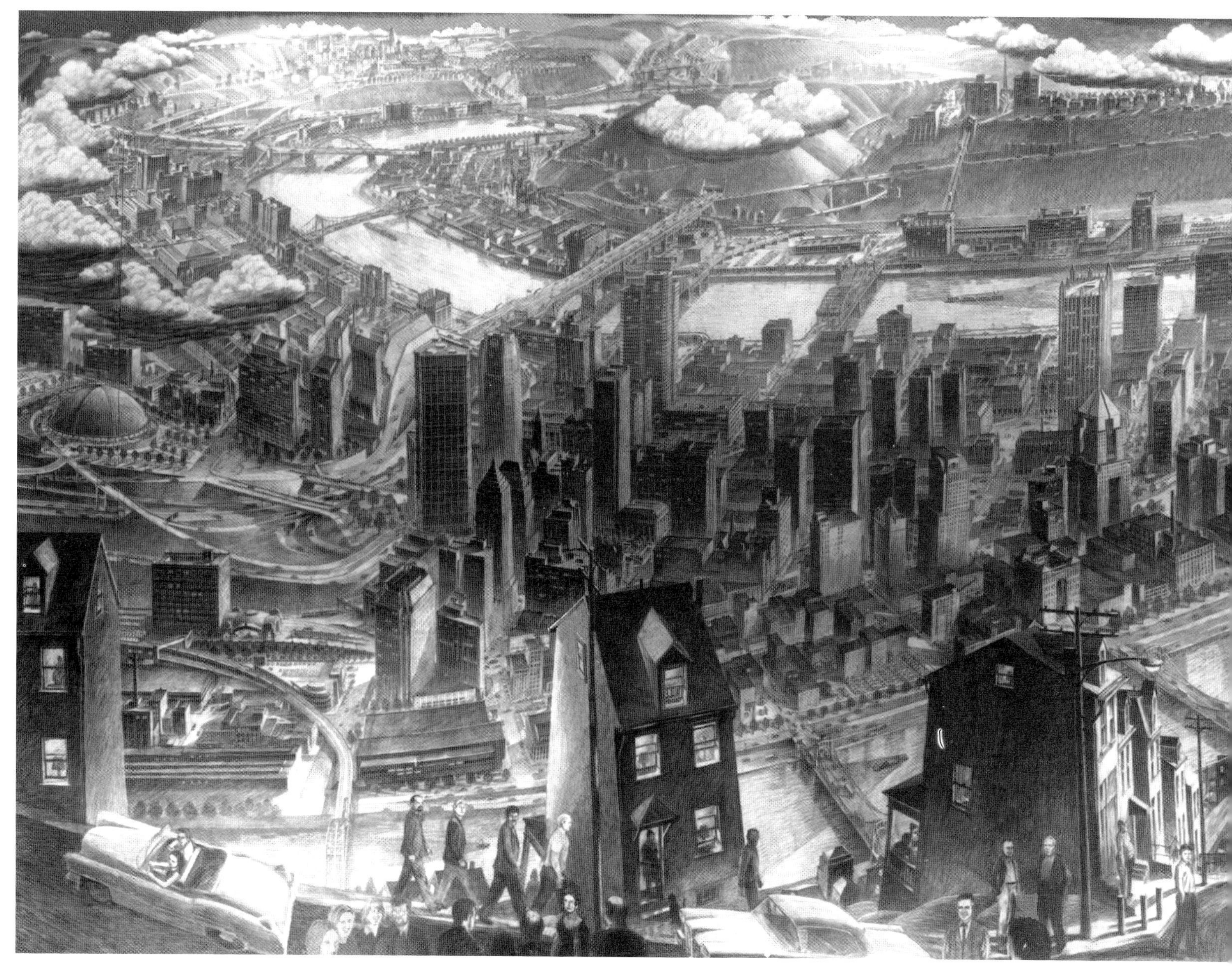

Spring Hill. Deloitte Consulting Mural, 1998.

The mural is centered in Spring Hill.

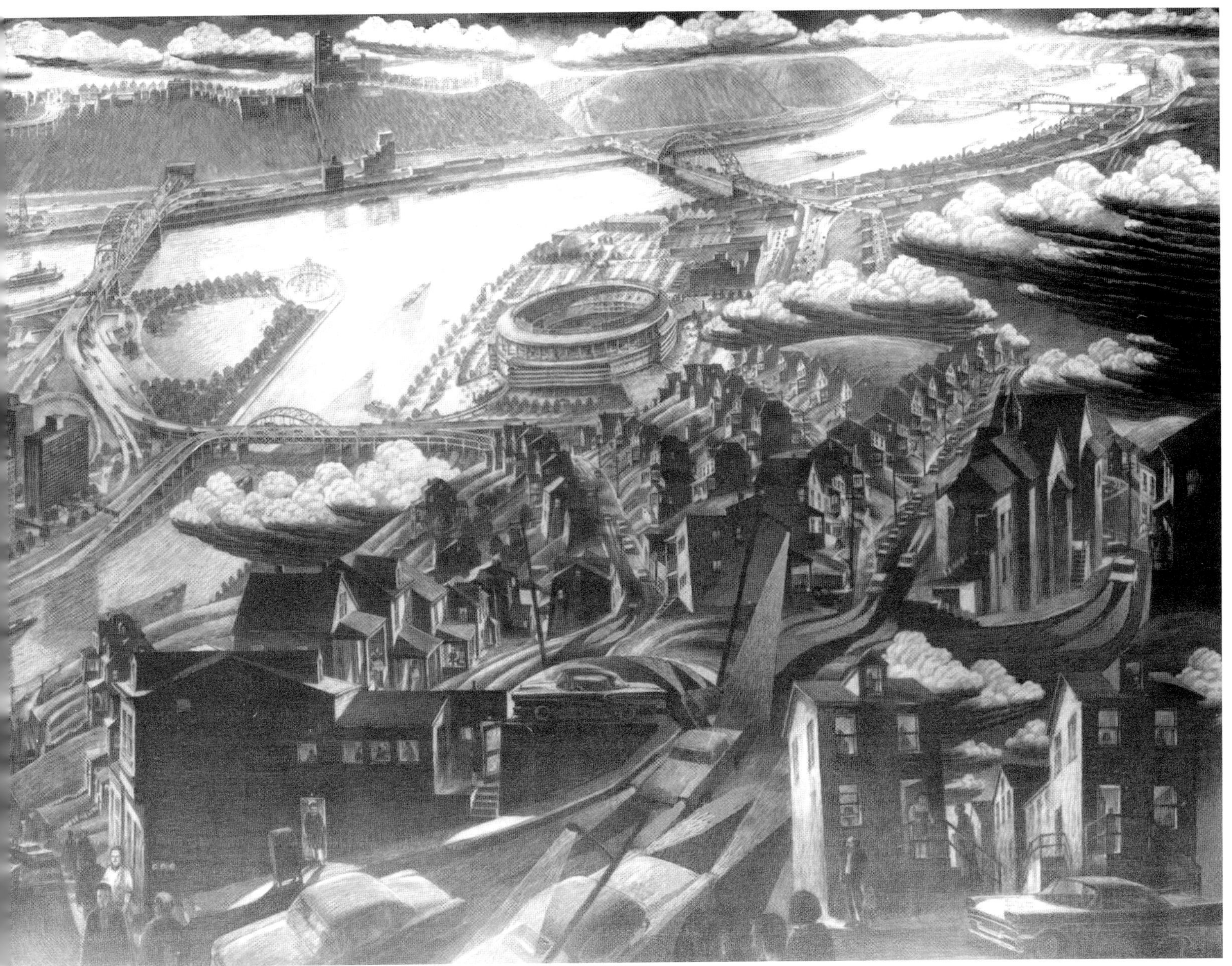

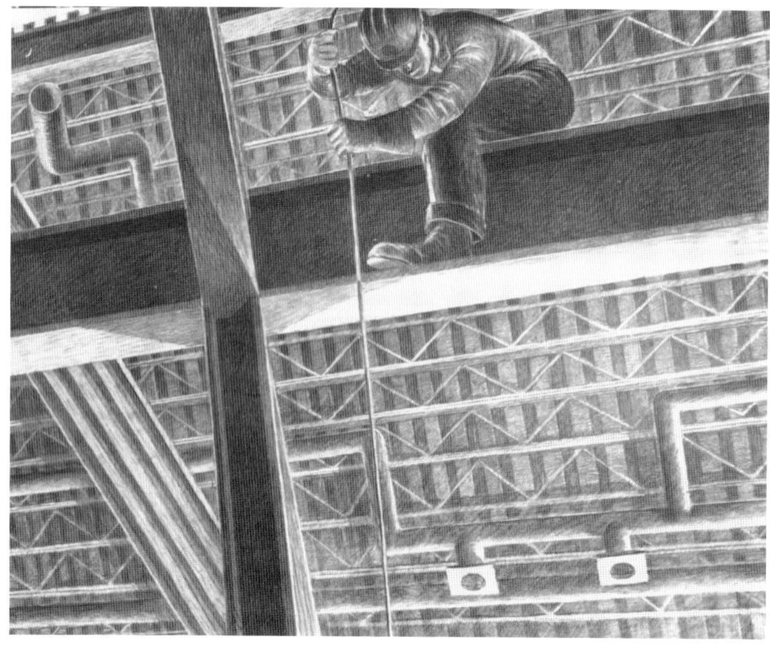

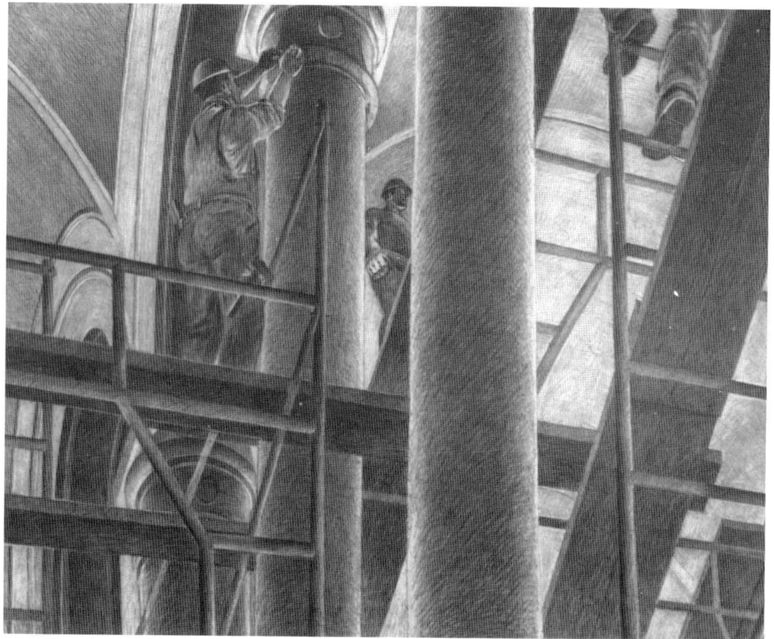

Mascaro Mural, 1999.

Both sides emphasize the vertical dimension of the space.

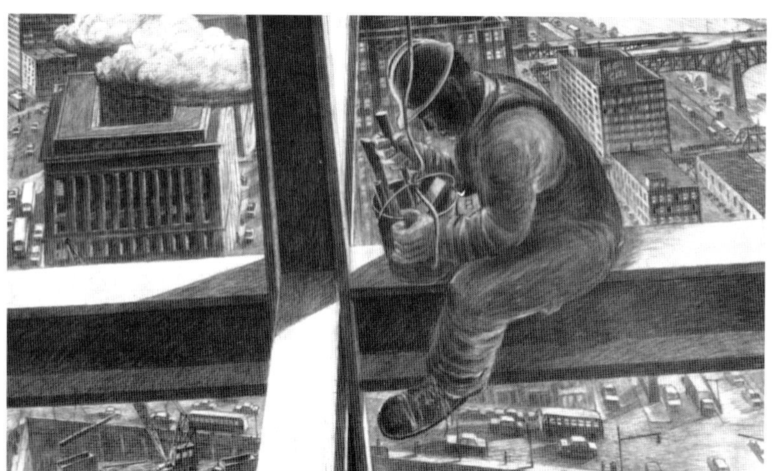

clients come in the door, I want them to say two things. I want them to say, 'Wow!' and I want them to say, 'They build things here!'" This content, together with the steep sight lines, led quickly to my approach.

I developed the view as a steep view up through two fictitious building sites—one on each side of the space. The one on the left imagined a historic restoration of the kind Mascaro has often done. It looks upward through a grid of workers on scaffolds. The other shows a view up through the steel cage of a new building.

Both of these steep views gave me an opportunity for using JT's ability to draw figures skillfully in perspective (JT had continued to work for me on and off). Ironworkers are shown walking the beams at dizzying heights while cranes are lifting other beams into place. Both sides emphasize the vertical dimension of the space, and once again I used the decelerated perspective I had used in the University Center mural to make the convergence believable for viewers down below. Woven through these views of construction is a background Pittsburgh landscape featuring many of the buildings completed by Mascaro and highlighting the Italian roots of the Mascaro family.

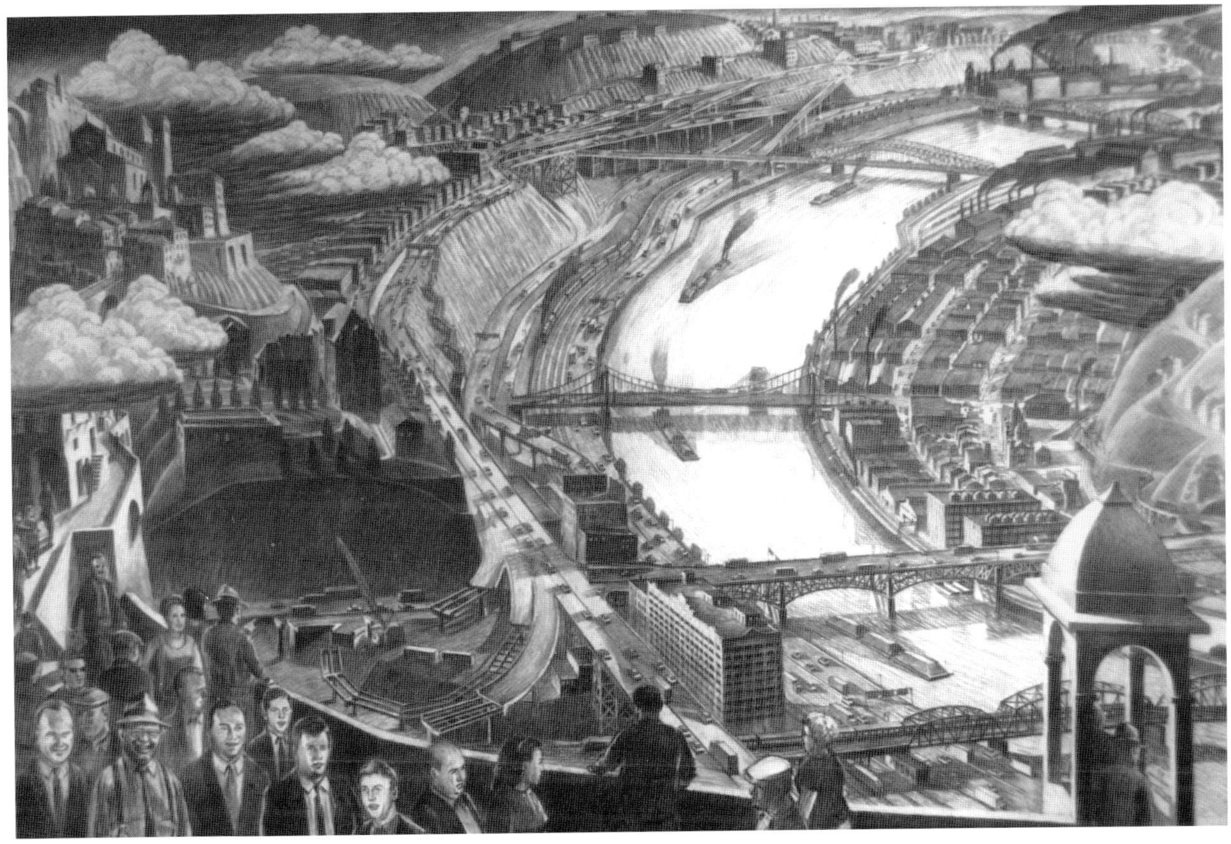

Mascaro Mural.

The background shows the Pittsburgh landscape and highlights the Italian roots of the Mascaro family.

Finding Mema: The Past and Future Day

Forbes Field from the right-field stands. World Series, game 1, 1925. *(Courtesy Pittsburgh History and Landmarks Foundation.)*

Because of the photograph's detail, I wanted to know exactly where he and Mema had sat.

I*t was as if* I had just gotten off the train with my father and been delivered by my Aunt Mary to see Mema once again. Only this time, my grandmother was younger and more stylish, and my father was still a young man.

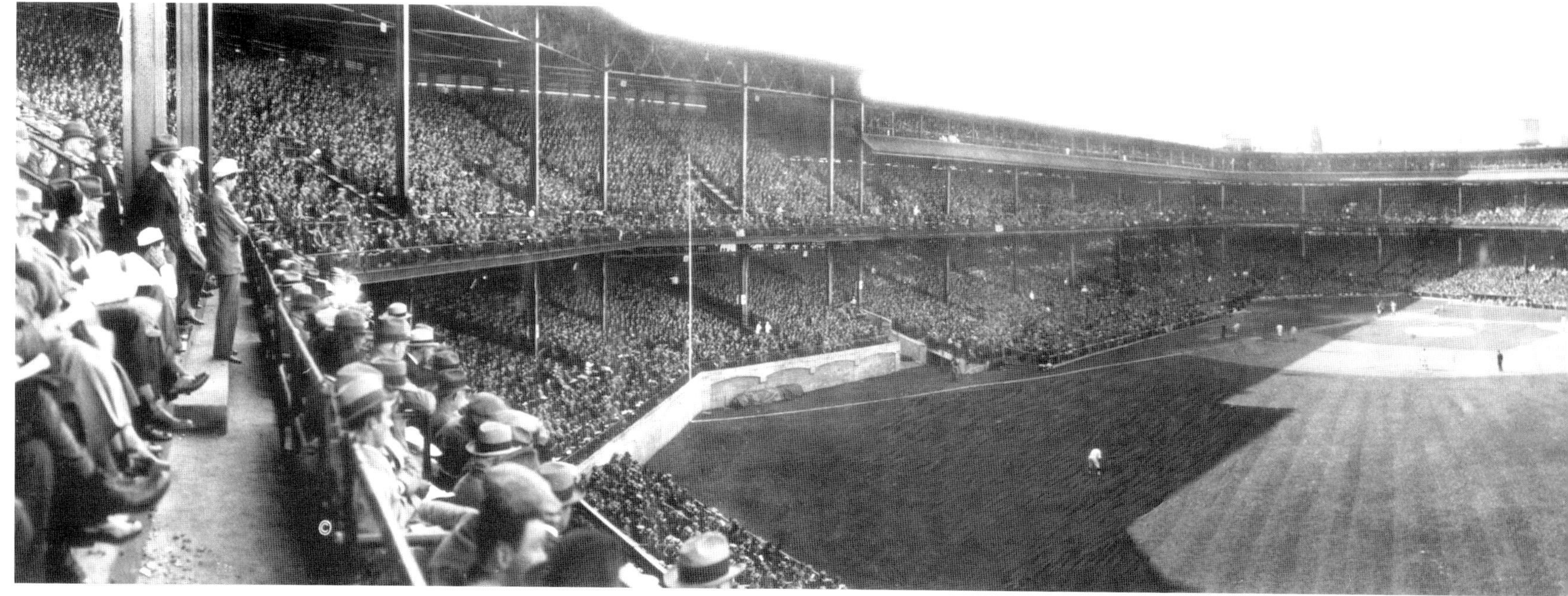

It was December of 1997. I had gone to an exhibition of photographs of Pittsburgh called "Pittsburgh Revealed" at the Carnegie Museum, an exhibition filled with evocative black and white images of the Pittsburgh industrial landscape from photographers such as Lewis Hine, Luke Swank, and Todd Webb. But the photograph that brought me back to this exhibition again and again was a large, panoramic view of Forbes Field taken from the right-field stands during the first game of the 1925 World Series between the Pirates and the Washington Senators.

It is a dramatic view filled with personal details and small stories. The museum kept a small set of portable steps available nearby, and each time I went, I climbed these so I could study the photograph from close up. Most of the fans are men wearing hats. In the lower-right corner in the bleachers behind the outfield wall, a fan can be seen sneaking a friend into the game by hoisting him up over the outside wall.

Many years before, my father had told me he had attended this game, and

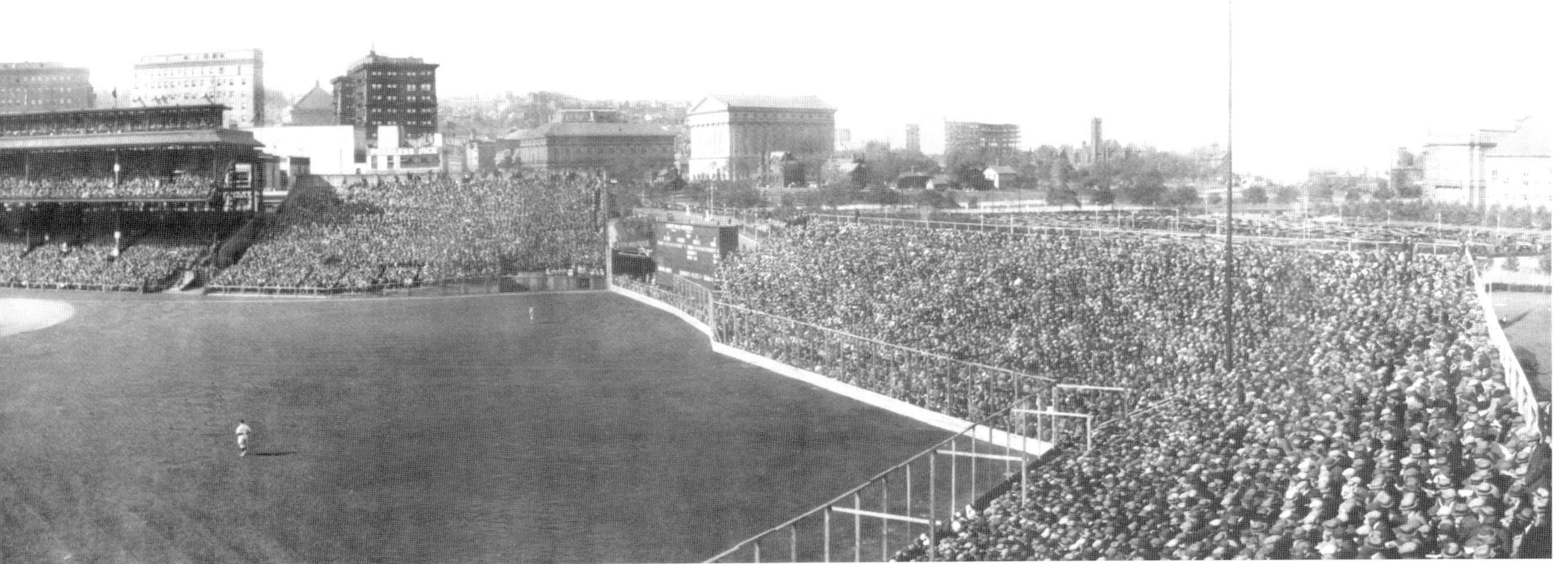

so, between trips to the museum, I told him about this photograph I had found and asked him to tell me more about the game.

"Mema took me," he said. I'd never known Mema had taken him. I'd always just assumed it was a father-son outing. "It was cold and drizzly when we stood in line for the tickets, but it cleared up later in the day. The great Walter Johnson pitched superbly, and the Senators won the game."

But because of the photograph's detail, I wanted most of all to know exactly where he and Mema had sat. "We were in the upper deck," he said, "four or five rows from the top and about in line with the first base line."

It was just where I had hoped they would be.

Using a magnifying glass, I found them quickly. There were, after all, very few women in the stands. Several rows from the top I found my father, a very handsome looking fourteen-year-old boy. Next to him is Mema, in a black hat with a feather.

Next week, I will start a drawing of the McKees Rocks Bridge, which has caught my eye recently. I will drive over the bridge many times—from one end to the other. It is the approach to this bridge over the "Bottoms" that fascinates me. I will see the churches and houses and backyards that it passes over. I will take my sketchbook—it is winter still—and I will draw it quickly. I will record the to-and-fro and up-and-down of its passage. And then in my studio I will complete the drawing from memory in charcoal.

It will be dark. In my memory of my visit to Mema, Pittsburgh is always dark. It will be light. In my memory from my visit to Mema, the light always flares out in Pittsburgh. From this bridge, I will see once again the city that so fascinated me in my childhood, the city forever caught between shadow and light, the city of coal, water, fire, and steel.

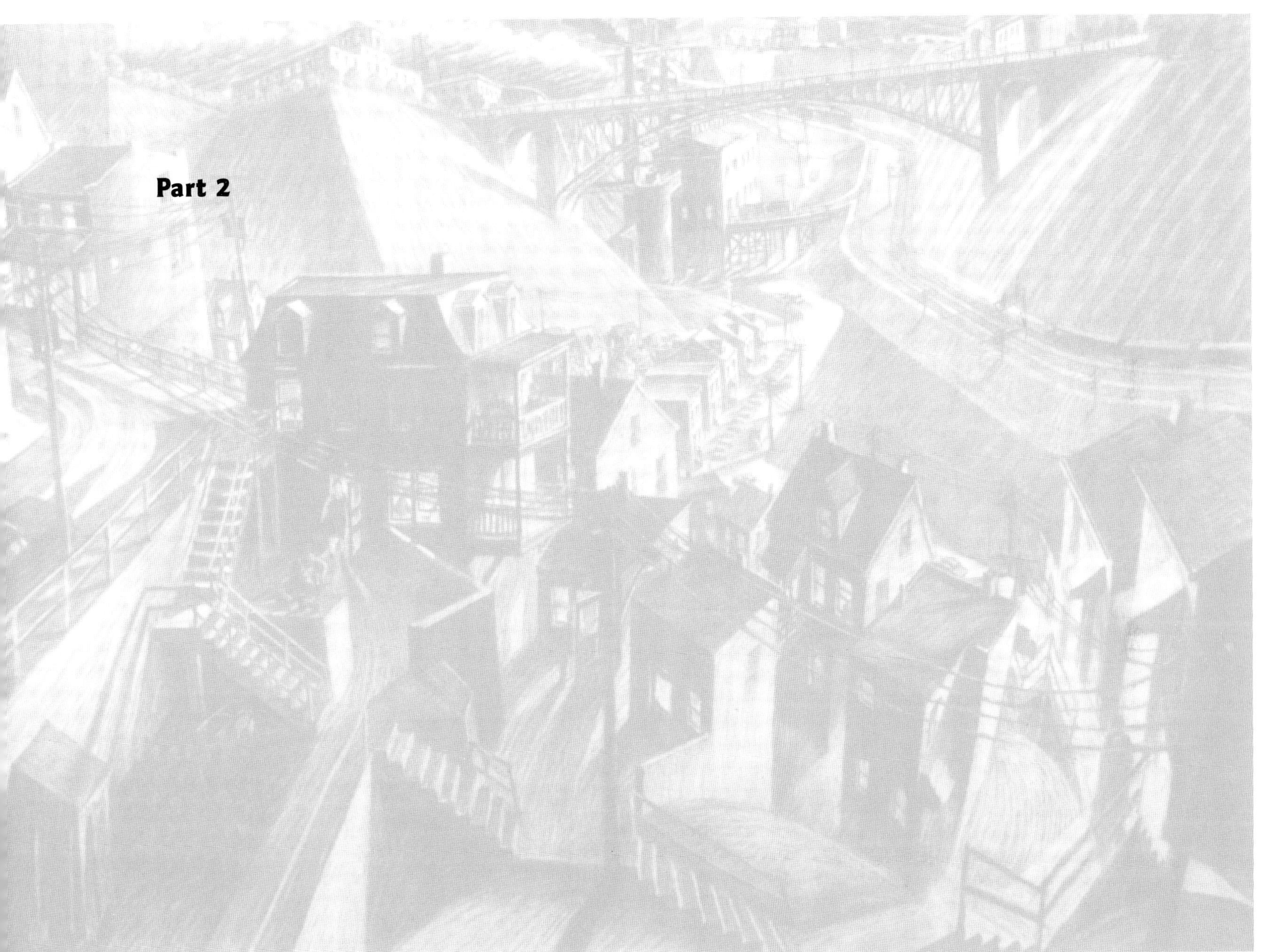

Part 2

The City and Its Neighborhoods through Time

Words by Pittsburgh Writers, Art from the Murals

Oakland

Carnegie Museum

It was a great town to grow up in, Pittsburgh. With one thousand other Pittsburgh schoolchildren, I attended free art classes in Carnegie Music Hall every Saturday morning for four years. Every week seven or eight chosen kids reproduced their last week's drawings in thick chalks at enormous easels on stage in front of the thousand other kids. After class, everyone scattered; I roamed the enormous building.

Under one roof were the music hall, library, art museum, and natural history museum. Late in the afternoon, after the other kids were all gone, I liked to draw hours-long pencil studies of the chilly marble sculptures in the great hall of classical sculpture. I sat on one man's plinth and drew the next man over—until, during the course of one winter, I had worked my way around the great hall. From these sculptures I learned a great deal about the human leg and not much about the neck, which I could hardly see. I ate a basement-cafeteria lunch and wandered the fabulous building. The natural history museum dominated it.

I felt I was most myself here, here in the churchlike dark lighted by painted dioramas in which tiny shaggy buffalo grazed as far as the eye could see on an

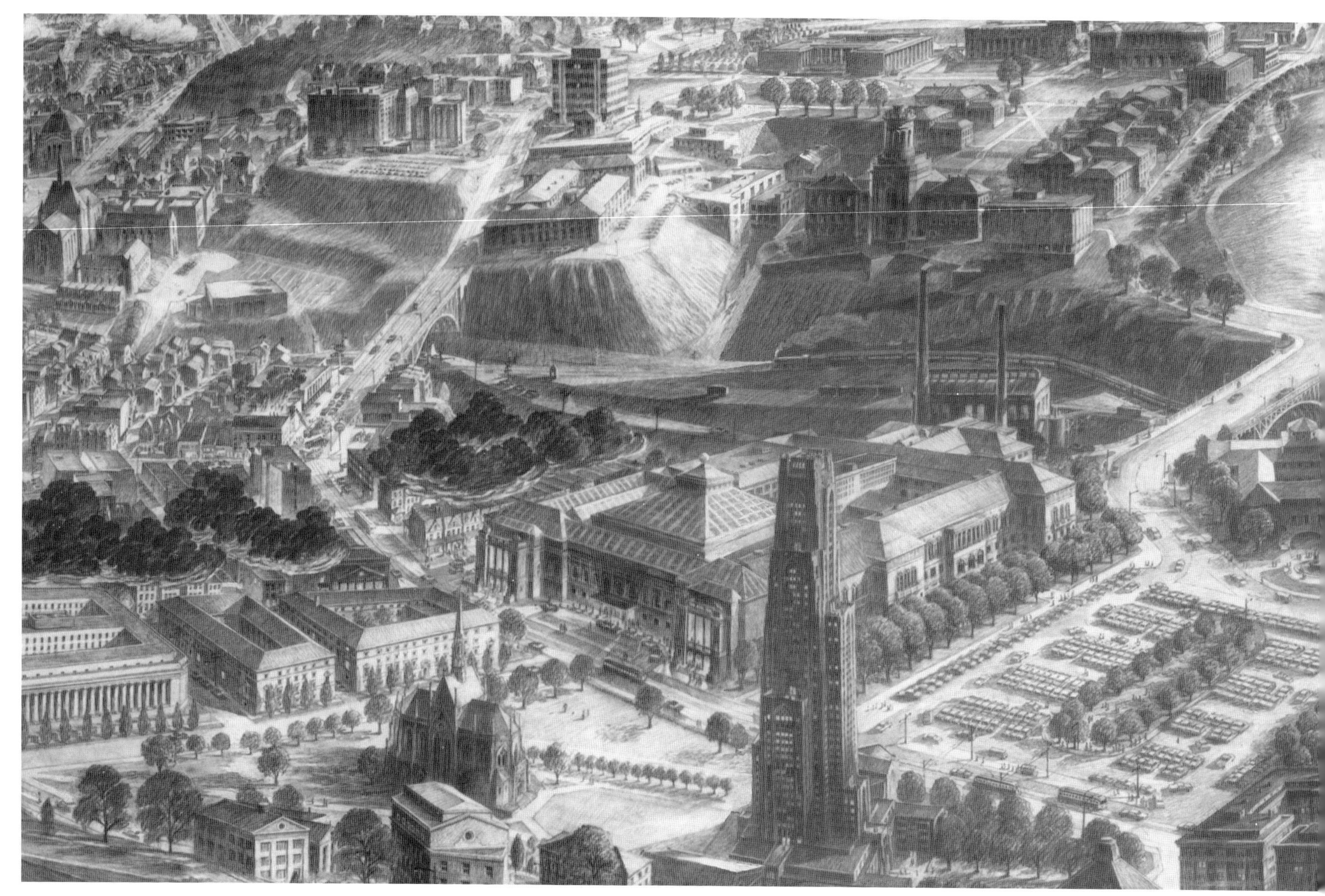

Oakland panorama, East Wall. University Center Mural. (Photo: Ken Andreyo.)

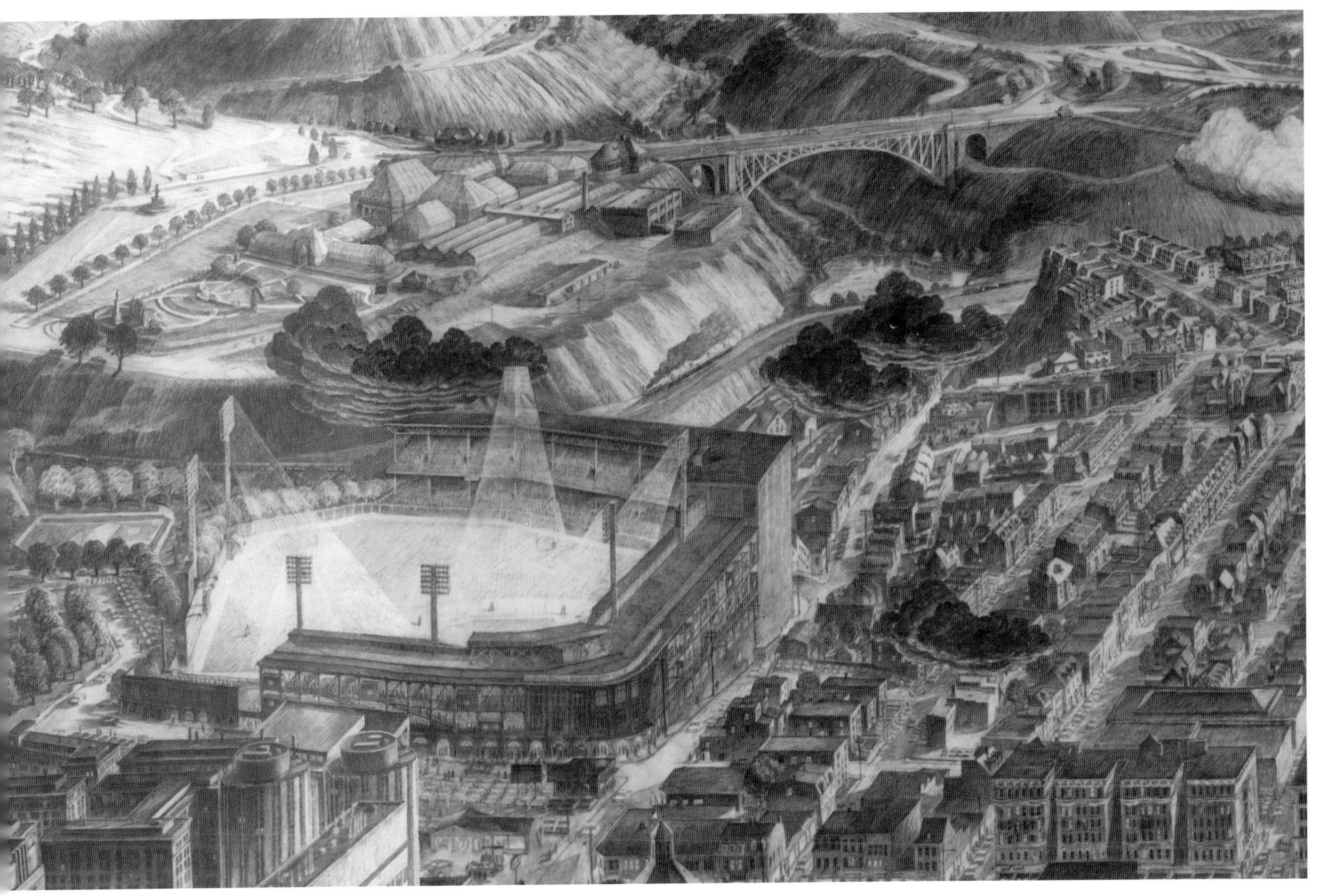

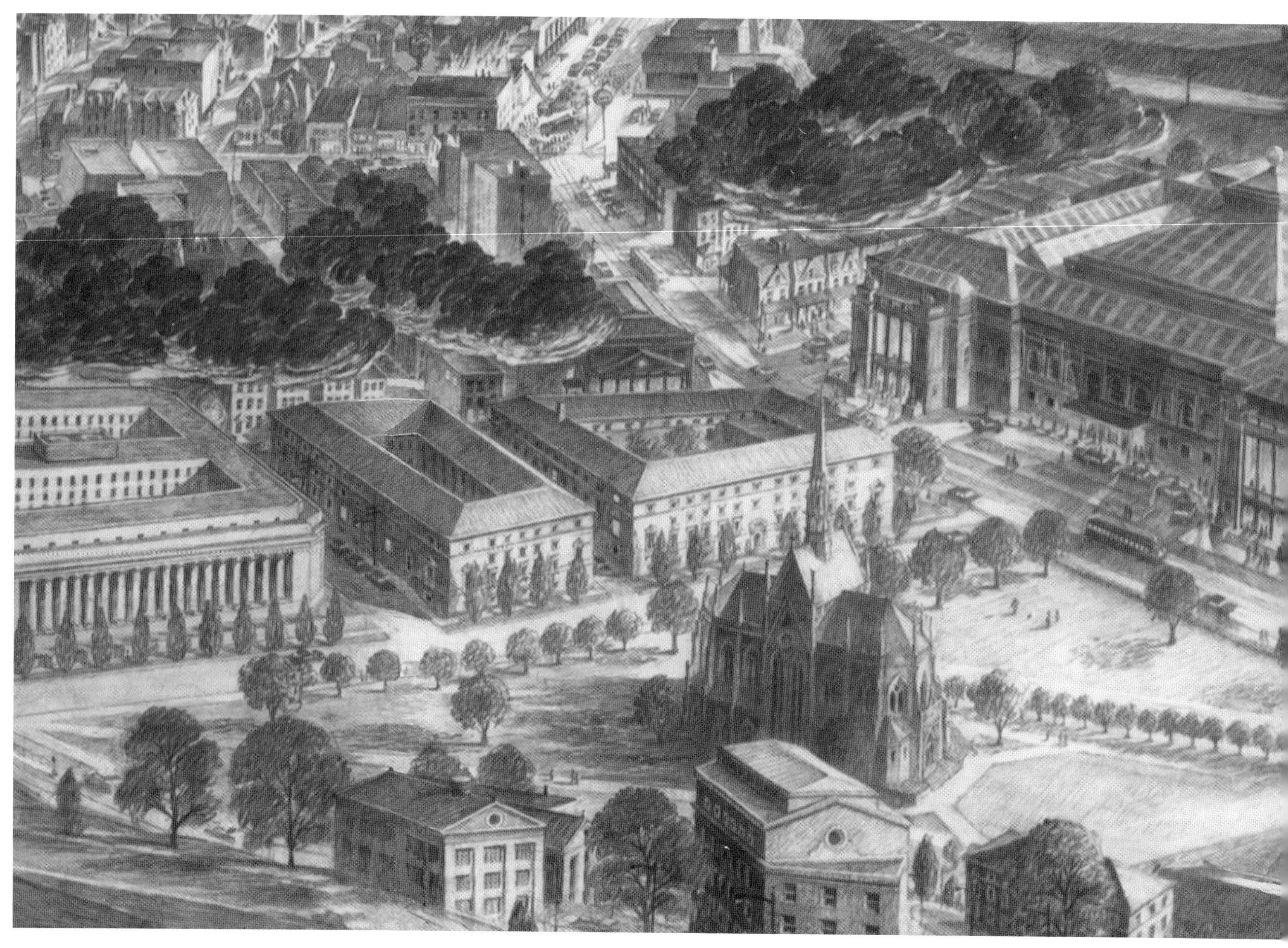

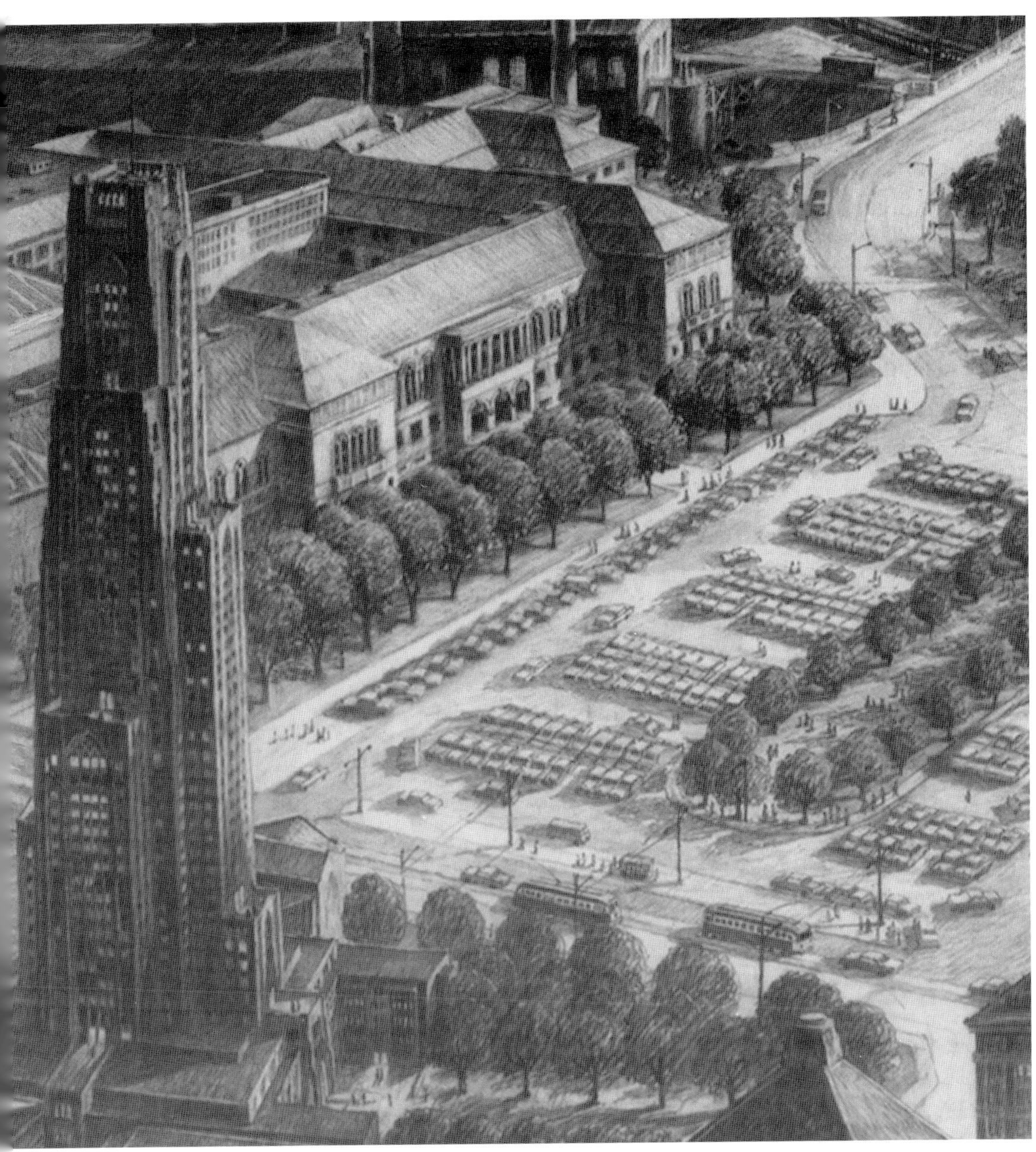

Carnegie Museum, East Wall. University Center Mural.

(Photo: Ken Andreyo.)

Under one roof were the music hall, library, art museum, and natural history museum.

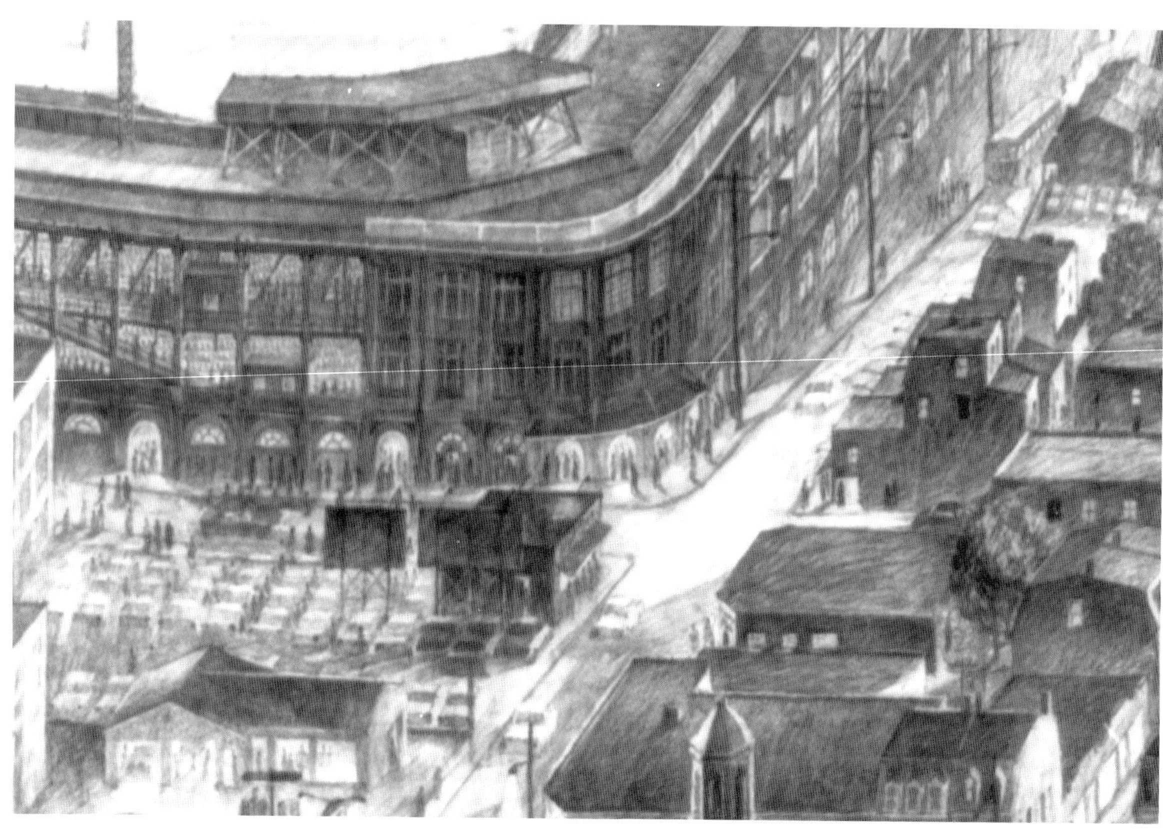

Forbes Field, back of home plate. East Wall, University Center Mural. (Photo: Ken Andreyo.)

enormous prairie I could span with my arms. I could lose myself here, in the cavernous vault with the shadow of a tyrannosaurus skeleton spread looming all over the domed ceiling, the skeleton shadow enlarged the size of the Milky Way, each bone a dark star.

—ANNIE DILLARD, *An American Childhood*

Forbes Field, 1960

Church bells still were ringing at 11:30 P.M. as the goggle-eyed city partied. The only orderly celebration may have been, in fact, the "official victory party" for the entire Pirates' organization in Webster Hall Hotel. The only out-door space spared from the horn blowing and bell clanging was antiquated Forbes Field, major league baseball's second oldest park. A gentle fall breeze rippled the ivy clinging to the left-field wall. There at 3:36.30, New York's Yogi Berra

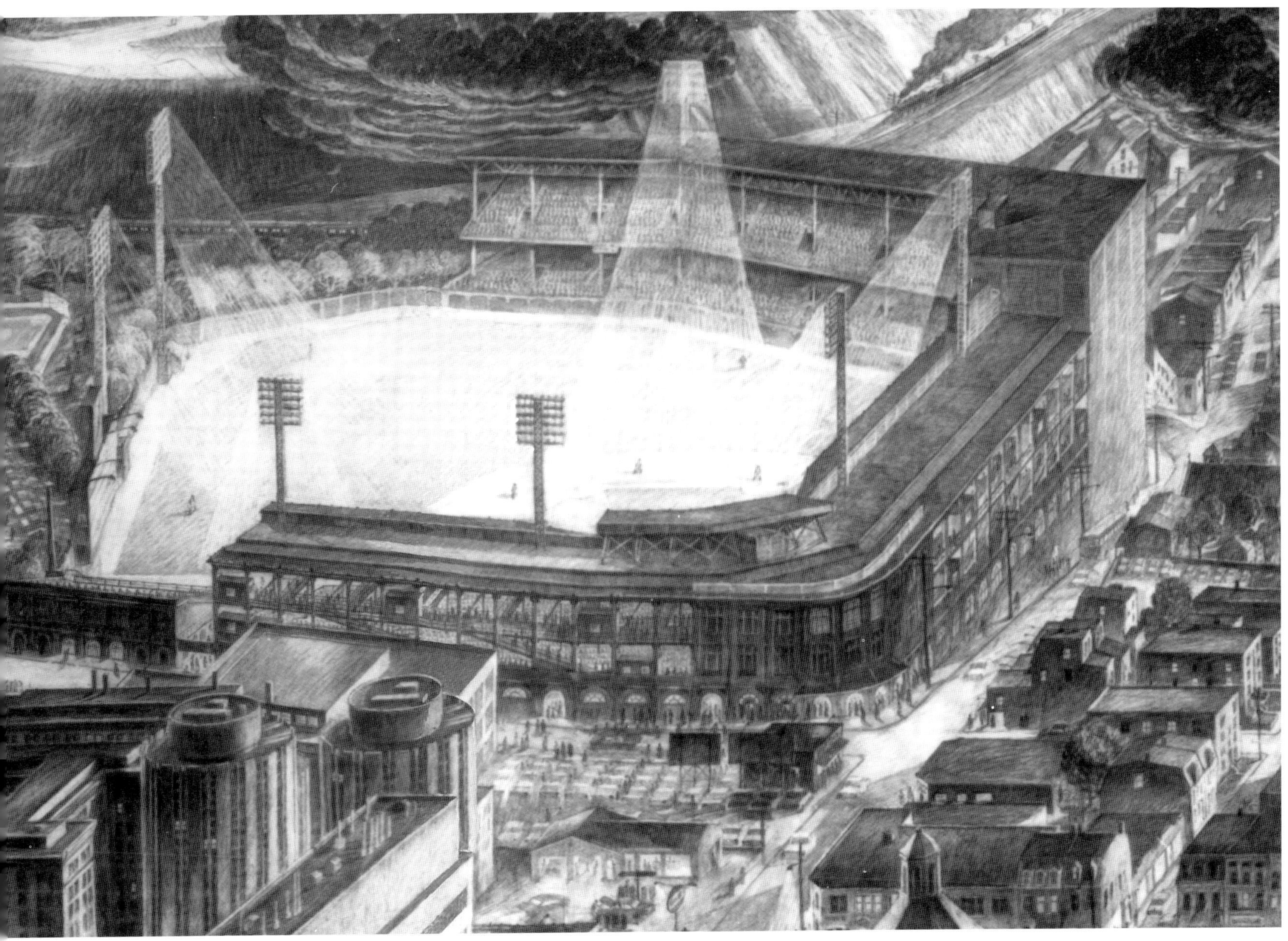

Forbes Field. East Wall, University Center Mural. (Photo: Ken Andreyo.)

The only outdoor space spared from the horn blowing and bell clanging was antiquated Forbes Field, major league baseball's second oldest park.

had pivoted to watch a baseball sail over the fence. No. 9, Bill Mazeroski, had hit it. And he was dancing, waving his cap, and circling the bases in the slight formality that stood between Pittsburgh and its first World Championship since 1925.

—DICK GROAT AND BILL SURFACE, *The World Champion Pittsburgh Pirates*

Green Weenie

You could buy a Green Weenie from your favorite Forbes Field vendor. You could shake it, and you could make some serious noise; official Green Weenies had lots of little particles inside. The idea, Bob Prince said, was to shake hundreds and thousands of Green Weenies at the other team's pitcher. He went on the air to warn the pitcher, fair and square, that "The Green Weenie Whammy will getcha."

—TOM MCMILLAN, "When Prince Was King"
(courtesy *Pittsburgh Post-Gazette*)

Chasing Foul Balls

I used to stand out and hope that they would hit a foul ball over the fence so I could run after it and catch it. Finally one day one of the kids got brave and pulled one of the planks off the back of Forbes Field. Just was big enough for kids to get through, and we all went in, underneath the right field bleachers. And that's the first time I got a sight of Forbes Field. Inside. Good.

—REVEREND HAROLD TINKER, center fielder, Pittsburgh Crawfords,
"A Map of Memories"

Living with Meg across from Forbes Field

Meg and I married in 1967, and soon thereafter, we moved into a first-floor duplex apartment along Bouquet Street opposite Forbes Field, where we would live for three years. It was within walking distance of Carnegie Tech, where I was studying architecture. That was the feature we emphasized for both sets of parents. The real reason we moved there was baseball.

Our apartment was up a steep climb of steps from Bouquet Street. From

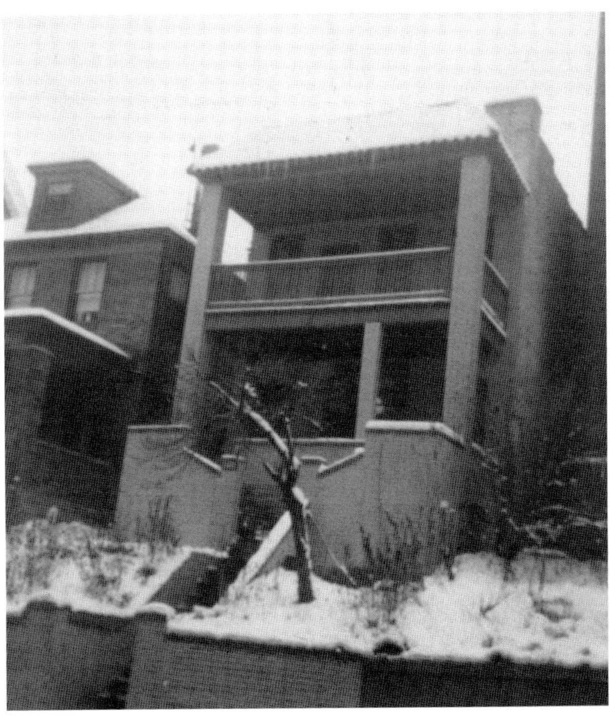

260 Bouquet St., 1967–1970.

Our apartment was up a steep climb of steps from Bouquet St.

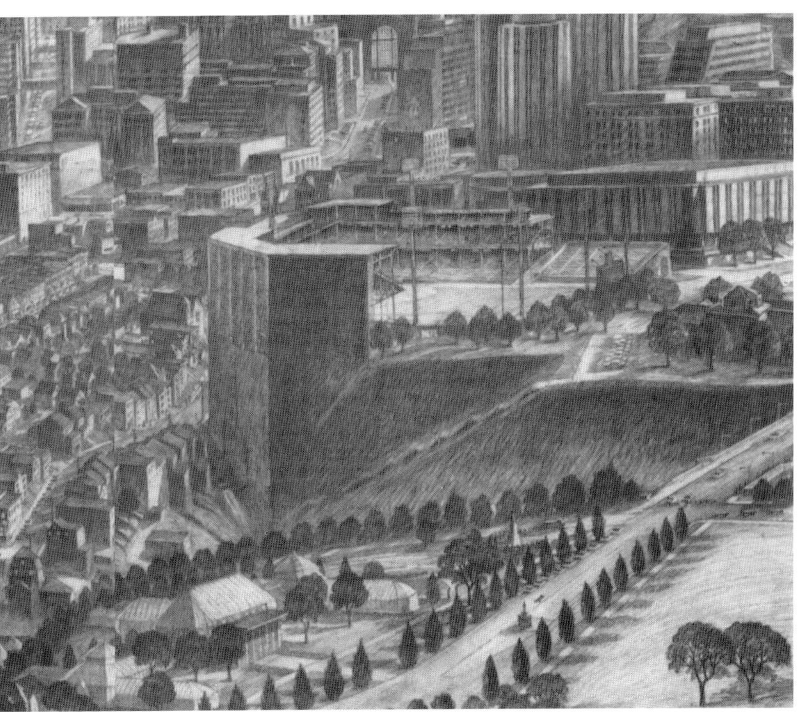

Forbes Field. East Wall, University Center Mural. (Photo: Ken Andreyo.)

The real reason we moved there was baseball.

our front porch we had a good overview of the street and, more important, the players' entrance directly across from us. We were close enough to the grandstand that fans taking a break between innings along the outside rail could call down to us if we were sitting on our porch. Our neighbors in the second-floor apartment were high enough to see over the lower grandstand and into the field, where they had a good view of second base.

Downstairs we had to be content with a somewhat confused sense of the events of Forbes Field on the basis of sound alone. A Saturday afternoon promotion, which would fill the nearby right field stands with several thousand Cub Scouts cheering every wiggle and waggle, would distort our impression of the game's progress. That first summer Meg and I woke up one Saturday morning (our bedroom faced away from the field) startled by lions roaring and elephants trumpeting off in the distance. The previous evening the annual Police Circus had moved in and the outfield was now a parking lot of caged beasts.

Bouquet Street was fast becoming a student ghetto, but it still had the flavor of the first-generation Italian neighborhood it had once been. At the end of Bouquet Street, down the city steps below Dawson, where Meg and I often took evening walks, we could still hear Italian. Our neighbors on one side were from L'Aquila, near Rome. The grown sons, Mario and Chi-Chi, still lived at home—one ran the bar up the street—and the parents spoke little English. We talked to the sons and gestured to the parents, porch to porch.

On the other side was the First Spiritualist Church, which conducted regular séances and where people often gathered in a weed-filled backyard to await contacts. The only effect the spiritualists might have had on our lives was the size of the vegetables we grew in our otherwise unfertile backyard. One carrot we pulled from the garden that first summer measured three inches in diameter. We cooked it nevertheless. It had the consistency of wood and might have been used to kill vampires.

Most of that first summer we spent painting the house and building furniture. We had much to prepare for, because Meg was pregnant. Just before Christmas that first year, our daughter Laura was born.

Winter across from Forbes Field brought an increase in the rat population. These were fearless rats grown huge on a summer of ballpark peanuts and Cracker Jacks. Several times I descended to the basement in knee-high boots, armed with a tennis racket, to do battle with them as they hissed at me from atop the central beam. And there were other pests. Our first upstairs neighbors were Korean. We had no contact with them except for the smell of cooking oil from their back porch, where they kept a wok. On Korean New Year they got drunk, fell down the stairs, and the next day moved out. On the day after that, the roaches moved out of their apartment and into every available space in ours, even our refrigerator.

However, when I think of this apartment, I think most of all of the summer evenings on the porch. We had two rocking chairs, a round table for mugs of beer, and a radio for Bob Prince, Nellie King, and Jim Woods to keep us up with the game. There was a band of young kids who used to gather in the street at the base of our steps waiting for foul balls to come over the roof. Bob Prince would alert them by radio if one were coming. It was important for them to know who had hit the ball, because one from a star player like Willie Mays or Roberto Clemente would fetch a higher price. Usually these balls would land on the tarmac or on a car roof and with high arching bounces lead the band of boys on a chase down Bouquet Street or sometimes all the way to the base of the hill down Joncaire.

Once and only once did a ball land on our porch. I was alone in my rocker, drinking a beer and listening to Bob Prince, so I had advance warning. I looked up as the ball flew out of the glow of the light stands overhead and landed right beside me, where it rattled back and forth between the house and the brick parapet wall. I took my time. I considered it mine already, a gift from God and much welcomed, because, in all the games I had attended, I had never once caught a major league ball. I put my beer down and went over to the ball, which was now rolling toward the steps. Just as I leaned over to pick it up, a hand from one of the street boys hooked around the parapet and grabbed the ball away.

The radio alerted us when the game reached the seventh inning stretch, and the Pirates opened the bleacher gate so fans could exit easily. If the game was still close, we would gather up Laura from her bed, put her into a basket, where she would continue to sleep soundly, and head over to the bleachers for the two innings that remained. The left-field bleachers were a wonderful place to view a game. They were close to the action, because they paralleled the third-base line.

It was on one of these free visits to Forbes Field that we witnessed the "throw." Usually when I think of Roberto Clemente, I think of the catlike tension and precision with which he prepared to face the pitcher. But if there is a single play I remember, it is his one errant throw. It was the only error I ever saw him make. Someone hit a long line-drive deep into right-center field. Clemente caught up with it on perhaps the third bounce, at the 436 ft. sign near

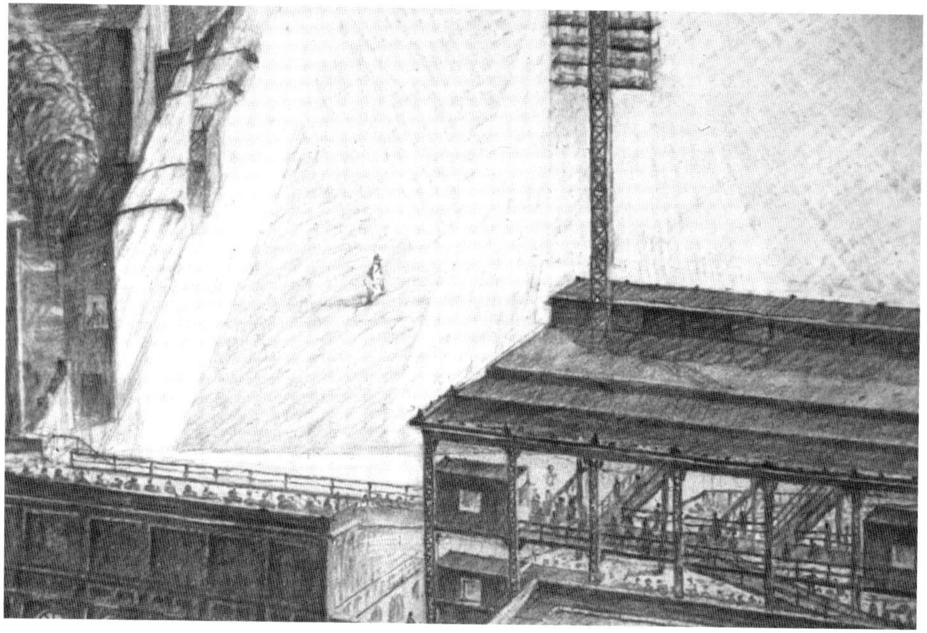

Forbes Field bleachers. East Wall, University Center Mural.

(Photo: Ken Andreyo)

The left-field bleachers were a wonderful place to view a game.

the outfield exit gate, and in one motion he whirled and threw toward third base. Clemente threw almost straight-armed, as if throwing a javelin. His throw started out on a low line, but then it started to rise. And it kept on rising: over the third baseman's head, over the coach's head, over the dugout, and far up into the stands, still rising and rising with an energy internal. The runner trotted home. No one clapped. No one booed. There was no response. No one had known a throw could travel that far.

There were also interesting bleacher regulars. There was the man who ran the scoreboard. On hot days inside that green metal oven, he was often visible, stripped down to his underwear, through the opening of an as-yet unrecorded inning. There was a bald man and his wife, who ran the food concession. It was an informal concession, just a terrace cooker for hot dogs and several stacked cases of Coca-Cola. When we took Laura to night games, she would occasionally wake up, and her outstretched arm or foot startled the bald man, who had assumed our basket on the bench was a picnic dinner.

From my rocker on the porch, there was a sequence to each baseball game only part of which concerned the actual play. The smell of popcorn and peanuts was the first sensation. Then the players began arriving. Most of them parked in a lot under the right-field stands and walked up the long slope to the players' entrance across from us. During the three years we lived on Bouquet Street, 1967–1970, the "walk of the arriving players" changed quite a bit. It was during this interval and after the assassination of Martin Luther King that the black players began to dress more assertively. By 1970 the walk had the feel of a fashion runway. Doc Ellis, who would later become infamous for pitching a no-hitter while on LSD, got the most commentary from the porch sitters up the slope for his pink suits. Willie Stargell had some great white ones. Roberto Clemente remained a more classic dresser.

About three hours before game time, the hot dog stands opposite the main gate would open. If I stood up, I could see their open awnings from my porch. Then came a gathering crowd, a hush, the national anthem, the booming voice of Art McKennan announcing the lineup and the game itself.

A few minutes after the game, a bus would pull up outside the players' entrance and wait for an hour to pick up the visiting team for the trip back to the hotel. The engine was kept running to keep the air conditioning up, and a crowd would gather. Sometimes I would go across the street myself to wait for a close-up of the visiting players and their groupies under the heat-wash of the air conditioner's exhaust.

The park didn't close down totally until well into the night, when the clean-up crew was done sweeping away the peanut shells and crushed cups.

Occasionally there was a turnabout in our role as observers. Long rain delays brought bored fans to the edge of the stands, where they looked back at us. The rickshaw-like porch swing that I made for Laura and painted electric pink got a lot of comments. Meg, while pregnant with Laura, was once called, "beer belly." But most of the comments were directed at our upstairs neighbor, who had a huge tangle of hair, built a quasi-religious shrine with candles on his porch, and was for these fans the very Antichrist.

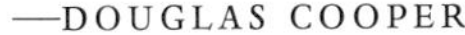
—DOUGLAS COOPER

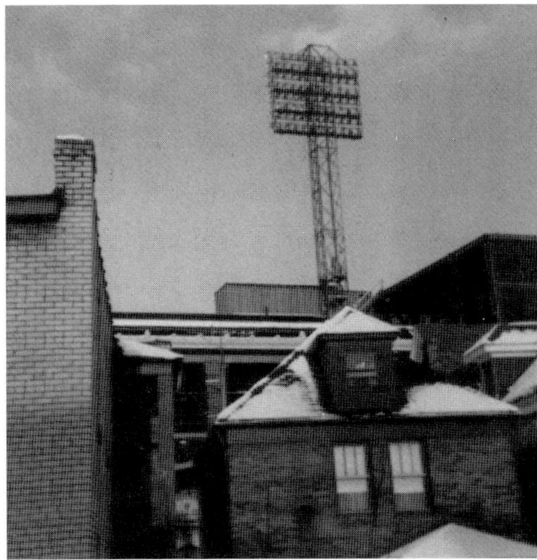

Backyard, looking toward Forbes Field, 1967–1970.

Then came a gathering crowd, a hush, the national anthem, the booming voice of Art McKennan announcing the lineup, and the game itself.

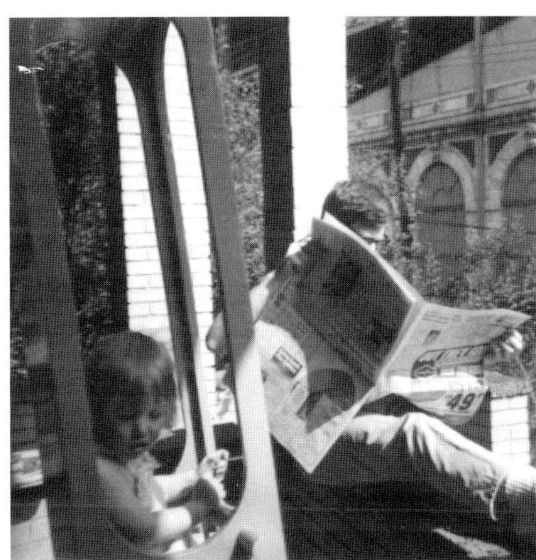

Front porch, looking toward Forbes Field.

The rickshaw-like porch swing that I made for Laura and painted electric pink got a lot of comments.

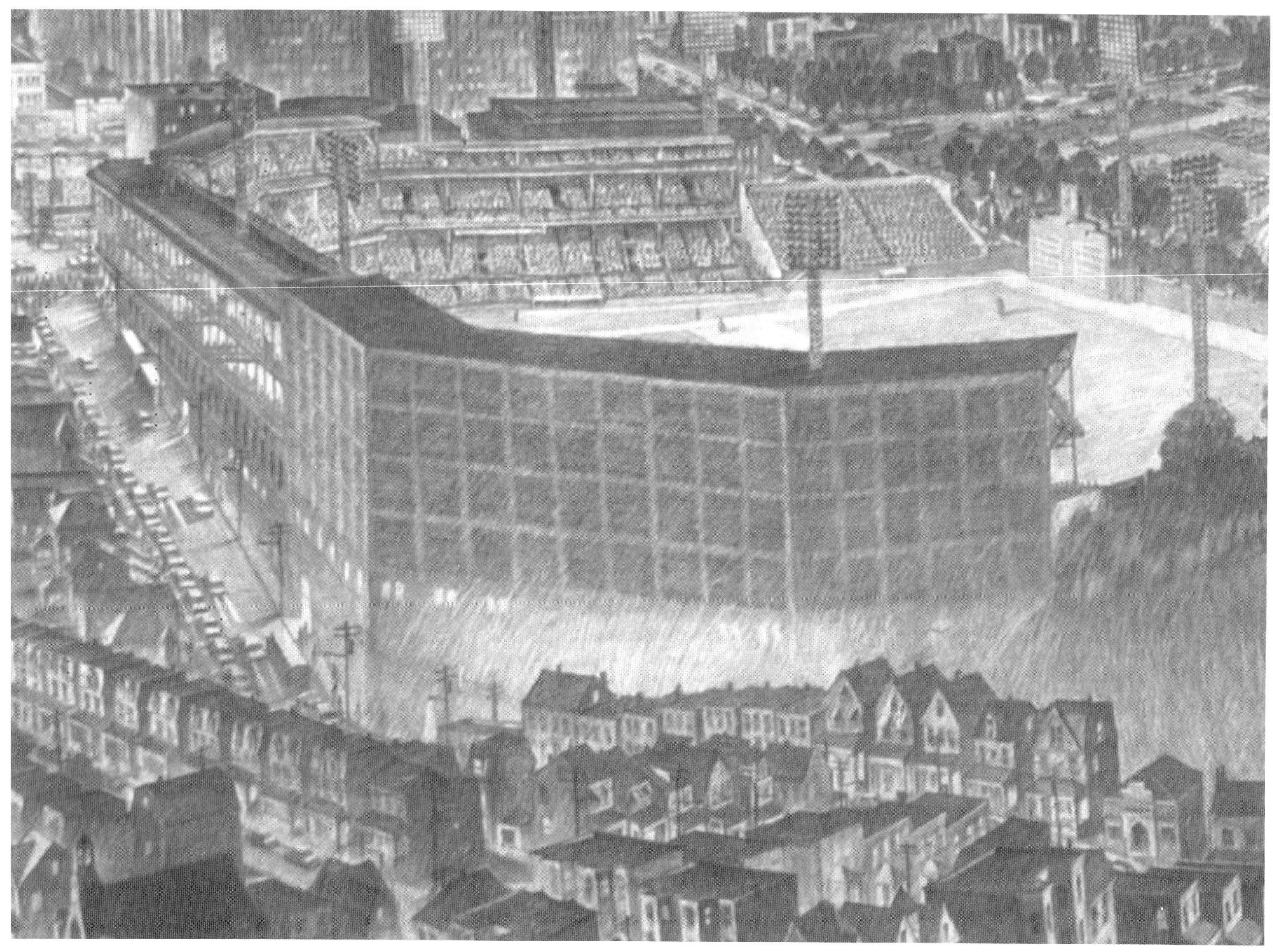

Past Summers, 1997. (Private collection.)

The gem of Bouquet is the churchlike St. Lorenzo di Gamberale Mutual Benefit Association.

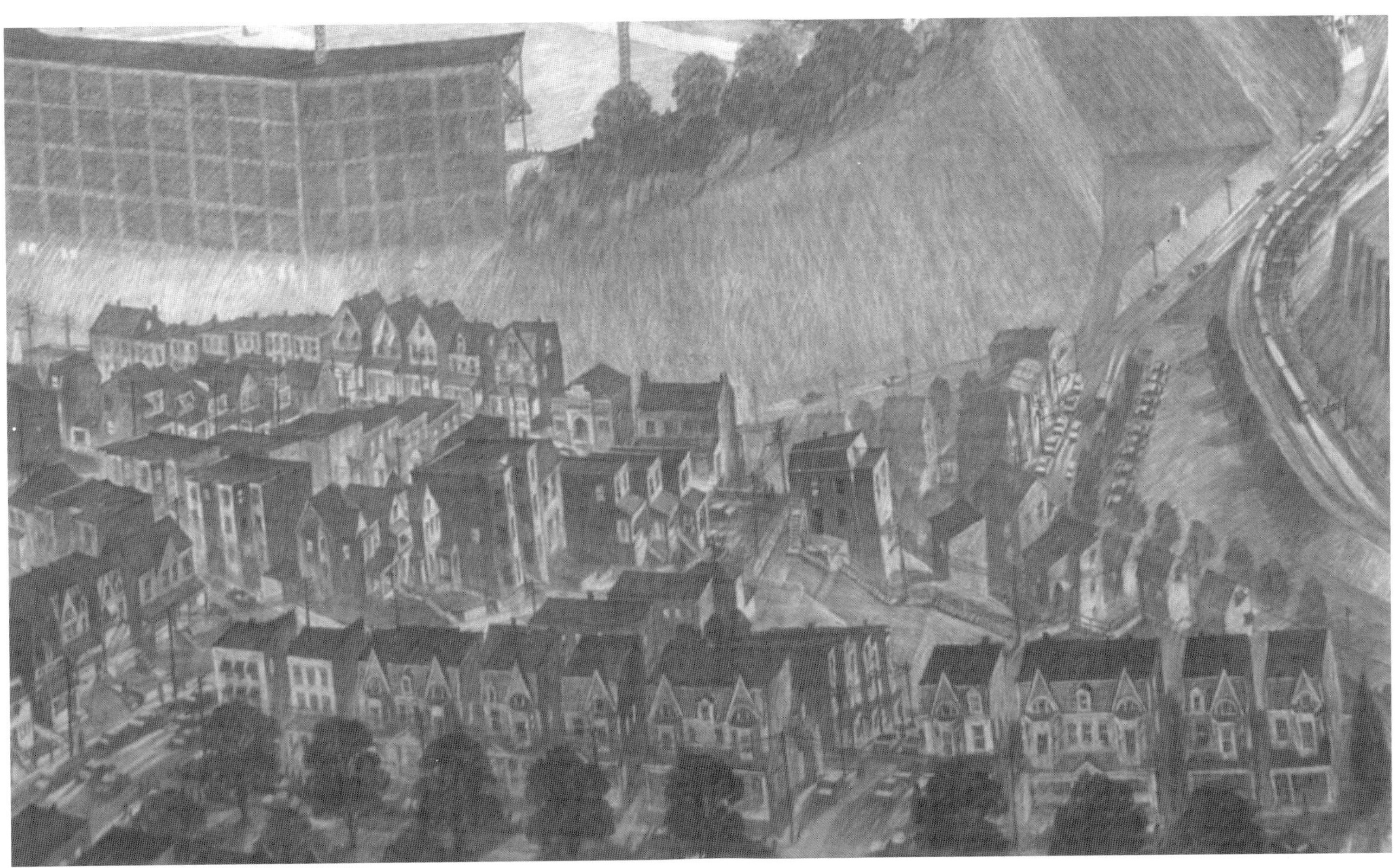

Past Summers.

A descent into this haunting gully is a sobering conclusion to any study of Oakland.

St. Lorenzo

The gem of Bouquet is the churchlike St. Lorenzo di Gamberale Mutual Benefit Association. Built in 1938 as the social center of an Italian community that established itself a century ago on this street and in Junction Hollow below, the hall is emblazoned with twin reliefs of dogs set in its scrubbed-brick façade. Its members still live in homes precariously set on the slopes of Joncaire Street or along the footpath called Diulus Way. A descent deep into this haunting gully is a sobering conclusion to any study of Oakland, offering as it does a vision of the ancient terrain before the effects of human intervention.

—FRANKLIN TOKER, *Pittsburgh: An Urban Portrait*

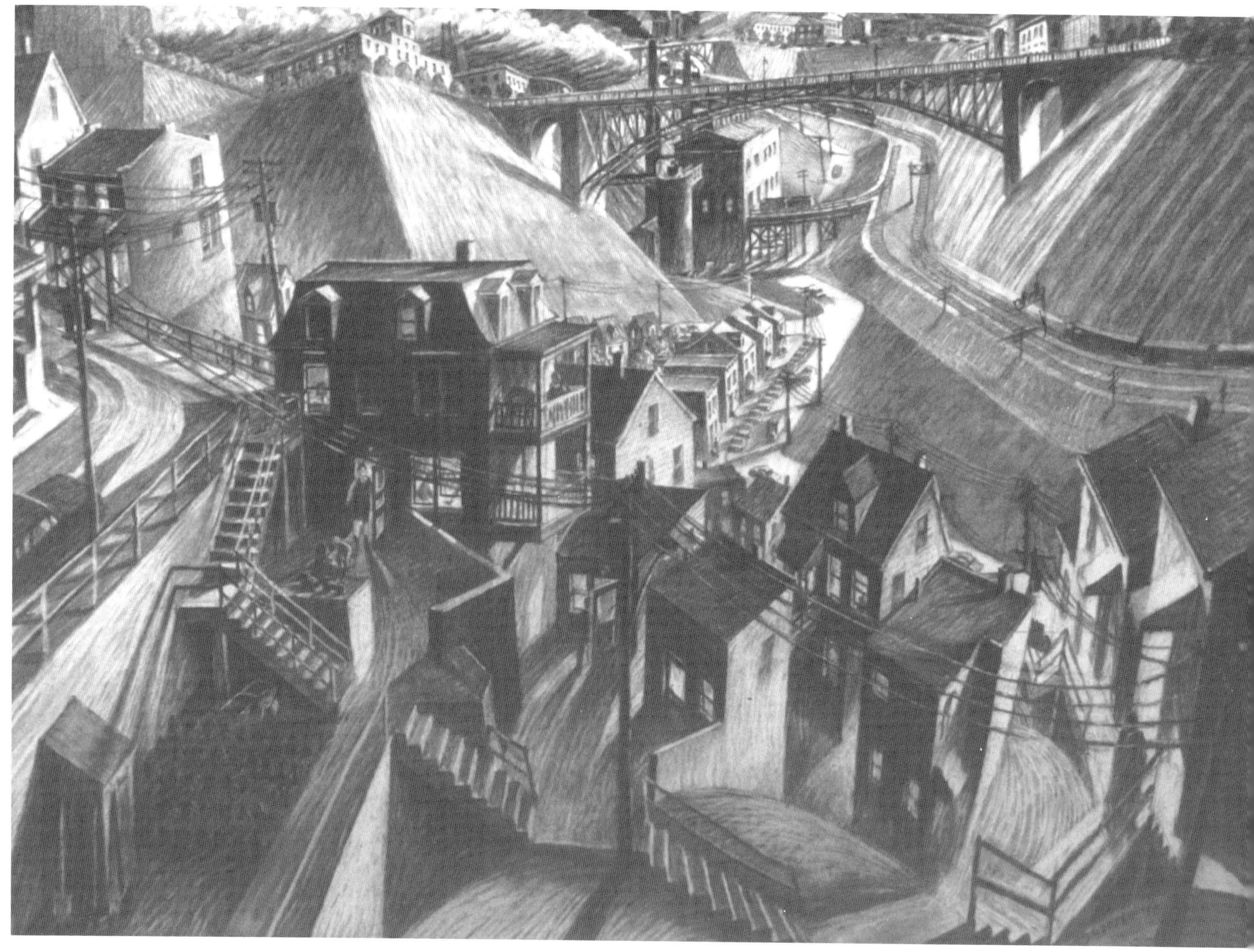

Down City Steps, 1998. 36″ x 48″. (Private collection.)

It was from a semisecret luncheon belvedere, the top step of a high concrete staircase that rose at least ten landings from the floor of the big hole, that I got my first long look at the Lost Neighborhood.

The Lost Neighborhood

No one ever satisfactorily explained to me the enormous hole, bridged in three separate places by long iron spans, that makes the whole southeastern end of the Oakland section of Pittsburgh into a precipice. Between the arrogant stupid prow of Carnegie-Mellon University and the ugly back end of the Carnegie Institute, between the little shrines to Mary in the front yards along Parkview and the park itself, lies the wide, dry ravine that contains essentially four things: the Lost Neighborhood, the Cloud Factory, train tracks, and a tremendous amount of garbage.

It was from a semisecret luncheon belvedere, the top step of a high concrete staircase that rose at least ten landings from the floor of the big hole, that I got my first long look at the Lost Neighborhood: the mysterious couple of streets and row or two of houses—a diorama, which one sees only from above, if one ever notices it. I had probably seen it once or twice during my four years in Pittsburgh, but had never known of the half-dozen ancient staircases scattered throughout South Oakland that led down to it, nor realized that there were people really living in it. There were even a school and a baseball field; you could see the tiny shapes of children running bases down there at the bottom of Pittsburgh.

—MICHAEL CHABON, *The Mysteries of Pittsburgh*

The Cloud Factory

Yes, the Cloud Factory. Haven't you ever noticed it? When you walk across the Schenley Park bridge, there, from the park into Oakland, you pass above the Cloud Factory. What does it do? we used to wonder. Why do these great clouds, perfectly white and clean, white as new baseballs, come out of that building by the tracks? Cleveland and I would be all stoned and out of school and we'd loosen our neckties, and there would be the Cloud Factory, turning out a fresh batch of these virgin clouds.

—MICHAEL CHABON, *The Mysteries of Pittsburgh*

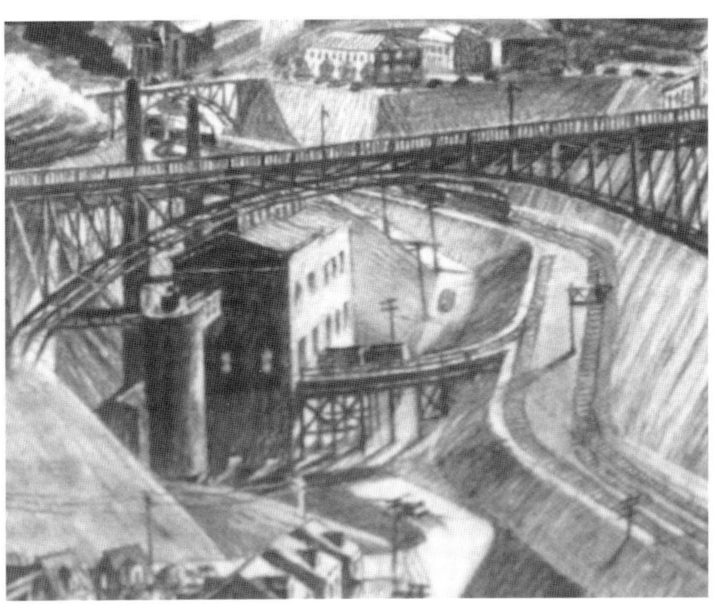

Down City Steps.

Yes, the Cloud Factory. Haven't you ever noticed it?

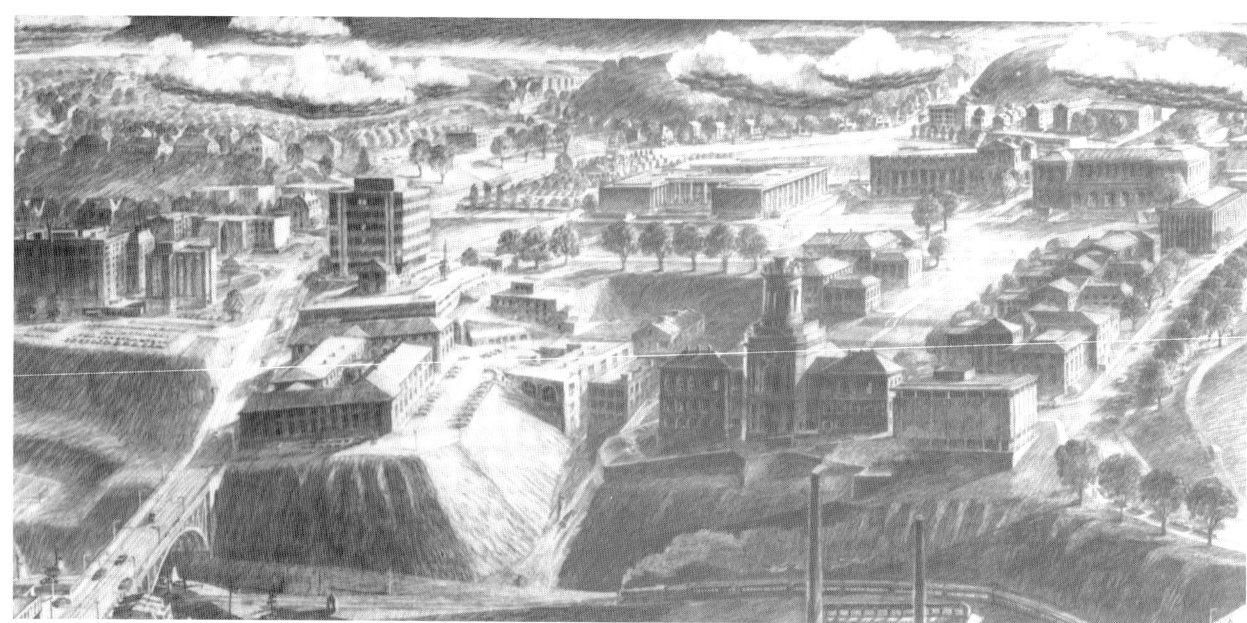

CMU campus. University Center Mural. (Photo: Ken Andreyo.)

Henry Hornbostel designed CMU's campus after the pattern of the 1893 Chicago World's Fair.

CMU Campus

Henry Hornbostel designed CMU's campus after the pattern of the 1893 Chicago World's Fair, a double range of buildings on a midway. But he sought a balance between monumentality and utilitarianism, translating Beaux Arts symmetry and order into something congenial with Carnegie's idea of education. The buildings, in industrial brick, observe functionality as their first principle. Rumors still circulate that Carnegie intended to transform the campus into a factory if the school didn't fulfill its role. In fact, the slope of the long, handsome corridor of Baker Hall—the building on the left as you face west entering the main quadrangle—was not intended to facilitate production-line movements, but simply to accommodate the slope of the hill. . . .

The focus of the campus—if you can take your eyes off Pitt's Cathedral of Learning—is the 1912 Hamerschlag Hall, dominated by a classically garbed smokestack. Hornbostel saw the campus as a ship as well as a factory—architects generally mix metaphors—and that inspired the 1899 placement of a bronze prow ornament from the armored cruiser USS Pittsburgh on the western brow of Hamerschlag Hall's hill.

—BARRINGER FIFIELD, *Seeing Pittsburgh*

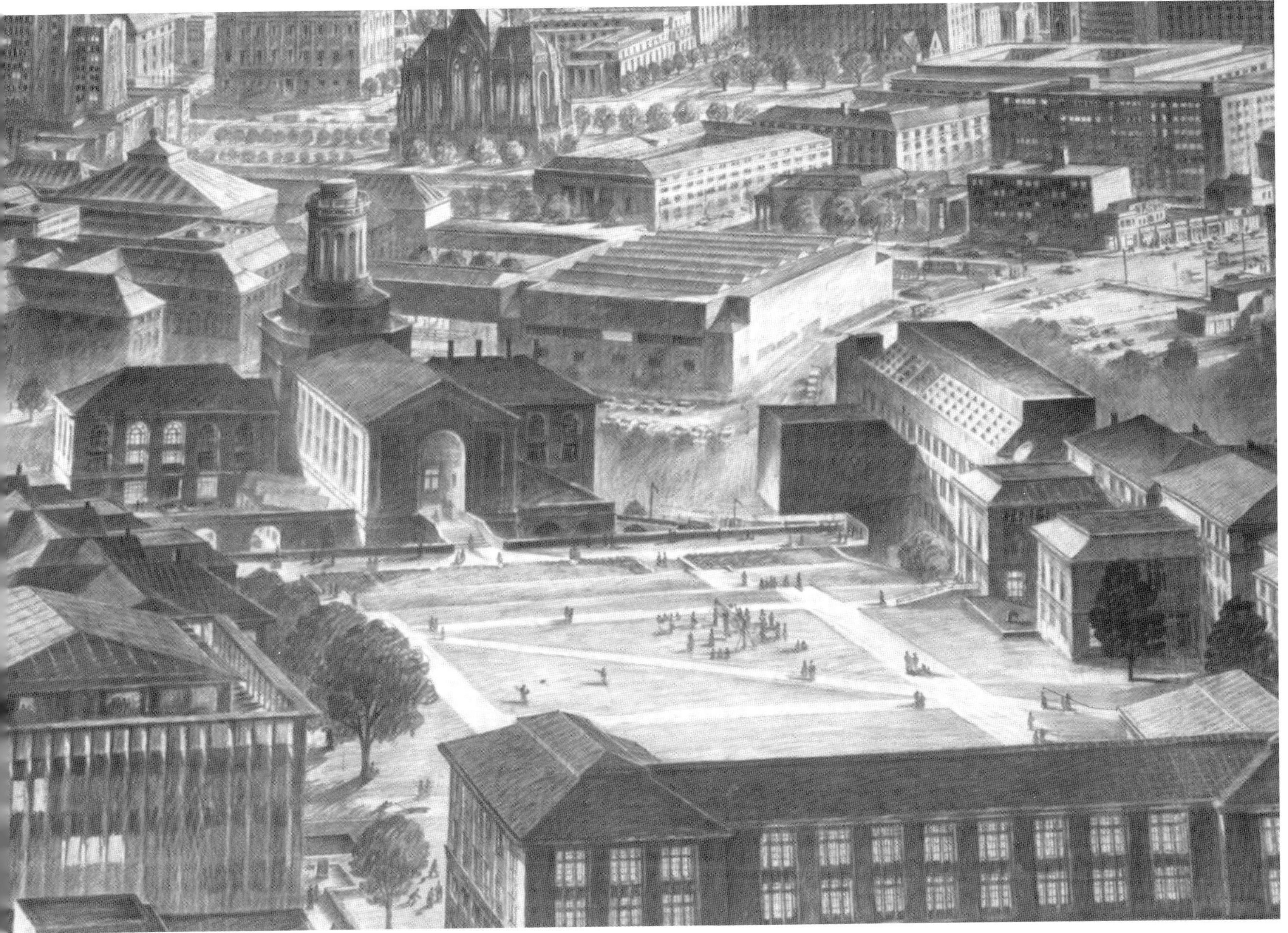

CMU campus. University Center Mural. (Photo: Ken Andreyo.)

The focus of the campus—if you can take your eyes off Pitt's Cathedral of Learning—is the 1912 Hamerschlag Hall, dominated by a classically garbed smokestack.

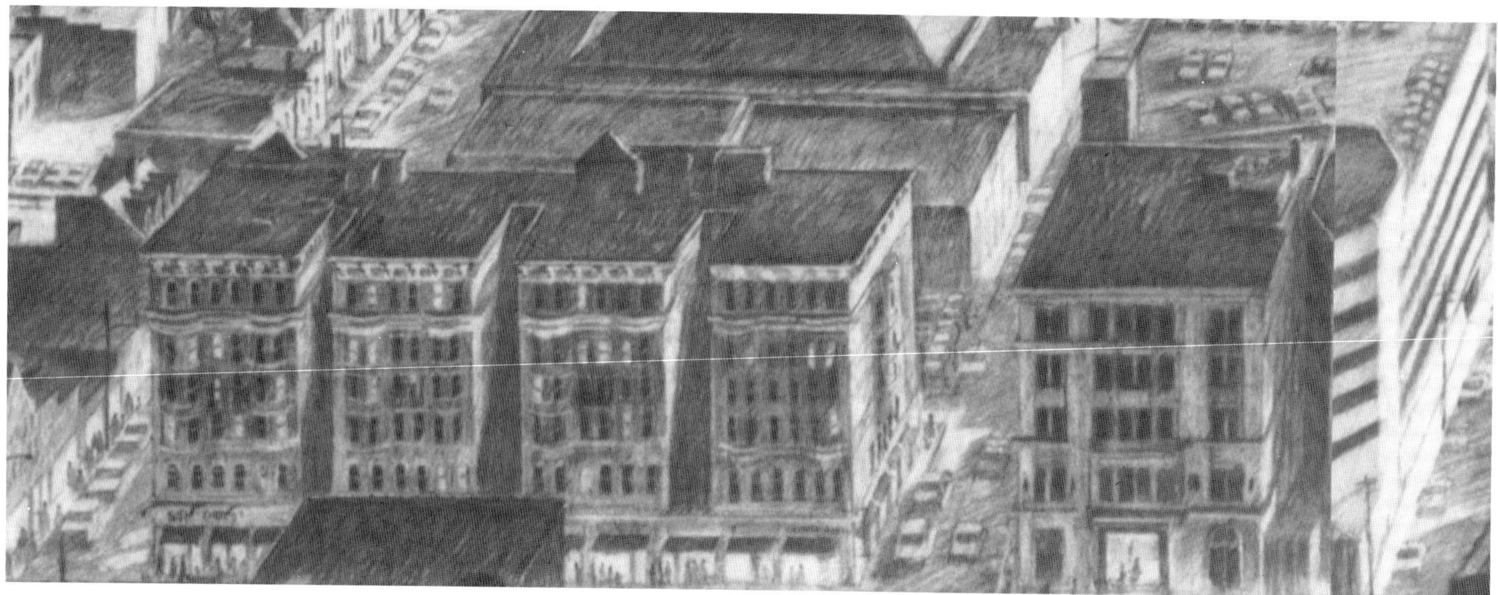

Iroquois Building. University Center Mural. (Photo: Ken Andreyo.)

This was the first example in Pittsburgh of the large, more or less "palatial" apartment house rather on the high-rise order.

Iroquois Building

This was the first example in Pittsburgh of the large, more or less "palatial" apartment house rather on the high-rise order, although the chief dimension of these facades is still lateral. Flat houses of this order were already well-established in New York, beginning with Hardenburgh's Dakota Apartments of the 1880s, and they reflected a marked change in American living habits, especially of the upper classes after the mid-nineteenth century. In 1898 the Schenley Hotel had already established in Oakland the image of the large high-rise urban hotel that could also be "residential." Wealthy Pittsburgh manufacturers and industrialists often lived there during the winter.

The broad width of the Iroquois was treated by Osterling with some restraint as regards ornament. Except for a heavy cornice there is a minimum of classical detailing on the Forbes facades. There are four projecting wings facing Forbes; on the ground floor are shops, and the entrances to the apartments were at one time between the wings, except that of the center which was a shop.

Until about 1950, these long entry corridors were quite elaborate with much mosaic, dark oak woodwork, bronze maidens holding electric lights, and wrought iron elevator cages. In the early 50's these entries were removed and shops substituted. Much earlier the large apartments had already been split up into smaller ones, but since the building had ceased to be fashionable, it was partially remodeled for office space in the 1950's.

—JAMES D. VAN TRUMP AND ARTHUR ZIEGLER, *Landmark Architecture of Allegheny County, Pennsylvania*

Isaly's

Isaly's owes its commanding position as well as its function (it was an early take-out restaurant) to the automobile: its site was created when the Boulevard of the Allies bulldozed Oakland in half in the 1920s. There is a decidedly "Twenties" feel to the façade, which is covered in Art Deco terra-cotta tiles. But there is a solemnity to Isaly's in the bold piers that recall the Egyptian temple of Saqqara, whose excavation by the French was underway at that moment. Built as the main factory and showcase of the Isaly food chain, this radiant building was for years a temple to a different sort of cult: the chipped ham, Klondikes, and skyscraper ice-cream cones that were key ingredients of Pittsburgh's regional cuisine.

—FRANKLIN TOKER, *Pittsburgh: An Urban Portrait*

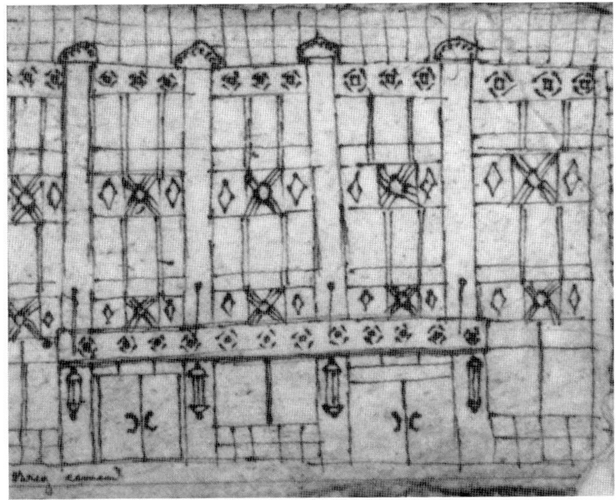

Isaly's (by Josephine Zielinski). Heinz History Center Mural.

There is a decidedly "Twenties" feel to the façade, which is covered in Art Deco terra-cotta tiles.

Isaly's. University Center Mural. (Photo: Ken Andreyo.)

. . . its site was created when the Boulevard of the Allies bulldozed Oakland in half in the 1920s.

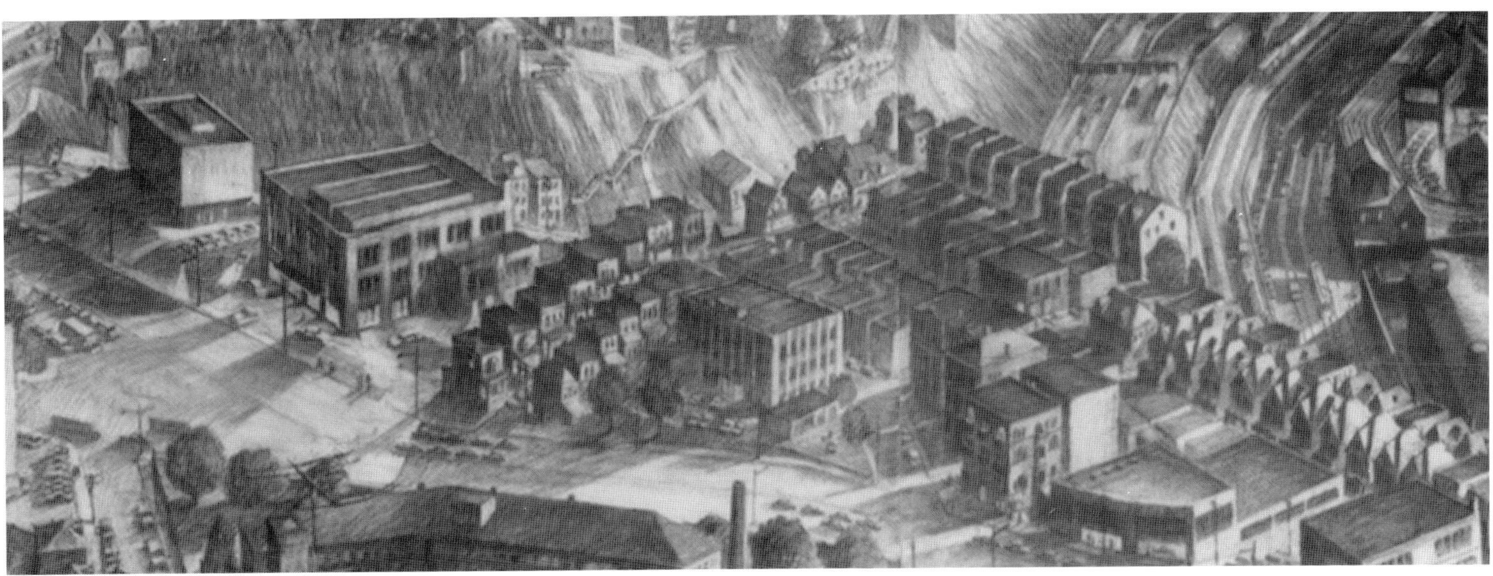

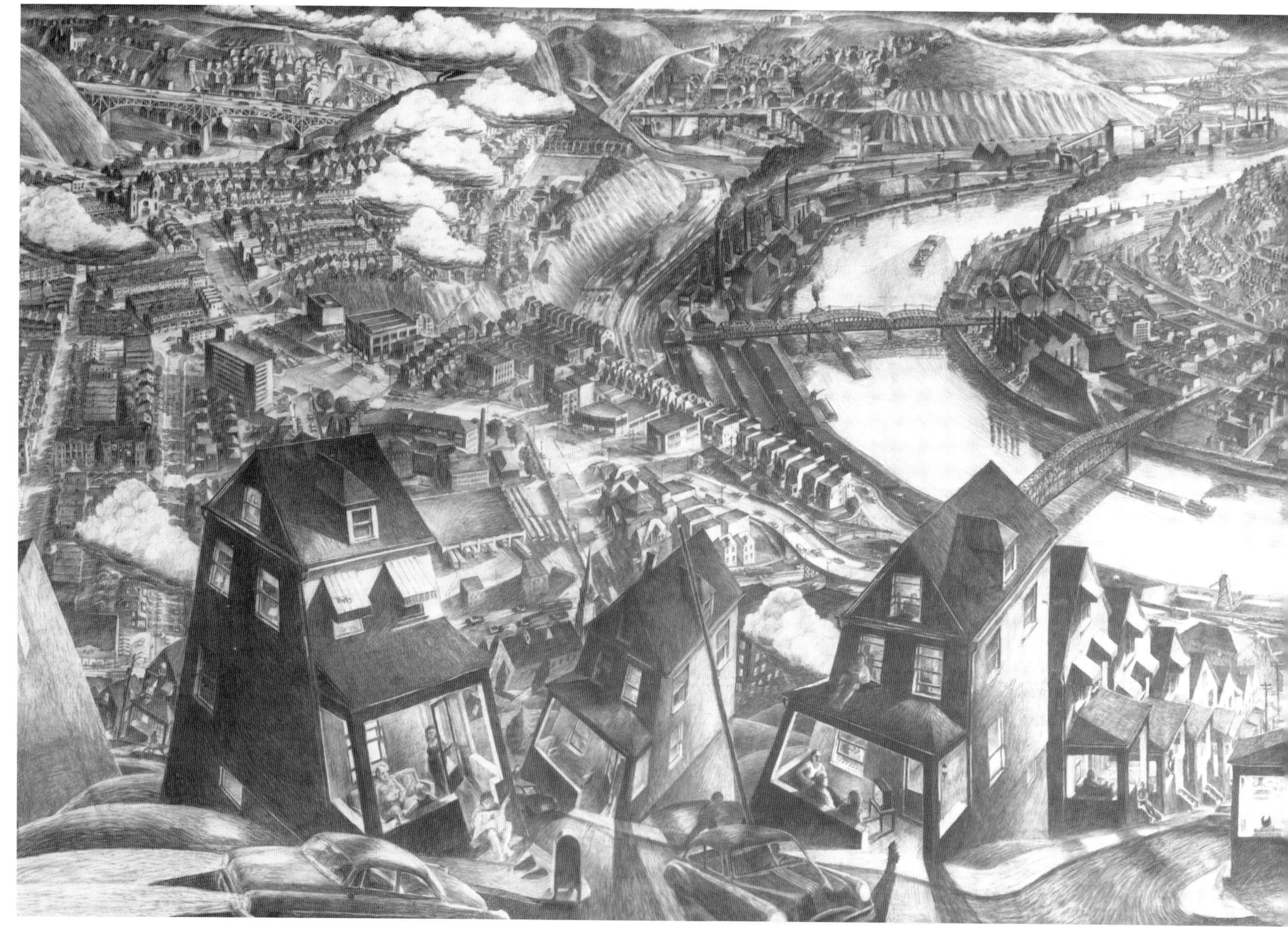

Overlooking the Jones and Laughlin mill from Robinson and Aliquippa. University Center Mural.

(Photo: Ken Andreyo.)

The sons may work a little further up than their fathers.

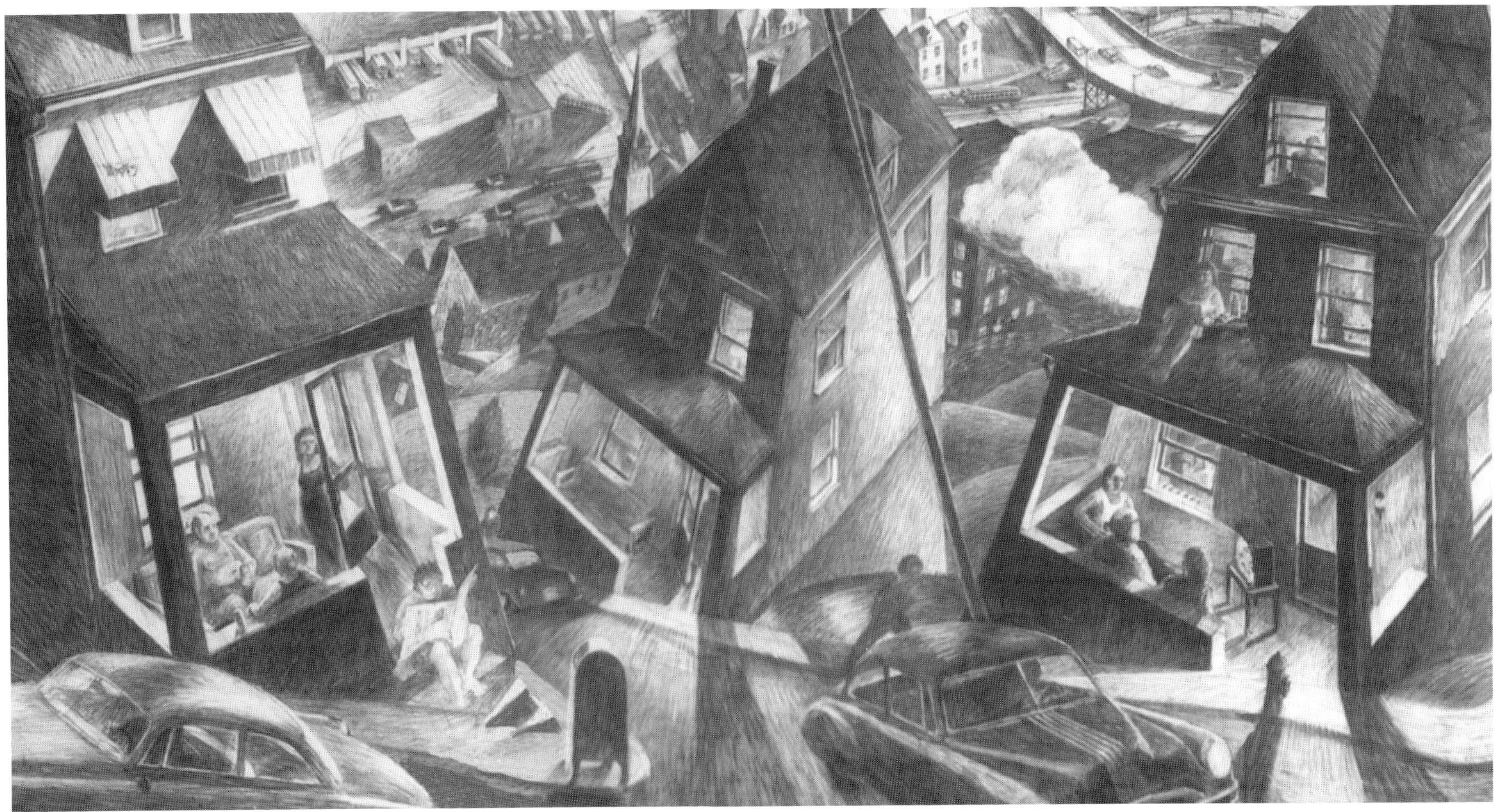

Corner of Robinson and Aliquippa. University Center Mural.

(Photo: Ken Andreyo.)

The mothers, too, expect that their daughters will eventually marry millworkers.

Sons and Fathers

The sons may work a little further up than their fathers; a man told me with pride that his son, who was a foreman, had secured for him a job in the mill, and a mother was eager to relate how her boy had taught the new assistant superintendent the way to do his work. Only rarely, however, do they secure an education that fits them for an entirely different kind of labor. The mothers, too, expect that their daughters will eventually marry mill workers.

—MARGARET BYINGTON, *Homestead: The Households of a Mill Town*

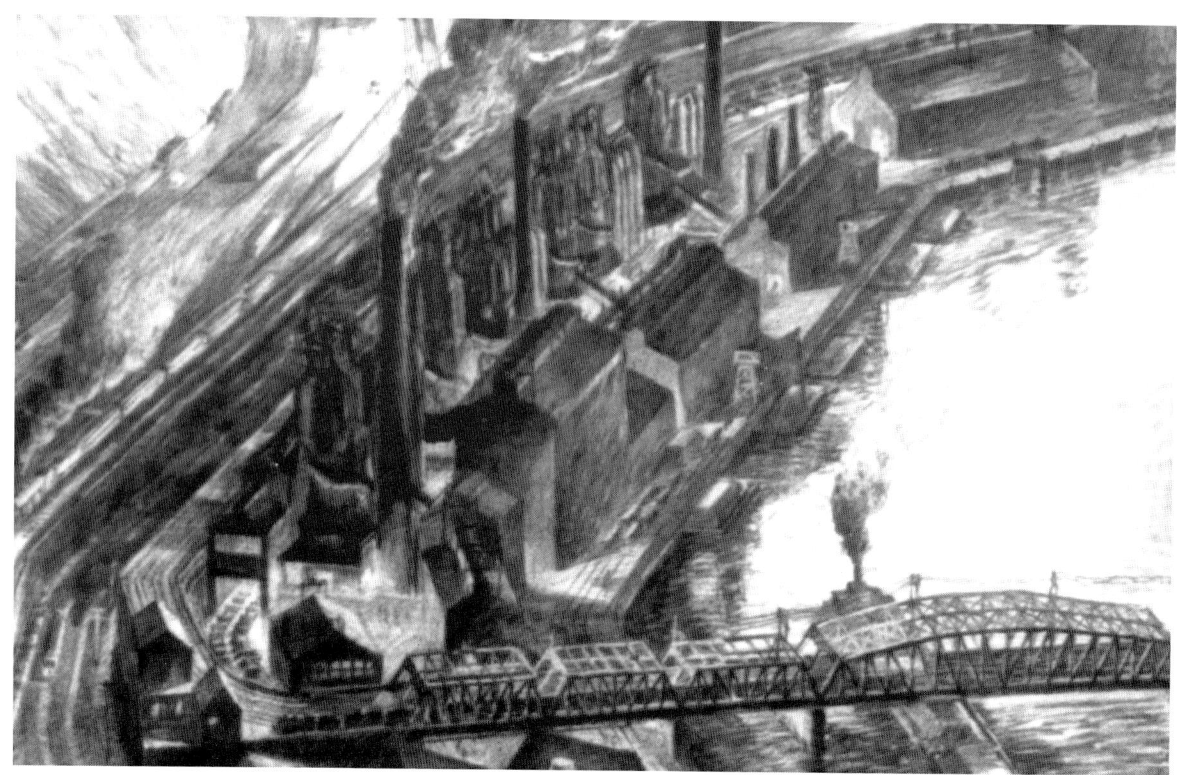

J&L Oakland and Southside works. University Center Mural.

(Photo: Ken Andreyo.)

I saw the full moon rippled into rags of light above a furnace stack.

Furnace Greens

I learned the pick and shovel, the sledge,
the post-hole digger, and the jack hammer.
I kept company with cranes,
backhoes, sheers, presses, and vats of acid.
My hand became a steel hook; my arms,
#10 cables; my joints, chain links.
My eyes turned into glass, plastic,
and wire mesh. I saw a man lose fingers.
I saw a hot strip of sheet metal jump the rolls
and sidewind across the floor
like a red snake. I saw the full moon rippled
into rags of light above a furnace stack . . .

—PETER BLAIR, "Furnace Greens"

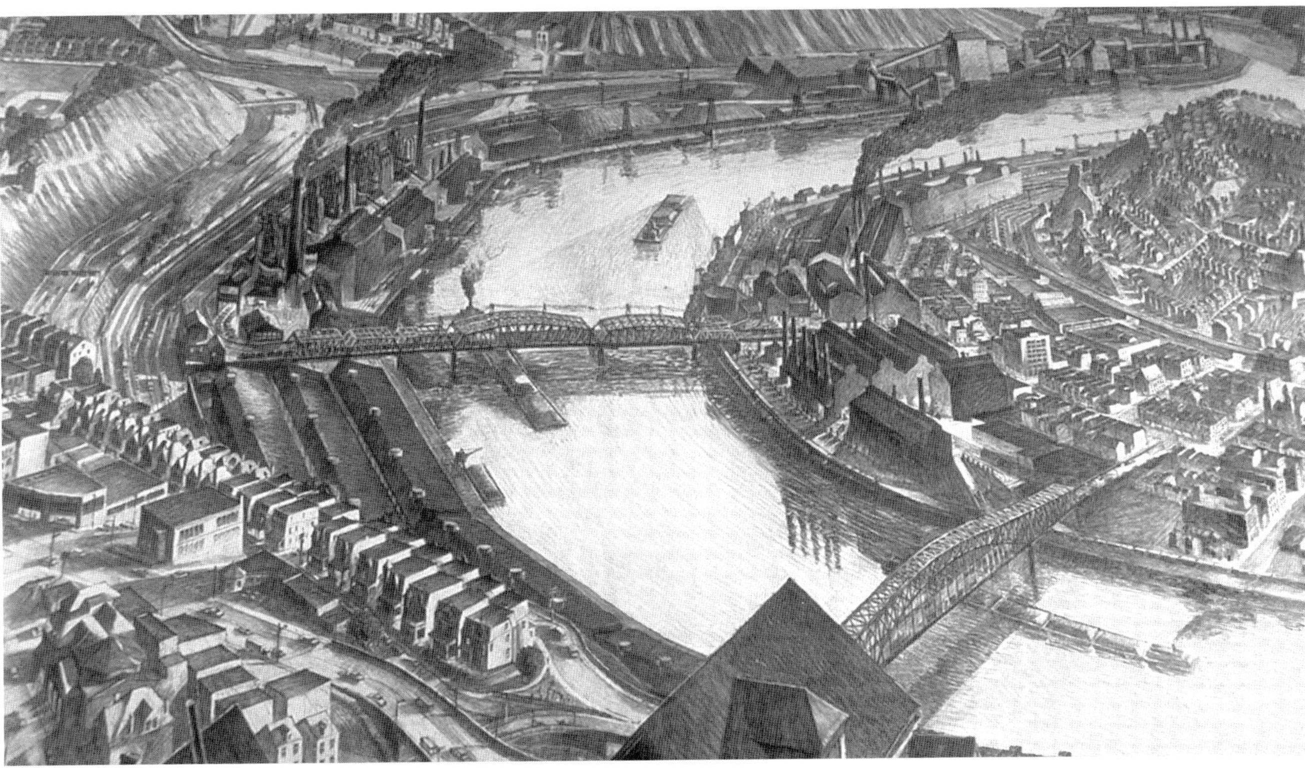

J&L Oakland and Southside works. University Center Mural.

(Photo: Ken Andreyo.)

Every two hours, the furnace is tapped.

Blast Furnaces

The blast of natural gas and heated air entered the furnace through tuyeres (pronounced tweers) linked to the huge bustle pipe that circled the bosh. Through a peep sight in the tuyere cap I could see the searing yellow white of the conflagration inside. As the burden descended, supported and fired from below by the blast, melted iron drained to the hearth. Flux combined with impurities in the ore to form slag, which accumulated on top of the iron. Rounding the furnace, I could see the taphole at hearth level, packed hard and tight with dirty, off-white clay.

Every two hours the furnace is tapped. As the moment for tapping approached, runners leading from the trough below the taphole filled with flame as natural gas was piped in to heat them before the cast. From a glass-enclosed control station the team leader directed an automated drill into the clay-packed taphole, five or more feet, then withdrew it, its bore red orange.

Liquid iron spilled forth. The area swelled with light. Sparks the size of a child's fist burst from the taphole and up from the iron runner. Cinder snappers dressed in silvers stood alongside, plunging long poles through the crust of cooling iron that began to form over the flowing metal, pulling them out aflame. Iron poured over the edge of the floor into a torpedo car below on its track, sparks and flames bursting from its mouth as the iron flowed. This was pig iron on its way to the BOP to become steel.

—LAURIE GRAHAM, *Singing the City*

Beau Posset

Not all of the people I worked with on the mural were from Vintage. I met Beau Posset through contacts I had made while I was drawing one November on the South Side slopes. It had been a particularly cold day, and a family who lived on Stromberg Street took pity on me and invited me in for some coffee. I asked if they knew anyone who had worked in one of the mills down below. They put me in touch with Beau.

Beau had worked in most of the J&L mills along the Monongahela River: the steel mill, the ironworks, and his then-current location, the Hazelwood Coke Works.

Beau told me about the inner workings of the South Side steelworks: where the open hearths were; how the "torpedoes," looking like kazoos filled with molten pig iron, were brought by train from the iron mill across the river; where cranes tracked overhead; and where they poured the ingots. Beau told me about the dangers of working in the mill and about one particular accident.

One day just before lunch, he had been talking with some of his co-workers. A boy barely out of his teens had been assigned to clear away some debris from below one of the ore bins. He was to use a small tractor called a "huff" even though someone had warned him that the huff had a suspicious clutch.

But the young man used it anyway. After lunch, driving under the bin, the clutch wouldn't disengage. It kept driving under the bin. The young man was beheaded under a low beam.

—DOUGLAS COOPER

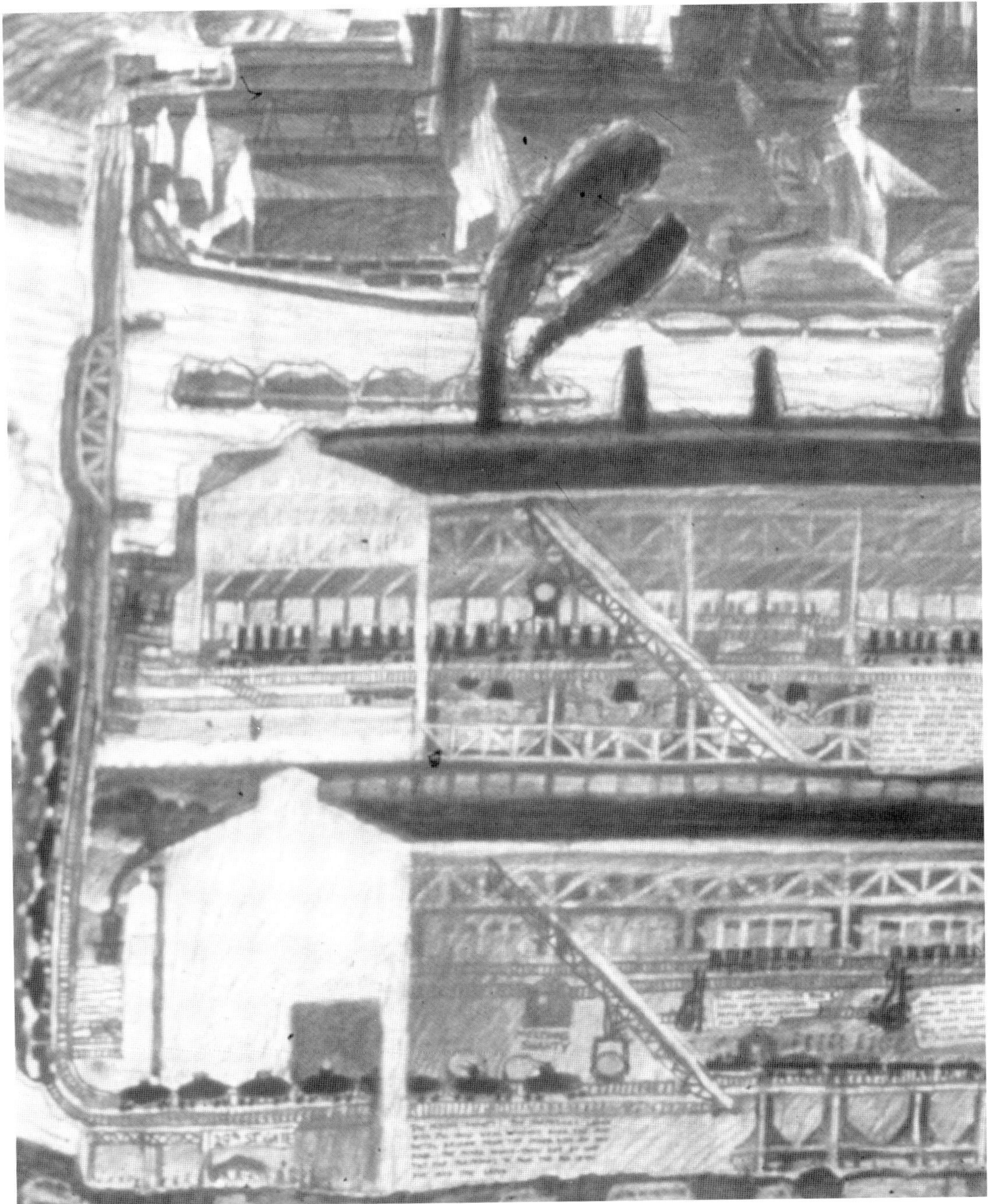

J&L Southside works. Heinz History Center Mural.

Beau told me about the inner workings of the South Side steelworks . . . how the "torpedoes" looking like kazoos filled with molten pig iron, were brought by train from the iron mill across the river.

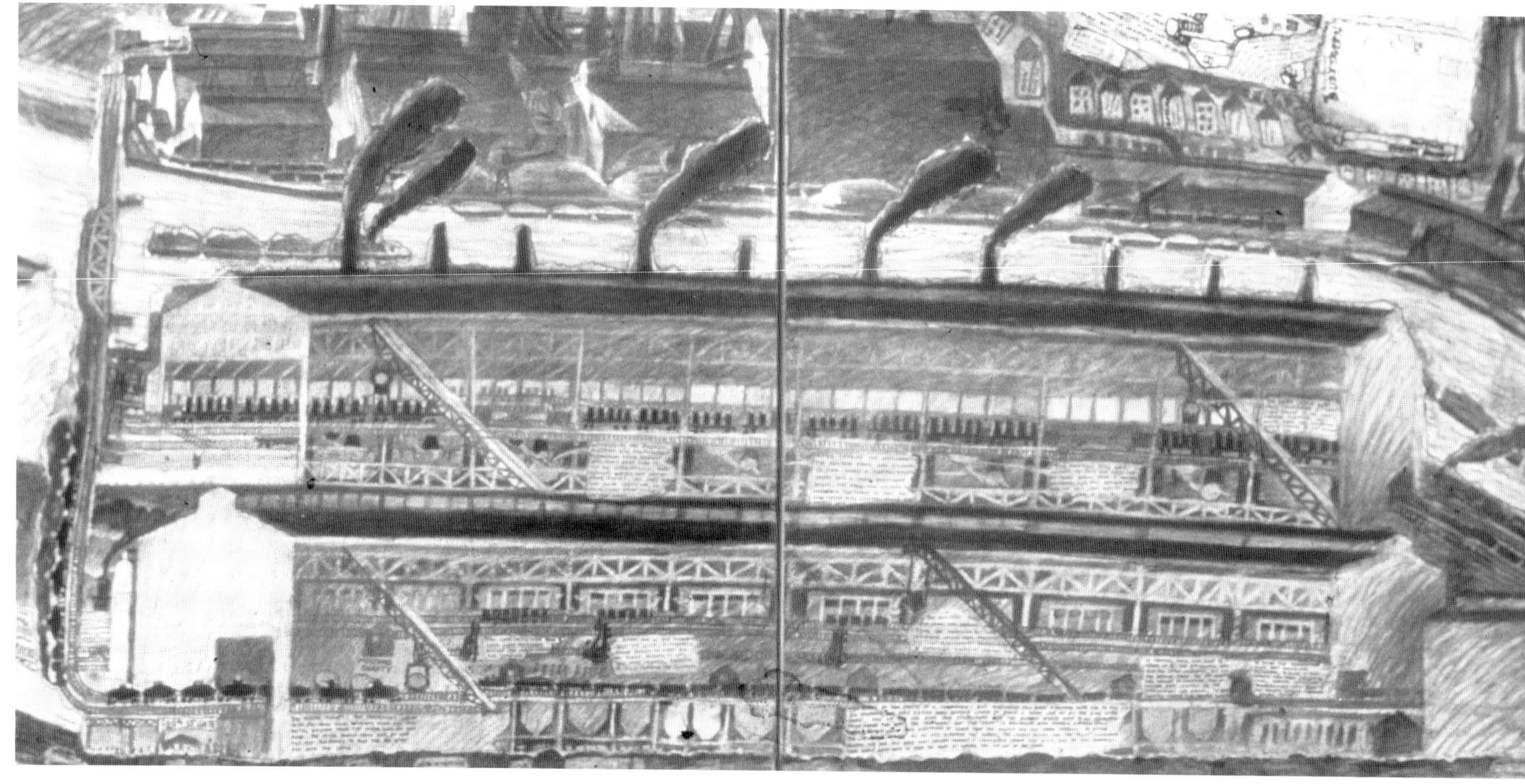

J&L Southside works. Heinz History Center Mural.

What was left in the ladle, bubbling like thick soup in a pot, was steel, perhaps the most useful product the world has ever seen.

At the Open Hearth

Everything was red and hot, as close to hell, the men said, as they hoped to get.

The men who worked the tapping hole at the open hearth wore thick protective coats, dark goggles, and heavy leather boots to protect against the heat and flames. A mixture of molten iron, limestone, and steel scrap bubbled at a temperature of three thousand degrees. After the mixture had cooked, the melter ordered that a sample be taken. A helper took a long, lancelike device, stuck it through a hole in the furnace, and removed a sample. If the mixture was adjudged good, a helper cleaned away the clay that dammed the six-inch tapping hole, took another long lance with a dynamic charge on the end, and—bam!—blew out the tapping hole. Out from the furnace into a huge ladle, amid fire, smoke, and steam, poured a great red-orange stream. Slag lighter than steel, a mixture of limestone and other unwanted elements, among them carbon and manganese, floated on the surface and overflowed into an adjacent pear-shaped iron pot. What was left in the ladle, bubbling like thick soup in a pot, was steel, perhaps the most useful product the world has ever seen, a product that made possible the Industrial Revolution and twentieth-century life.

—WILLIAM SERRIN, *Homestead*

Southside

Not Working

Why is it that every time the evening news decides to report on the area unemployment picture, they interview some bearded drunk in a seedy bar, or they question an overweight slob as he lounges on his living room couch with his equally fat wife. An uninformed viewer could easily think unemployment is a very pleasant and relaxing situation. Unfortunately, being un-employed is far from an enjoyable experience and the drunk and the slob are poor portraits of the thousands of area jobless. The fact is, unemployment is a full time job, and as many of you are finding out it's a tough job not working.

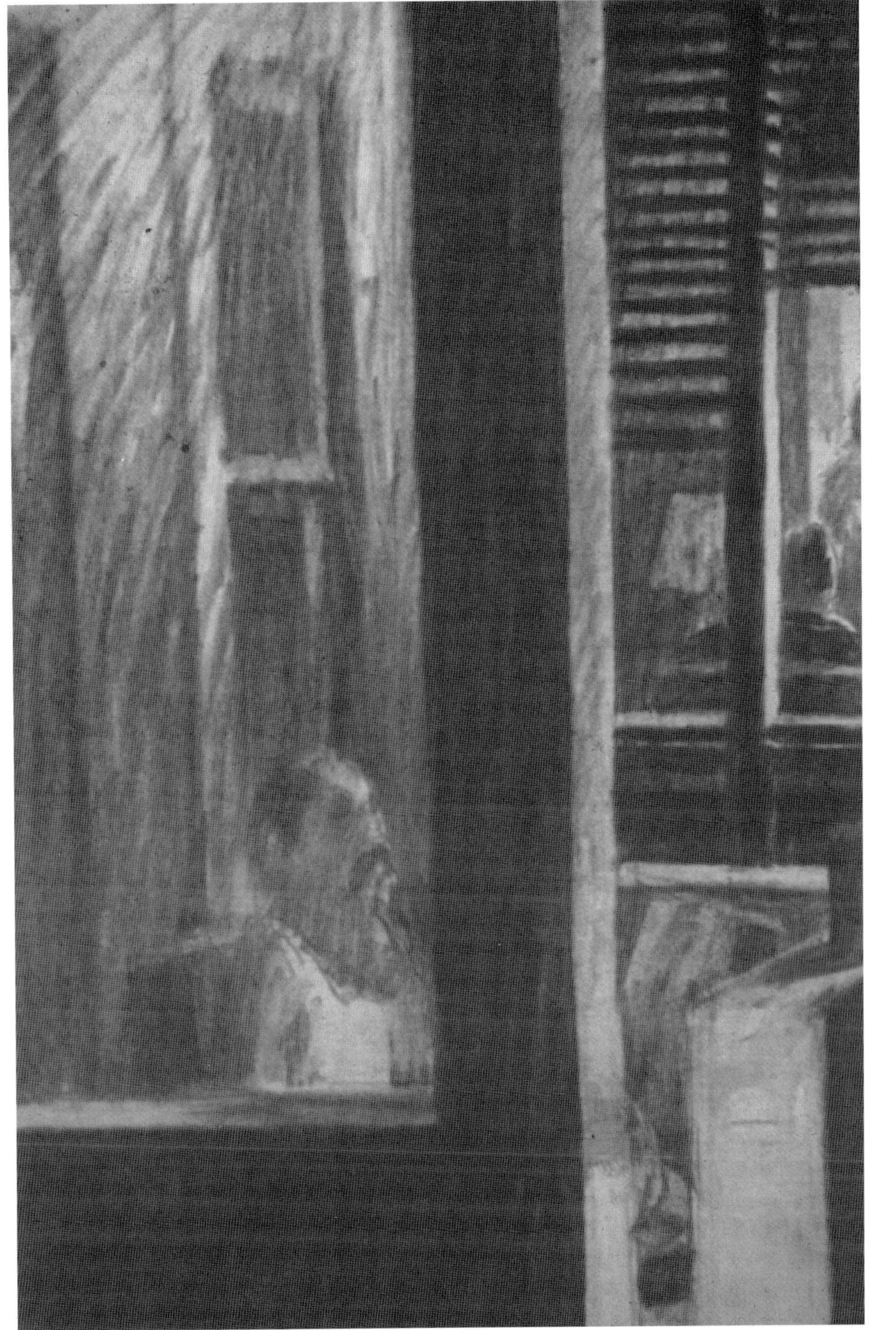

Porch at Holt and Barry Streets. Heinz History Center Mural.

The fact is, unemployment is a full-time job.

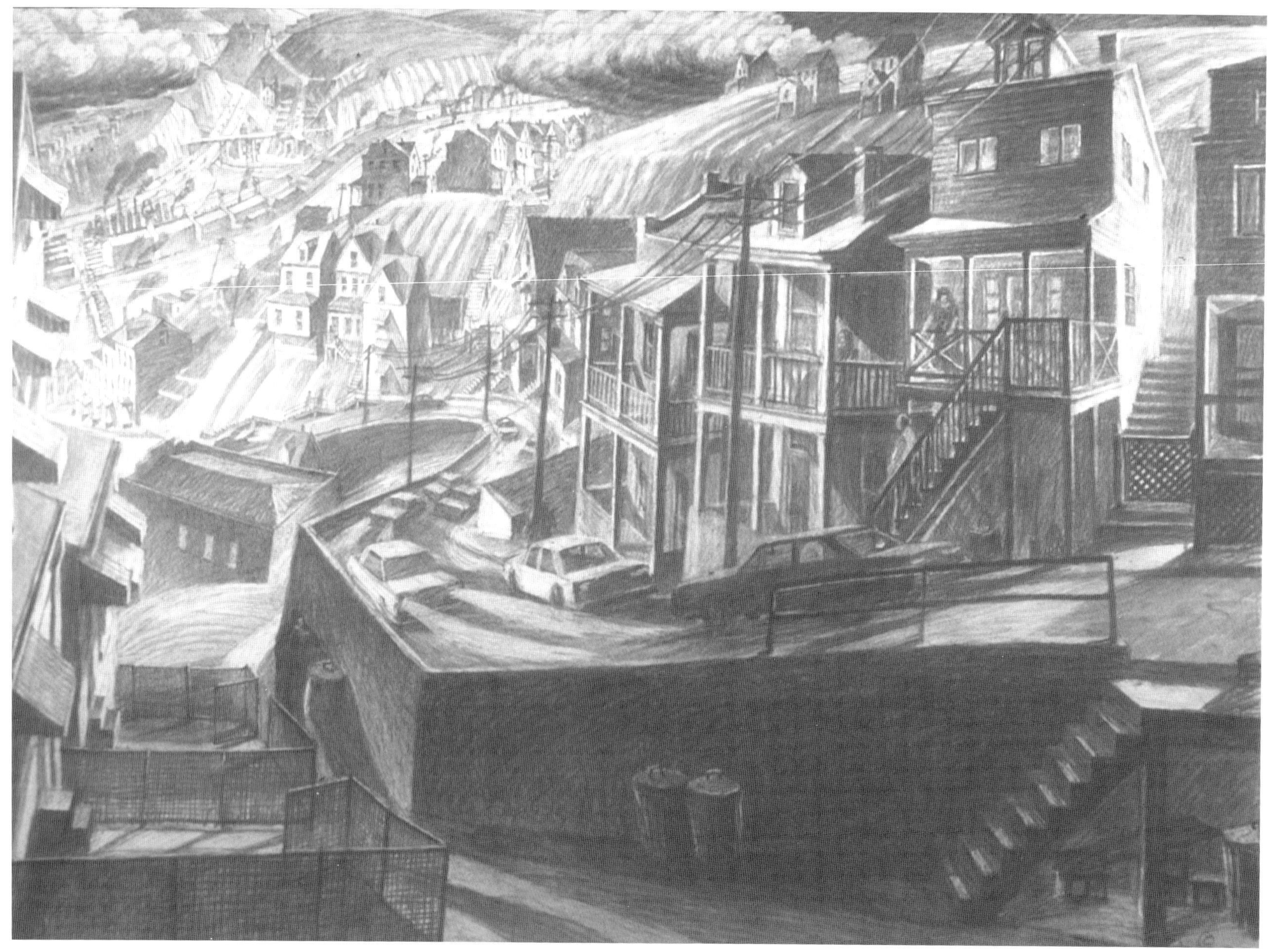

***Trash Day,* 1997.** 36″ x 48″. (Private collection.)

The walk to the mill was bitterly cold on winter mornings like this lowering Monday.

Unemployment starts out like any other new job. At first you're tentative, not sure of what you should be doing. The initial days are spent getting used to your new surroundings. You're a bit nervous because there seems to be so much to learn. You think you'll never get used to it, and begin to wish you were back at your old job. But you also know that you can't go back, that you must accept your new position.

—TOM LOFTUS, "Not Working Is a Tough Job"

The Walk to the Mill

The walk to the mill was bitterly cold on winter mornings like this lowering Monday. It was still dark when Paul and his father left the house. Wrapped in their greatcoats they kept their heads down against the wind and their hats pulled forward to protect their eyes from cinders.

Today was a particularly bad one for walking. The air was bitter, the sky an ugly dark gray streaked with black smoke from the riverside mills.

—MARCIA DAVENPORT, *The Valley of Decision*

Greenfield

Greenfield, December 7, 1941

For Mary Jane Kelly, the memory of the Japanese bombing of Pearl Harbor is forever tied to one place. Mary Jane had gone with some friends that afternoon to see Sun Valley Serenade with Sonja Henie at the Park Theater along Greenfield Ave. near St. Rosalia's. Just as they left the theater, they looked down the street and saw her brother talking excitedly in front of the Greenfield Grill. They went over to him and quickly learned of the bombing.

Mary Jane remembers nothing more of that day, nothing about what might have happened

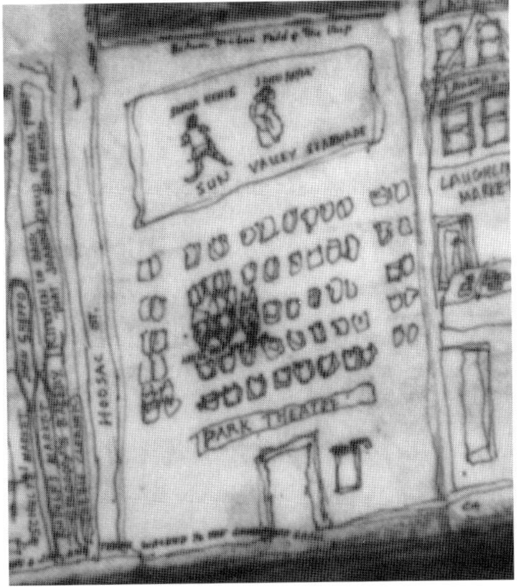

Park Theater. Heinz History Center Mural.

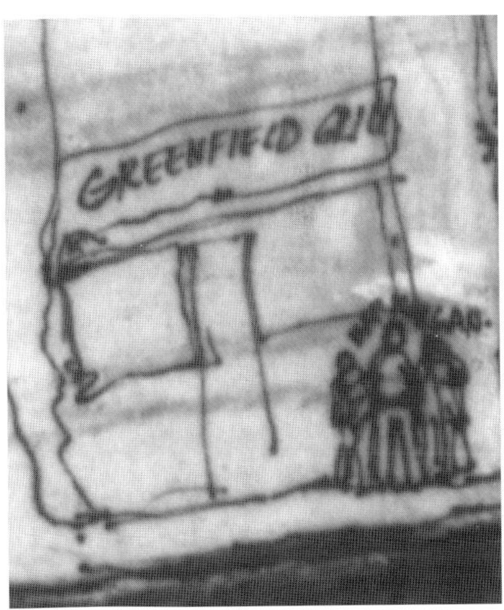

Greenfield Grill. Heinz History Center Mural.

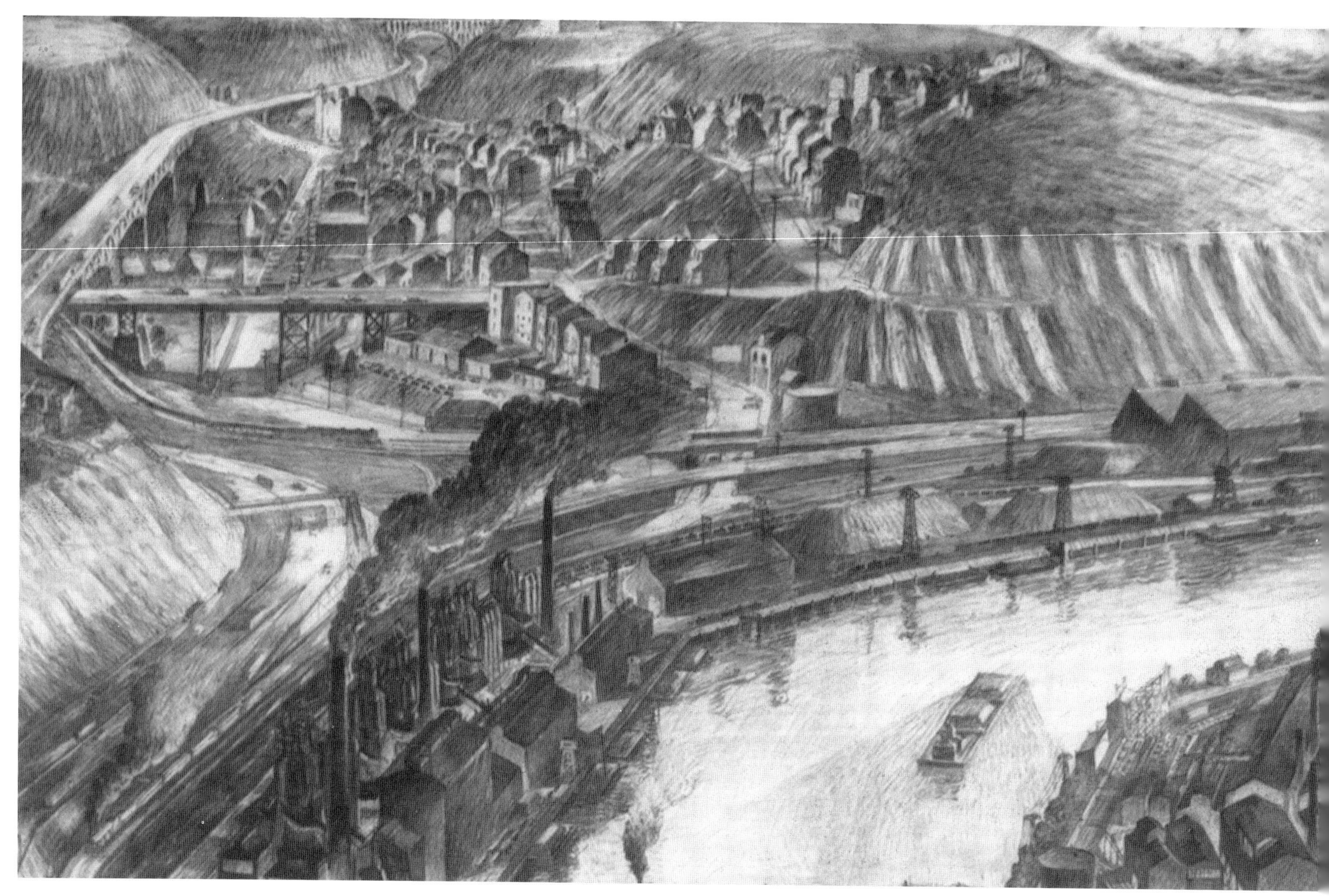

Greenfield and Hazelwood. University Center Mural. (Photo: Ken Andreyo.)

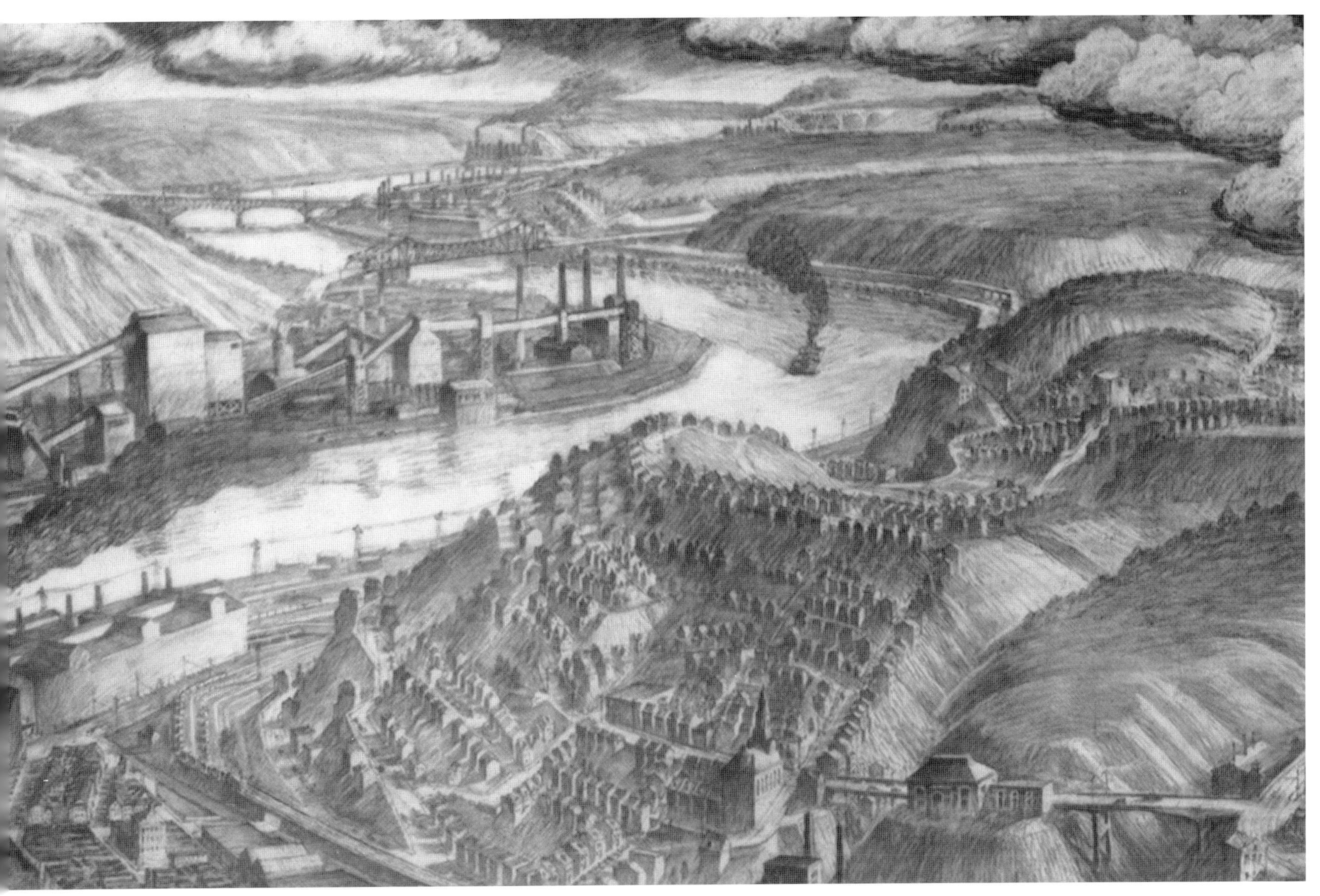

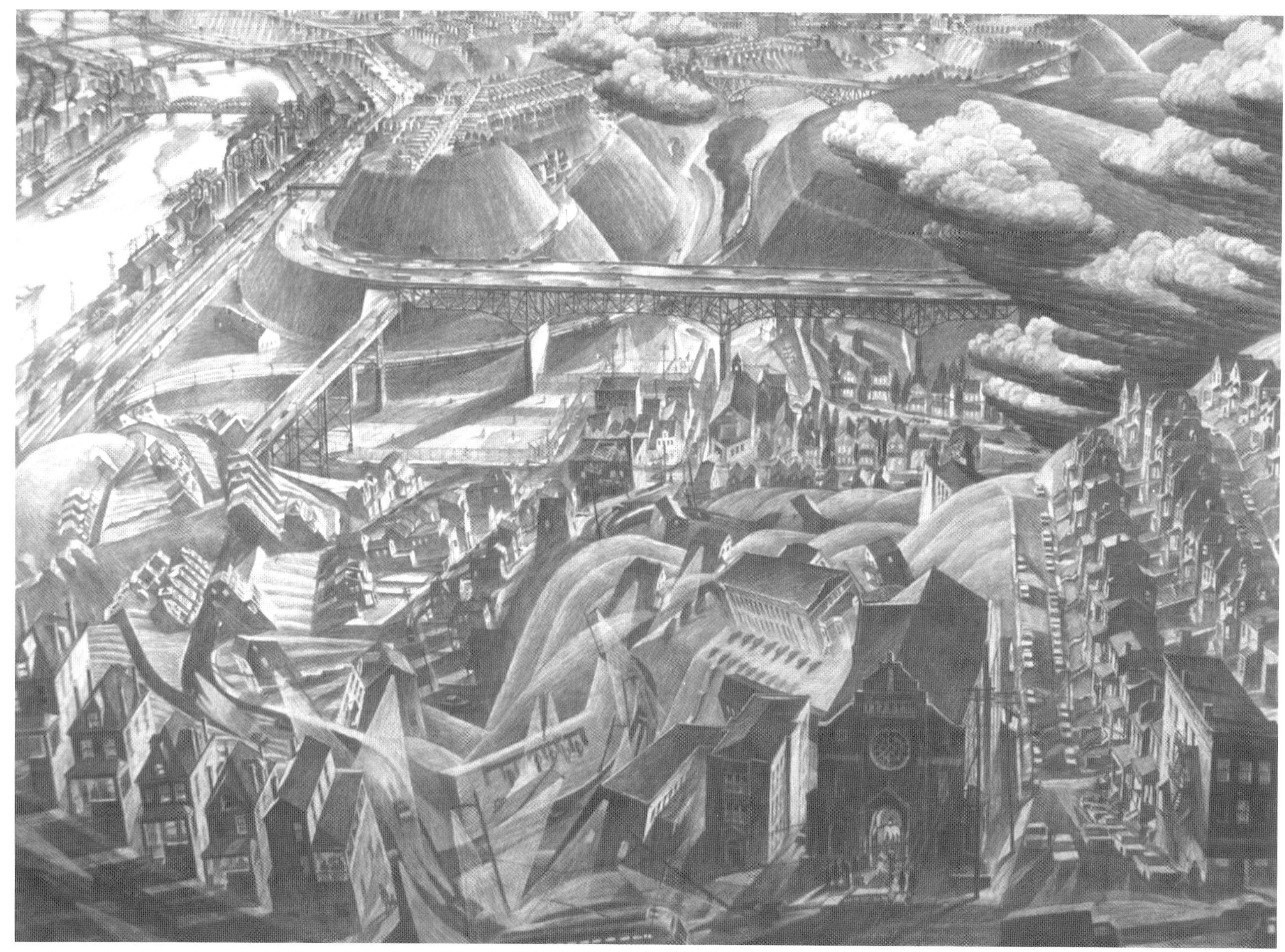

St. Rosalia, Saturday, 1997. 72″ x 96″. (Private collection.)

For Mary Jane Kelly, the memory of December 7, 1941, is forever tied to one place.

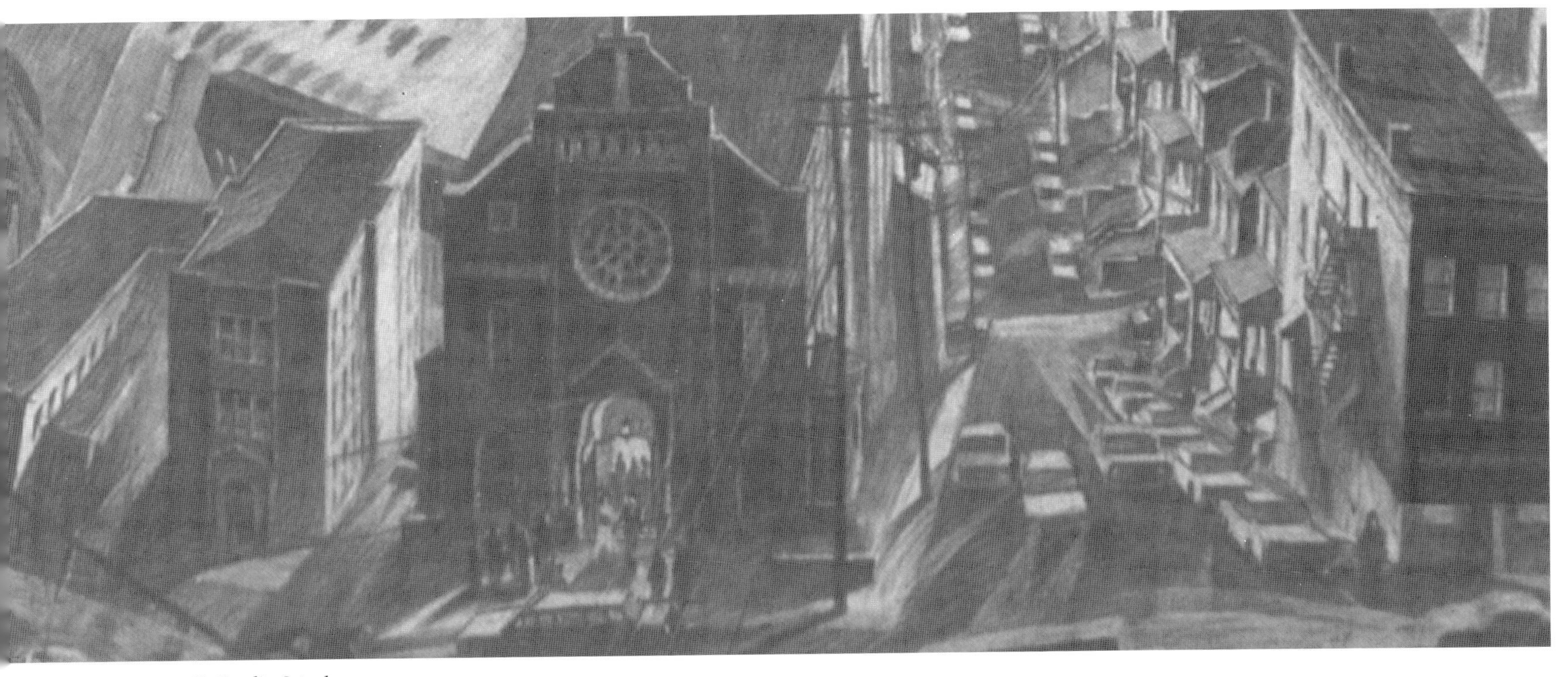

St. Rosalia, Saturday.

Mary Jane had gone with some friends to the Park Theater along Greenfield Ave. near St. Rosalia's.

after or about her parents' reaction to the news, nothing, only that moment of leaving the Park Theater and going over to her brother in front of the Greenfield Grill.

—STORY TOLD BY MARY JANE KELLY TO DOUG COOPER

Skip Hoists

The new automatic skip hoists and the equally new double-bell closure device were to make a great change in the blast furnaces. The ironwork shafts, topped by little shanties, of the old vertical skip hoists gave way to the inclined tracks, the cables and crawling buggies, of the automatic hoists; and the double

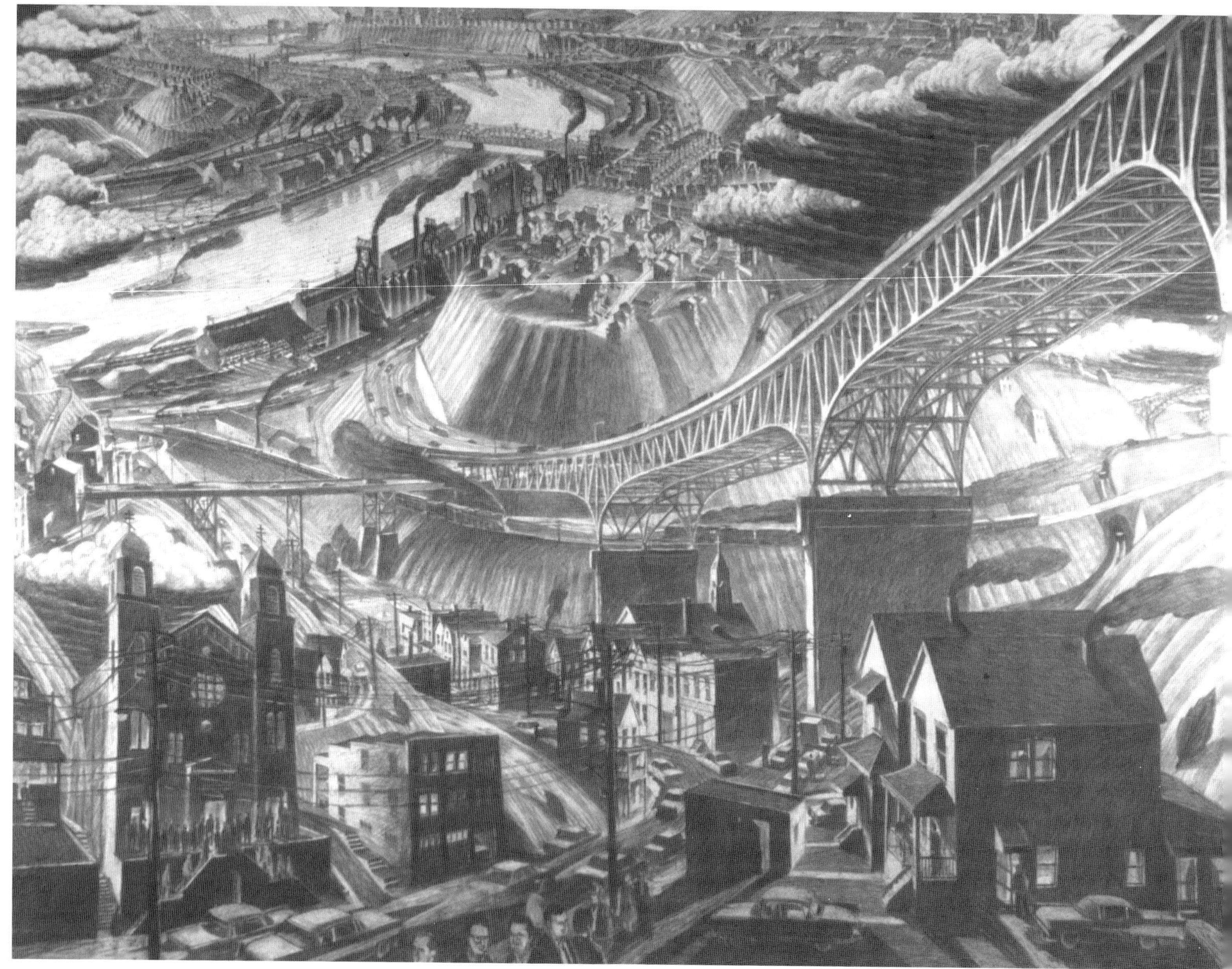

Under the Parkway Bridge.

They'd glance at the mill and wait for the flame and nothing happened.

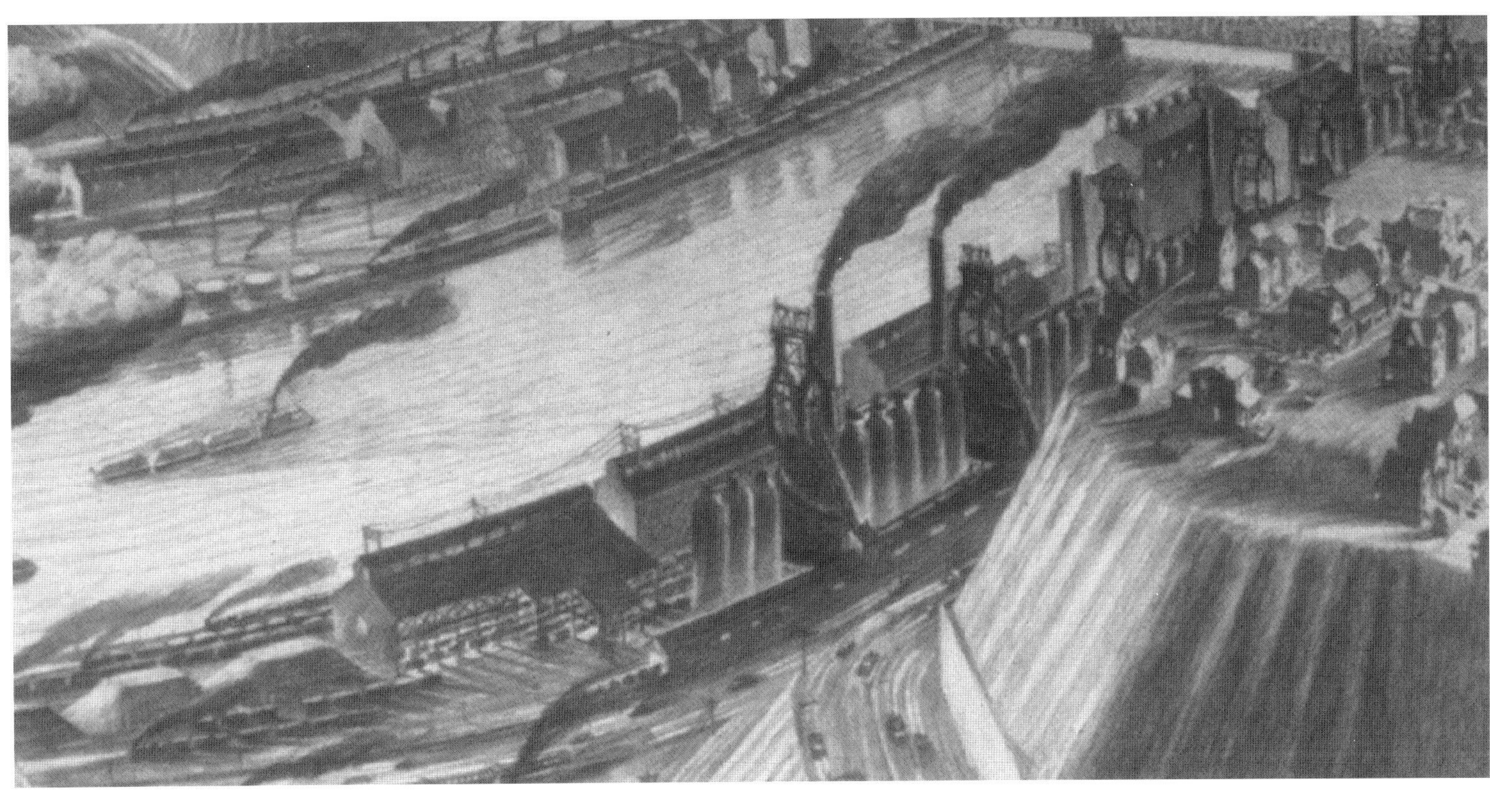

***Under the Parkway Bridge*, 1998.** 72″ x 96″. (Private collection.)

When the changes were made, the furnaces looked incomplete without the vertical shafts beside them.

bells put an end to the intermittent flames from the furnace tops. When the changes were made the furnaces looked incomplete without the vertical shafts beside them. People missed the periodic bursts of flame most of all. They'd glance at the mill and wait for the flame and nothing happened. The furnaces didn't look right, didn't look as though they were really working. At night it was as though the lights had been put out.

—THOMAS BELL, *Out of This Furnace*

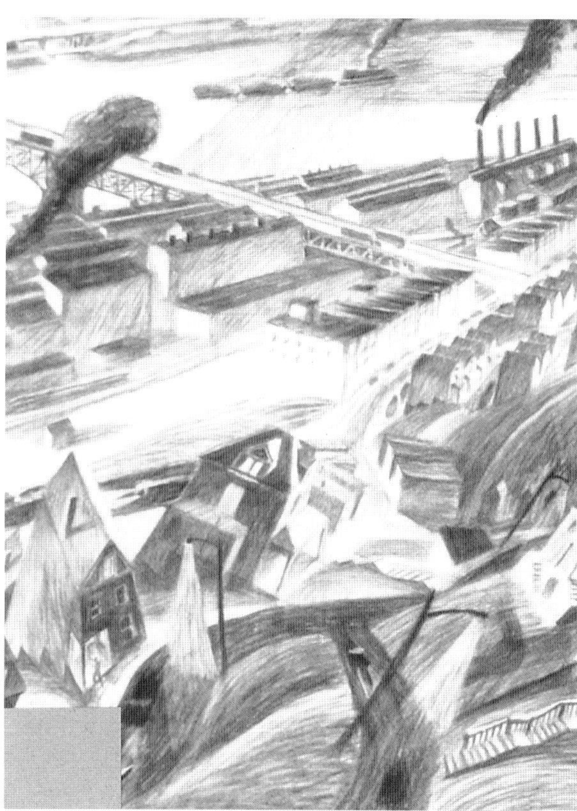

Homestead. Heinz History Center Mural. (Photo: Ken Andreyo.)

Homestead

Homestead Strike

Frick had smashed the unions at his coke ovens in Connellsville and some people said he meant to do a similar job in Homestead, that Carnegie had taken him in as much for that as because his blast furnaces needed Frick's coke. These were the same people who snorted disrespectfully when they were reminded that in books and speeches Carnegie had uttered some impressive sounds about democracy and worker's rights. Their suspicions were strengthened in May. While negotiations were still ostensibly in progress Frick had a tall fence built around the mill and erected searchlight platforms in the mill yard—hardly a peaceful gesture. The union men promptly named the mill Fort Frick. Going home one morning Kracha passed a group of carpenters working on the fence and heard a rougher call to one of them, "Do a good job on the fence, Charlie." The carpenter replied, "Ain't it a hell of a note? Like asking a man to dig his own grave."

—THOMAS BELL, *Out of This Furnace*

Until the morning of July 6, when they heard the warning blasts of the new steam whistle, no workers had trespassed on the company's property. Now hundreds of workers and townspeople stormed the works. Parts of the wooden fence that Frick had ordered built were pulled down, and the Homesteaders erected barricades

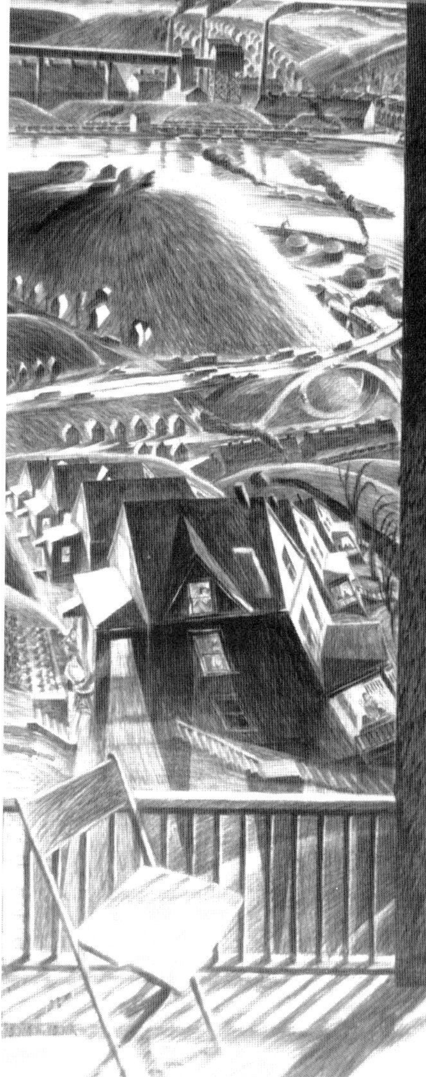

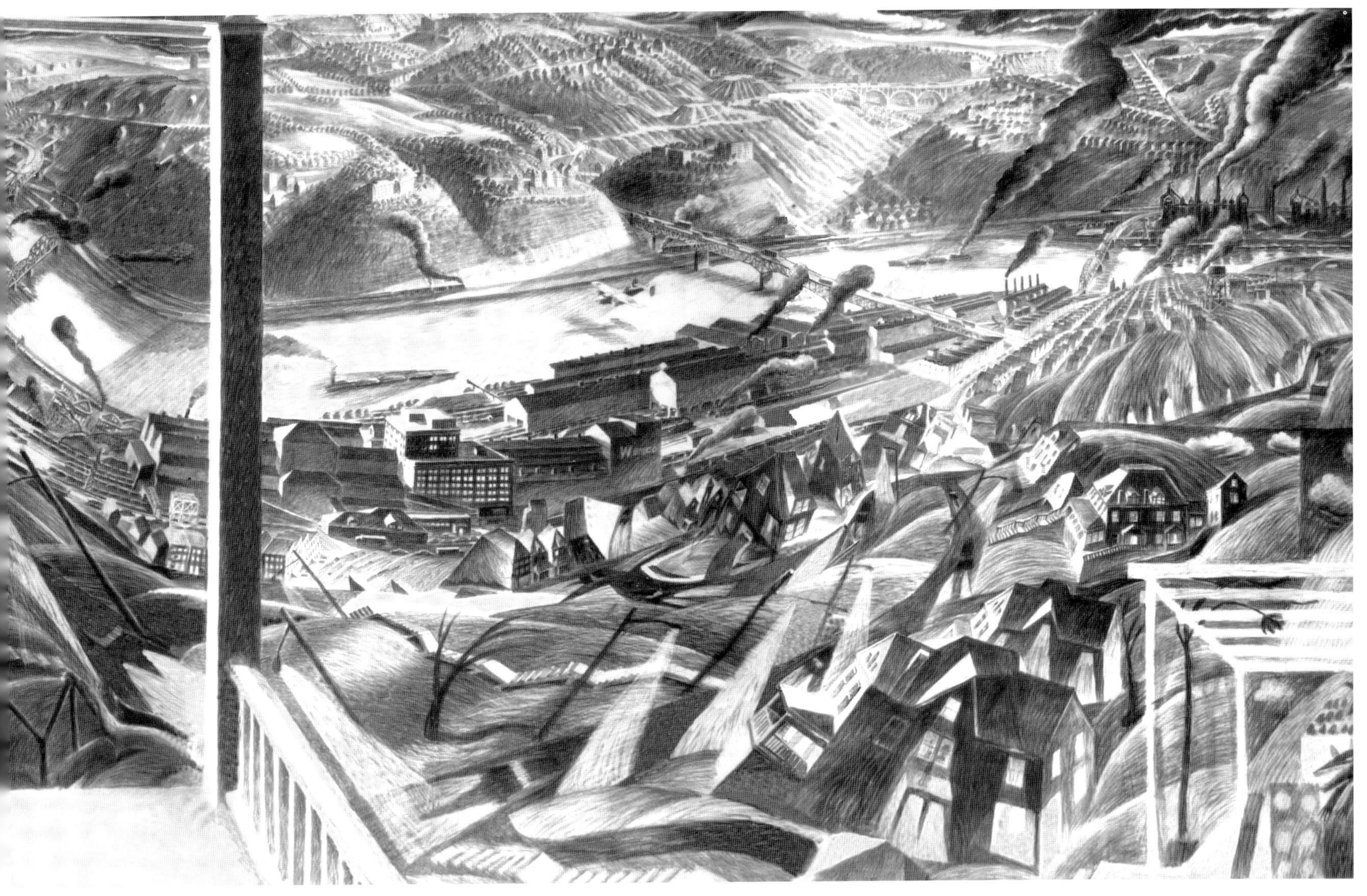

Homestead. 80″ x 178″. ***Heinz History Center Mural.*** (Photo: Ken Andreyo.)

and took up positions. Amsted Kemp, hired by the company to whitewash the fence, came to work early that morning, saw what was happening, and left town.

—WILLIAM SERRIN, *Homestead*

By the time he rose again the historic battle on the riverfront was several hours old. He breakfasted and then hurried to the upper end of the mill. Not far from the mill's general office building and nearly in line with the open end of Munhall Hollow, a roadway went down between the ten-inch mill and the boiler house to a dock at the foot of the pumping station where excursion boats docked in summer. Here, Kracha was told, two bargeloads of Pinkertons had tried to land and take possession of the mill. They were still there, effectively kept from landing by the union men barricaded on shore, and unable to leave because their tugboat had gone back to Pittsburgh.

—THOMAS BELL, *Out of this Furnace*

About 9:00 A.M., a great noise was heard—artillery! Workers across the river had obtained a cannon, loaded it with steel scrap, aimed it at the barges, and touched the piece off. A shot struck one of the barges, tearing a hole in the roof, but that was the best cannon round of the day. It was this shot, wide and long, that struck the worker Silas Wain in the mill yard and blew off his head. . . .

The firing continued. Whenever anyone, worker or Pinkerton, exposed himself, he was fired upon. At one point, it was believed, more than a thousand shots were fired within ten minutes.

—WILLIAM SERRIN, *Homestead*

Because the Homestead jail was too small to hold all the Pinkertons, the strikers marched them through the town, up the hill, to the skating rink. The women, the power behind the striking men, chanted, "Kill the murderers," and bludgeoned the unarmed Pinkertons with clubs as they were marched through the Homestead grounds. Children pelted them with rocks. A woman poked a

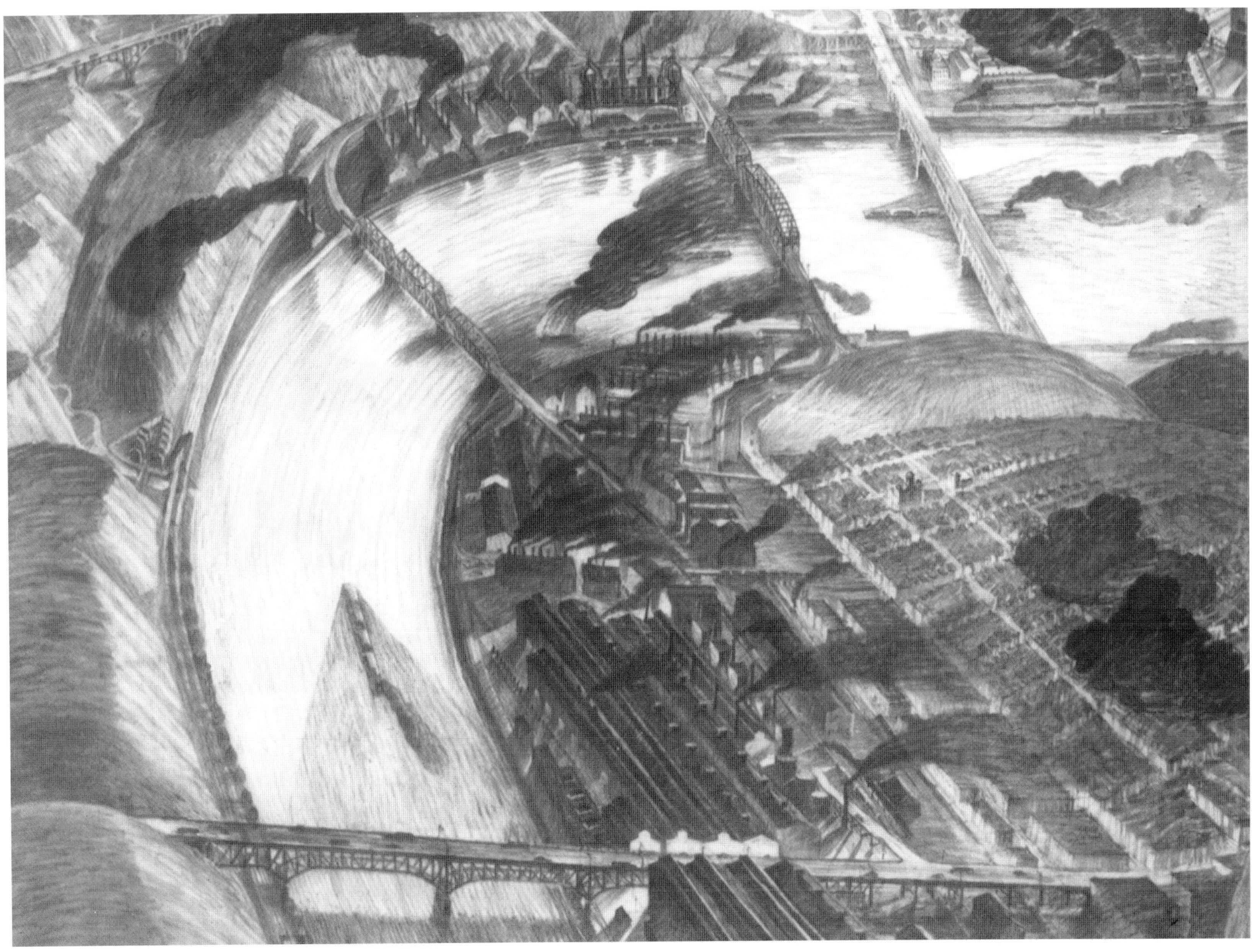

The Pinkerton barge aflame at the Homestead works. University Center Mural. (Photo: Ken Andreyo.)

About 9:00 a.m., a great noise was heard—artillery!

man's eye out with an umbrella. People kicked a guard who was on his knees begging for mercy, and clubbed him until he was unconscious.

—MARTHA FRICK SYMINGTON SANGER, *Henry Clay Frick*

The first of the dead was buried the next day. The mill was still down, the union men still in control. But on the Monday following the battle, General Snowdon came to Homestead with ten carloads of soldiers and camped on Carnegie Hill. The Homestead union leaders were arrested, charged with murder, riot and conspiracy. A notice was put up giving the men ten days to return to work, on the company's terms. Very few accepted the offer.

—THOMAS BELL, *Out of This Furnace*

Homestead in the 1950s

It seemed that nothing could stop the good times. In 1953, the corporation closed Open Hearth Number Three, "the Grand Old Lady of Victory Valley," as it had become known during World War II. Planned by Andrew Carnegie and Charles M. Schwab, and opened in 1901, OH Three consisted of twenty four furnaces—until World War II, more furnaces under one roof than at any steelworks in the world—with a capacity of seventy-five to one hundred tons apiece. In its fifty-two years of operation, OH Three turned out 148,000 tons of steel, including steel that the Homestead structural mills rolled into beams for the Empire State Building, the United Nations Building, the Delaware River Bridge, and the San Francisco–Oakland Bay Bridge. But production was not hampered by its closing. Open Hearth Four and Open Hearth Five remained open, and the works, after its wartime expansion, was larger than ever, numbering 450 buildings spread over 130 acres.

"The skies were red and blue from the steel production," said Richard Holoman, who went into the mill in July 1955 at $1.97 an hour. "Everybody was working. At Christmastime, everybody had a couple of bucks in their pocket. Christmas was good. Easter was good. The Avenue was booming, the town was booming. I'm telling you, it was a big, booming time."

—WILLIAM SERRIN, *Homestead*

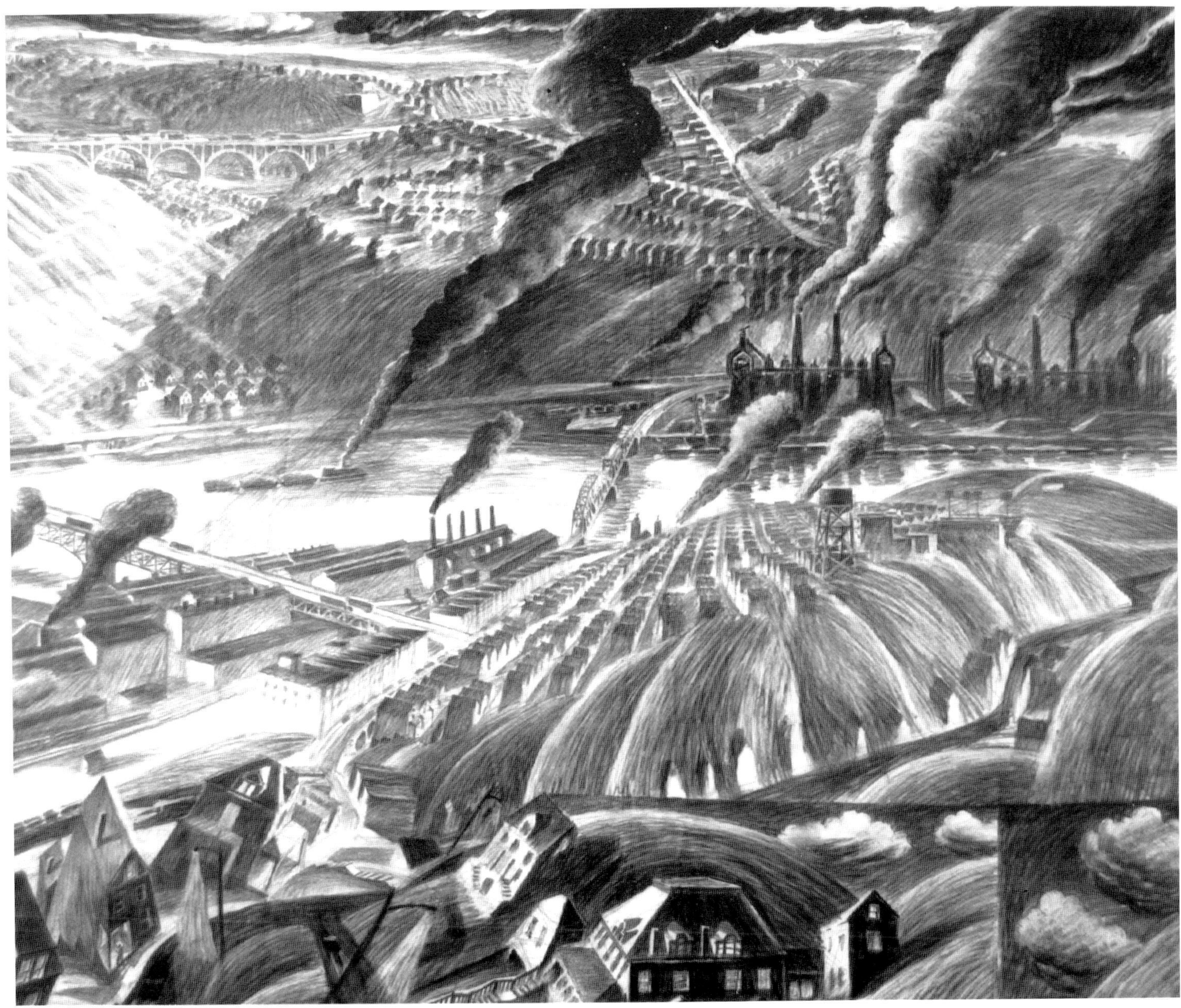

Homestead. Heinz History Center Mural.

It seemed that nothing could stop the good times.

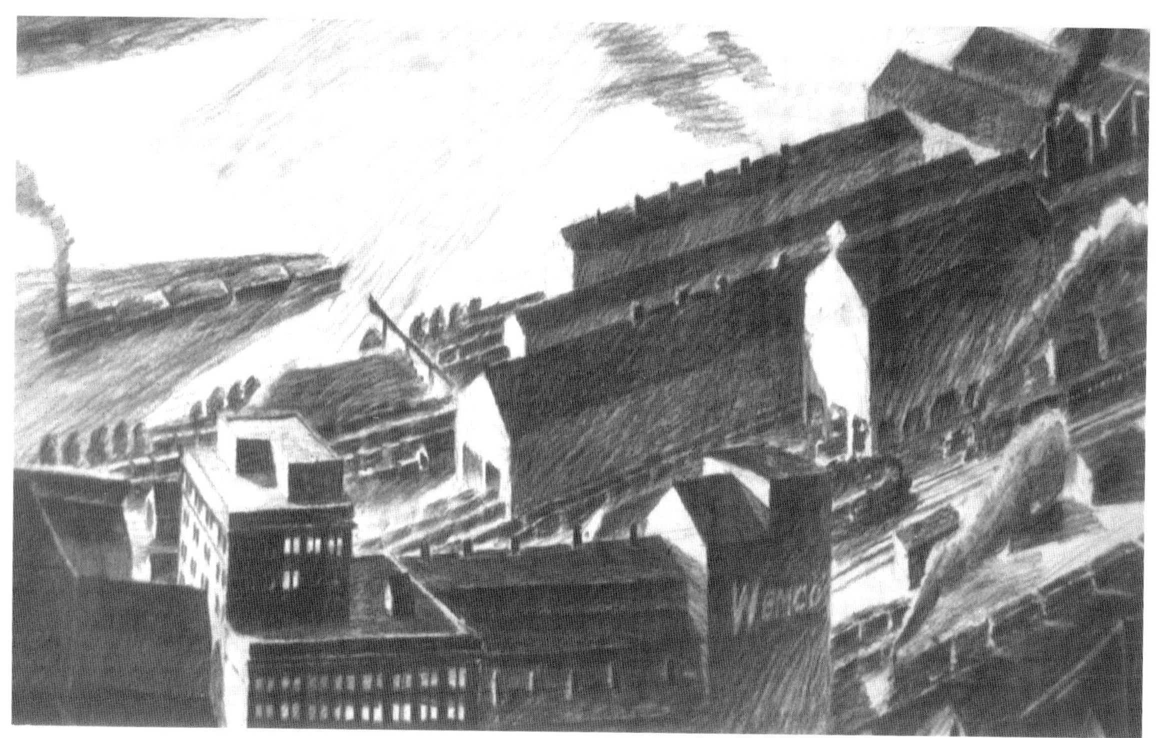

Mesta Machine Works. Heinz History Center Mural.

They brought him to the Mesta Machine Works.

Mesta Machine Works

When Nikita Khrushchev came to the United States in 1959, he was intent on seeing what he considered the defining elements of America, among them a farm and a steel mill. They brought him to Homestead, though not to the Homestead Works, which had been shut down by a nationwide steel strike, but to the Mesta Machine Works in West Homestead, manufacturers of steel machinery and, incidentally, the source of the fortune that fueled the career of international hostess Perle Mesta. The George and Perle Mesta house, with its adjacent ballroom (where her career began), still stands partway up the hill at 540 Doyle Avenue in West Homestead.

—LAURIE GRAHAM, *Singing the City*

Khrushchev's Wristwatch

Kenneth Jackey, a clerk ignoring security, stuck out his hand and presented Khrushchev a cigar, for which he had paid eight cents. Khrushchev was startled. What a splendid gesture! He wanted to give Jackey something in return. Stripping off his wristwatch, he handed it to Jackey. "It's yours," he said in Russian.

—WILLIAM SERRIN, *Homestead*

The Mystery B-25

A most puzzling occurrence, a mystery to this day, occurred on a cold gray day, January 31, 1956, when an Air Force B-25, on a mission from the West Coast to Washington, dropped out of the sky, glided west for a time over the river—the plane had lost its engines and was not making a sound—passed fifty feet above the High Level Bridge, and crashed into the Monongahela River. Traffic stopped on the bridge and in the yards at Mesta Machine as people, awestruck, watched the plane float downstream for a time, crew members huddling on the wing, then disappear beneath the cold, black water. Two servicemen drowned, four were rescued. The plane, as far as is known, was never found. Some say it washed downstream and broke up and that the parts are still there. Others believe it was on a secret mission and that the plane was somehow removed at night by American intelligence agents. The government has always remained silent on the matter—curiously so, some say.

—WILLIAM SERRIN, Homestead

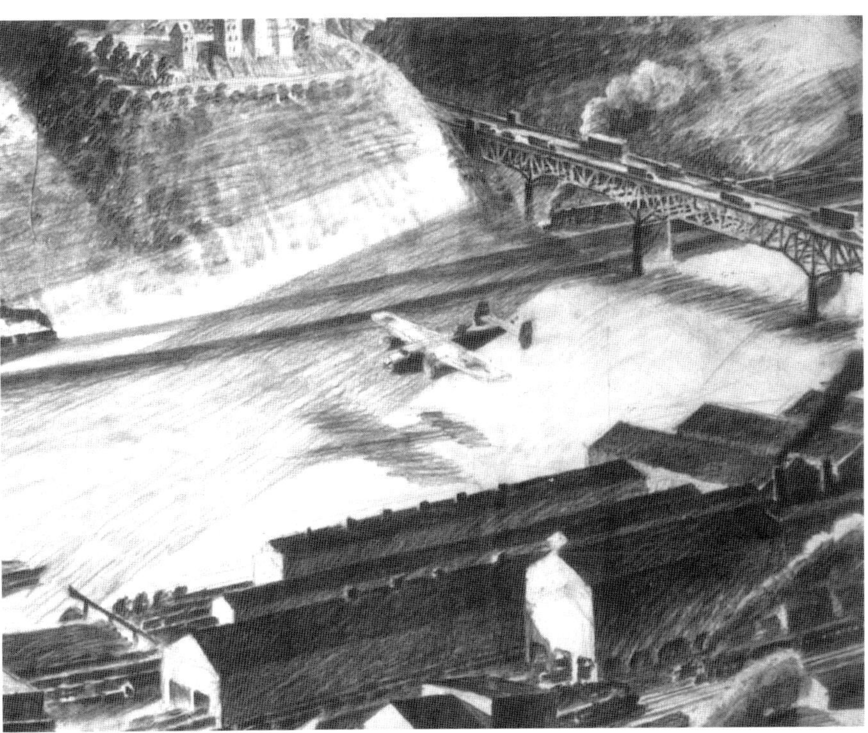

The crash landing of the mystery B-25. Heinz History Center Mural.

The government has always remained silent on the matter—curiously so, some say.

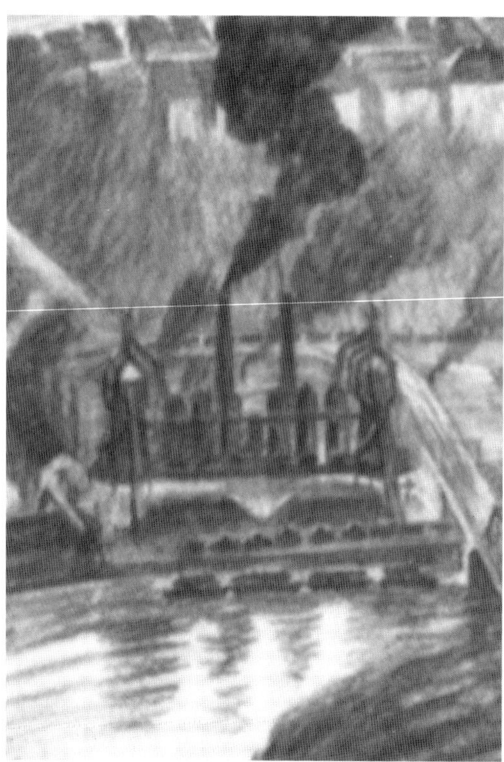

Carrie Furnace. University Center Mural.

"This saurian metal beast . . ."

Rankin, Braddock, East Pittsburgh

Carrie Furnace

This saurian metal beast under the cool sky is the body
we inhabit. To some guys, it's a woman: *more nights*
with Carrie than the old lady. In a steel shed
there's a six-inch hole a worker torched
in the wall: outside, large red lips chalked
around it say, *Kiss me on the other side*
where spread pink thighs surround it,
through the hole, a view of the furnace.

—PETER BLAIR, "Carrie Furnace"

A Hell of a Lady

A blast furnace is female for obvious reasons. She is charged with ore, then the ore is transformed in the fire of her voluminous belly. At the moment of birth molten iron bursts from her taphole amid a shower of sparks and light. "A blast furnace is temperamental as a woman," Manny said. "You feed her wrong, she gets constipated. You gotta treat 'em well."

—LAURIE GRAHAM, *Singing the City*

Braddock's Defeat

On the morning of July 9, Braddock's column reached a ford of the Monongahela River, two miles upriver from what is now Homestead, Pennsylvania. An advance party was sent across the river, and then, some time after noon, the main body crossed, drums and fifes playing "The Coldstream March." First came the Forty-fourth Regiment, the soldiers in red coats, bayonets gleaming in the sun, the king's colors snapping in the wind. Then sailors—brought along for their knowledge of ropes and knots, and to help with ferrying at the fords—barefooted, pants rolled to their knees. Then the artillery teams, brass howitzers and twelve-pounders, the pieces pulled by sweating, straining horses. Then wagons covered with white canvas, and cattle. Then Colonial soldiers, in blue, and, finally, in red, flags unfurled, the rearguard, the Forty-eighth Regiment.

All around were the sparkling blues of water and sky and the dark greens, sometimes almost black, of the forest. It was, Washington wrote years later in his autobiography, the most splendid sight he had ever seen. On the north bank of the river, the column re-formed. Commanders were confident. Some officers said they would not be surprised to hear the sound of Fort Duquesne, ten miles away, being destroyed by the French prior to retreat.

Then in the early afternoon, a quarter of a mile from the river, in a clearing, the advance guard saw a shocking sight: perhaps three hundred French soldiers and their Indian allies, many of the Indians almost naked, running at them down the narrow forest track. The British formed a line of battle across the trail. "God save the king!" a subaltern shouted.

British soldiers went down, wounded or dead. Some of the advance guard retreated and in so doing fell against the main column moving up. Confusion and disorder broke out. Some men fired upon their own ranks, killing or wounding many of their comrades. Some regulars took to the trees, but Braddock, his hat tied under his chin with a large white handkerchief, beat them with his broadsword. "Cowards!" he cried. The battle continued until the British and the Colonials retreated. Of the fifteen hundred officers and men who had gone into battle, one thousand had been killed or wounded. Braddock himself was mortally wounded.

He was carried from the field and across the river. "Who would have thought it?" Braddock said.

—WILLIAM SERRIN, *Homestead*

Edgar Thomson Works

The Edgar Thomson works marked Andrew Carnegie's decision to concentrate on manufacturing steel. Joseph Wall suggests that Carnegie's experience in bridge building may have convinced him that the age of iron was over. A brilliant engineer, James Eads, had specified steel for key portions of the bridge he was building over the Mississippi at St. Louis. The choice chagrined

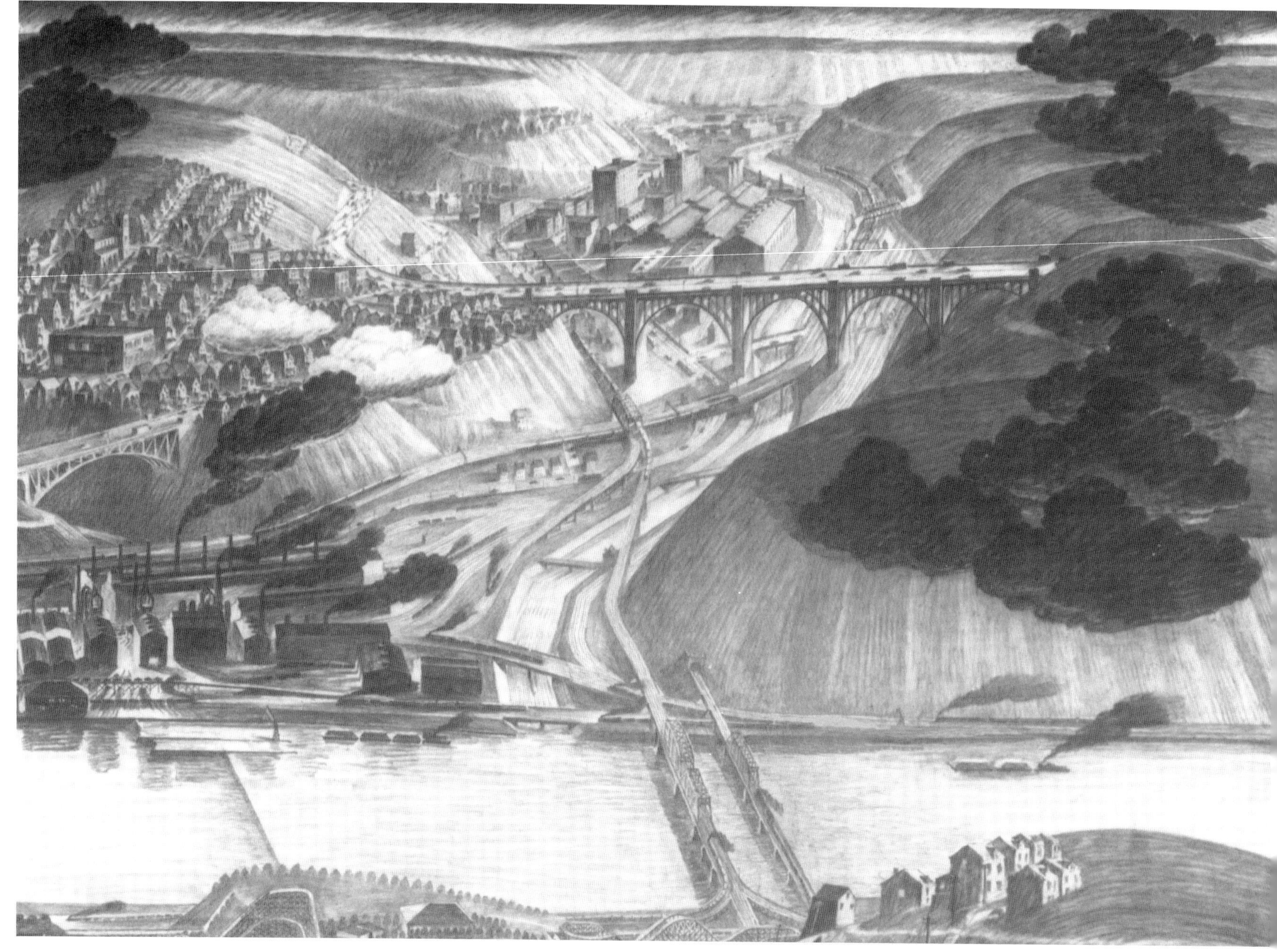

Edgar Thompson Works. University Center Mural. (Photo: Ken Andreyo.)

The importance of bridges had multipled with the rapid expansion of the railways.

Carnegie, whose Keystone Bridge Company built with iron. Engineers and scientists concurred that Eads was right in his insistence.

The importance of bridges in America had multiplied with the rapid expansion of railways which, in turn, meant nothing less than mastery of the continent. Carnegie named his works—in 1875 the most advanced Bessemer plant in the world—for an old colleague who happened to control the Pennsylvania Railroad. The Bessemer process made possible the economic production of durable rails, and therefore Carnegie expected railroads to be his best customers.

—BARRINGER FIFIELD, *Seeing Pittsburgh*

Westinghouse Bridge

The Department of Public Works (DPW) then took the knowledge gathered during construction of the Ohio River Boulevard arches to create what is perhaps the masterpiece of the DPW's bridge construction program: the spectacular, 1,598-foot-long, Westinghouse Memorial Bridge (1932). The 460-foot-long main span was the longest reinforced concrete highway bridge in the Western Hemisphere. Erected to eliminate chronic bottlenecks on the Lincoln Highway (U.S. 30), the bridge carries traffic high above the narrow and congested streets of East Pittsburgh and Turtle Creek.

DPW engineers considered numerous bridge designs for the location, including a cantilevered steel deck truss that would have been less costly than the bridge that was built. They settled on a reinforced concrete open spandrel arch because of its "superior architectural merit." The monumental bridge carries the highway 200 feet above the valley floor. Adding to the dramatic appearance is the extremely high "rise-to-span ratio" of the arches. The central span rises 153 feet over a 460-foot span. The great height is accentuated by the decorative end pylons that illustrate the achievements of industrialist George Westinghouse. (The Westinghouse air brake plant is located just to the south.) According to design engineer George S. Richardson, the bridge's monumental character, slenderness and simplicity were meant to bring order over the chaotic industrial valley, which was already crossed by three levels of transportation.

A trade journal described the Westinghouse Bridge as "spectacular in the service it renders, in the boldness of its design and erection, in the grace and symmetry of its architecture, and in its location over a busy industrial valley." It was compared with other engineering marvels of its era, such as the Hoover Dam, the George Washington Bridge, and the Holland Tunnel.

—GERALD M. KUNCIO, "The Golden Age in the City of Bridges" (courtesy of the Historical Society of Western Pennsylvania)

Under the Westinghouse Bridge

"I first made love under that bridge," a man announced from over my shoulder in a voice with too much "California Dreamin" to be believed. I had just drawn the Union Railroad trestle where it crosses the Pennsylvania Railroad's mainline under the shadow of the Westinghouse Bridge. It was the summer of 1993, and I was drawing a mural at the Carnegie Museum, a kind of work-in-

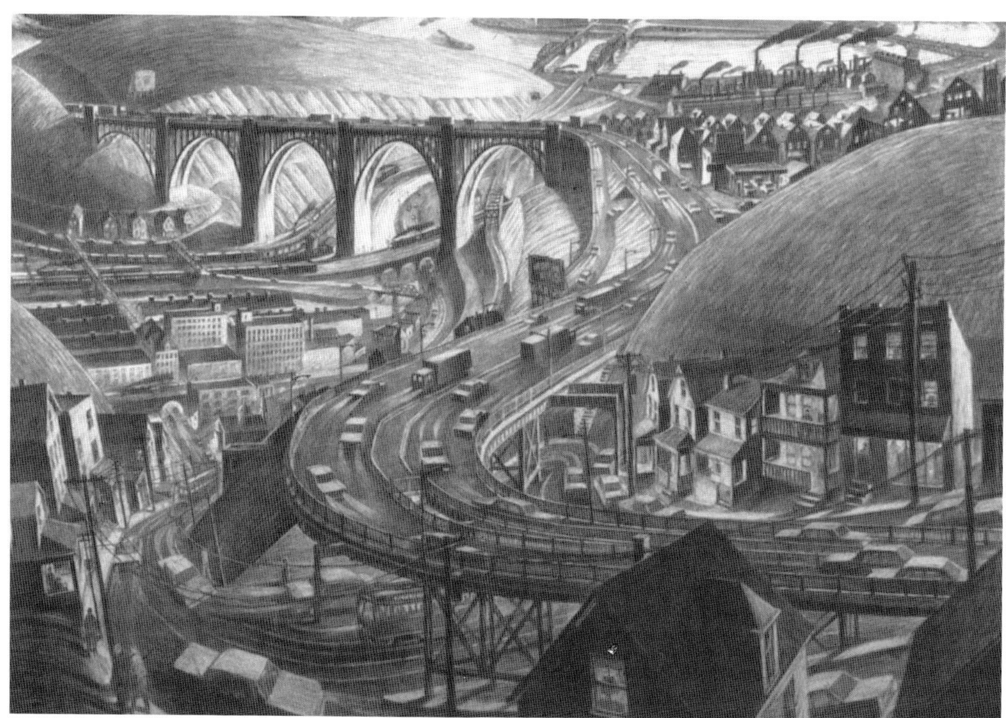

Route 30, Descending into East Pittsburgh, 1998. 48″ x 60″.

The bridge's monumental character, slenderness, and simplicity were meant to bring order over the chaotic industrial valley.

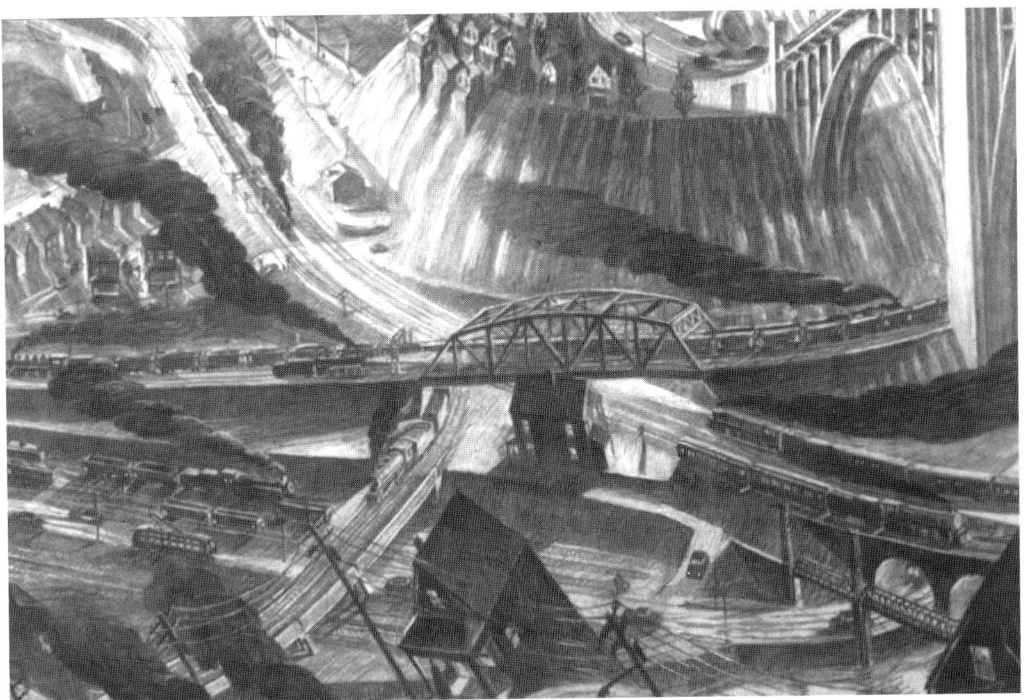

Morning Arrivals in Turtle Creek, 1997. 72″ x 96″.

(Private collection.)

"I first made love under that bridge," a man announced from over my shoulder.

progress show, in real time, in front of the public. People often came by and talked to me while I drew. I'd gotten used to it.

But there were four tracks in those days between the trestle abutments, I was thinking, and I could not imagine how or where this passionate event might have fit. There wasn't enough space. He was from L.A., I soon learned. What else should I expect?

But then he started talking about the Westinghouse Bridge and about his teenage years growing up in East Pittsburgh. Among his friends, he told me, there had been a rite of passage into manhood. Each of them had to climb down under the bridge deck, walk along the suspended inspection track, and then leap a yard or so across thin air to a concrete shelf at the bridge pier high up over the Pennsylvania tracks. There they painted their names. There he had painted his.

On his current visit back to Pittsburgh, he had gone under the bridge. Though he had not made the leap, he had made sure his name was still there.

—DOUGLAS COOPER

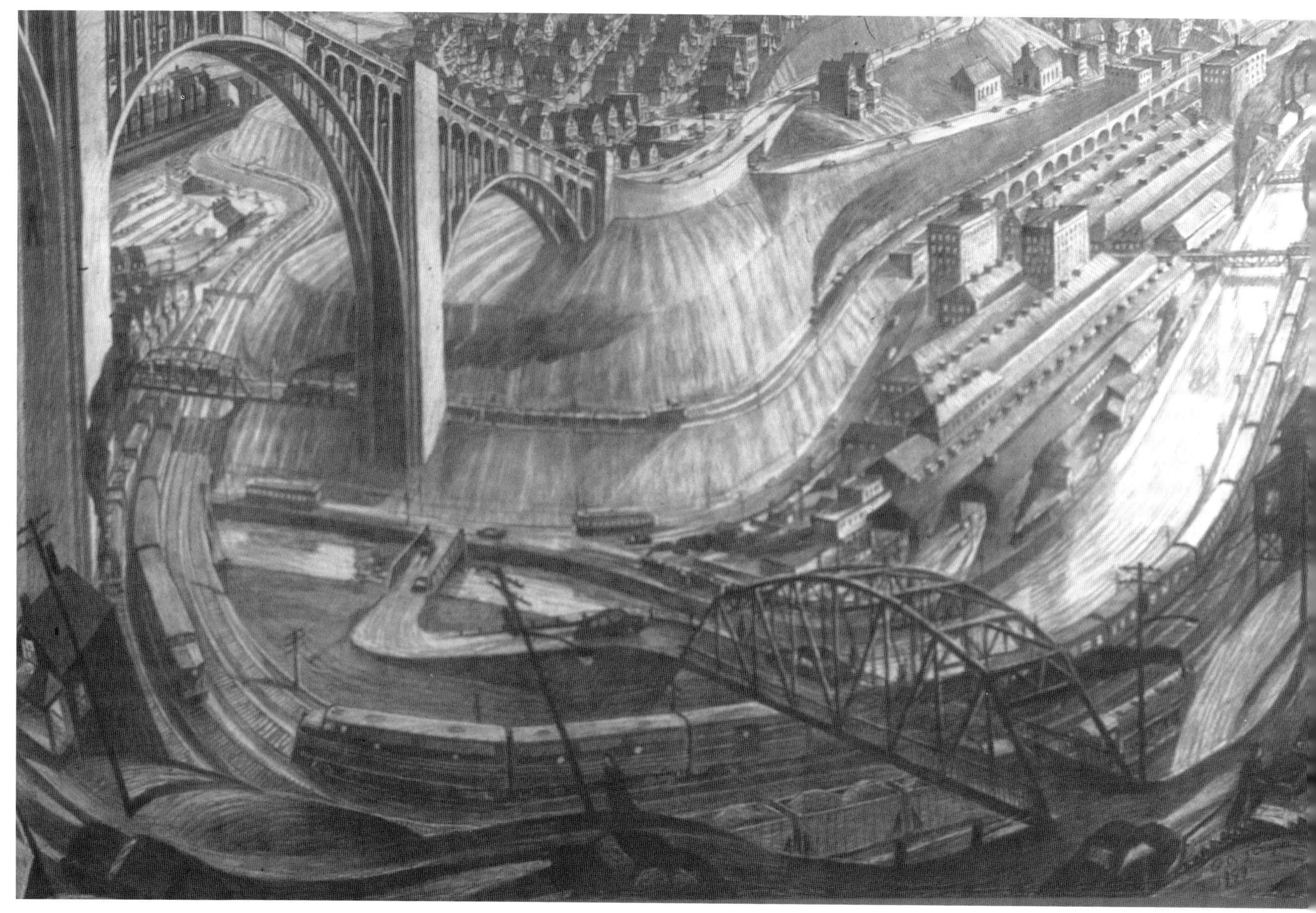

Morning Train under Westinghouse Bridge.

Two main lines led directly into Westinghouse Airbrake.

Russian Hill

After a short walk out Station Street, he charged the steep, red sandy slope. Hands and feet slipped on clumps of loose dirt and shale as he scrambled to the dirt trail above. His first quick steps and panting spooked a ringneck pheasant from nearby bramble bushes. Honking, it flew to the Wall side of the hill. Wall and Wilmerding were sister communities that stretched along Turtle Creek. Railroad tracks ran East and West from Wall, parallel on both sides of the creek, sepia colored from sulfur and other pollutants deposited by local industry. Two main lines led directly into the Westinghouse Airbrake and other mills further down the valley. Georgie had often heard it said: "If the Wall trackyards weren't there, then the Airbrake wouldn't be either." And without the Airbrake Plant, there would never have been a Wilmerding. Georgie had wondered where he'd be if that were so.

—GERALD MUSINSKY, "On Russian Hill," in *Mill Hunk Herald* no. 16, Spring 1985.

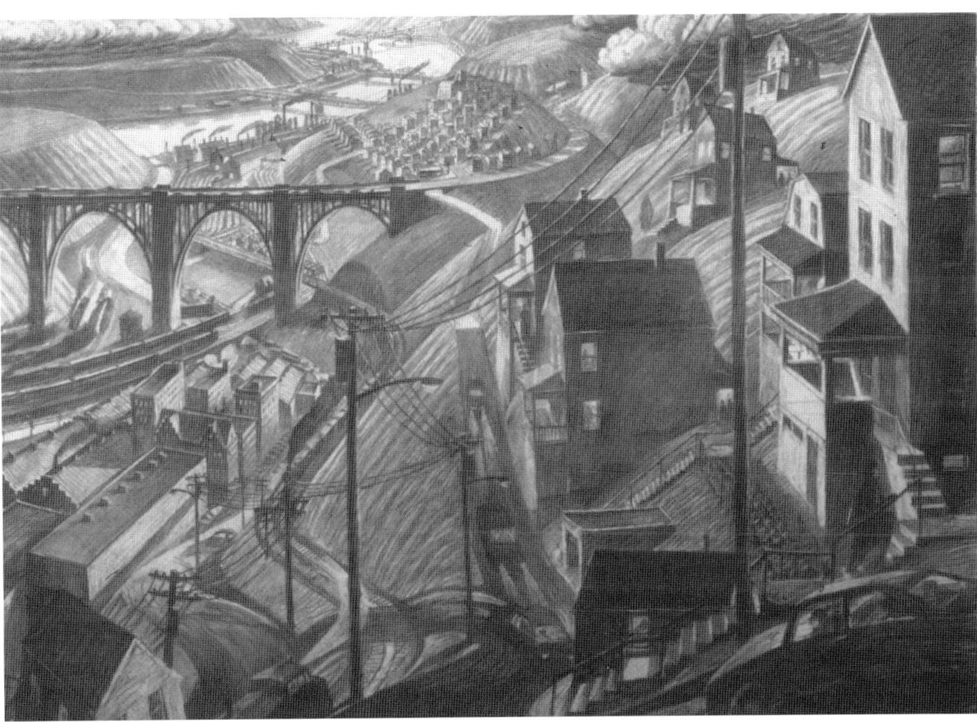

***Down to Turtle Creek*, 1998.** 36″ x 48″.

And without the airbrake plant, there would never have been a Wilmerding.

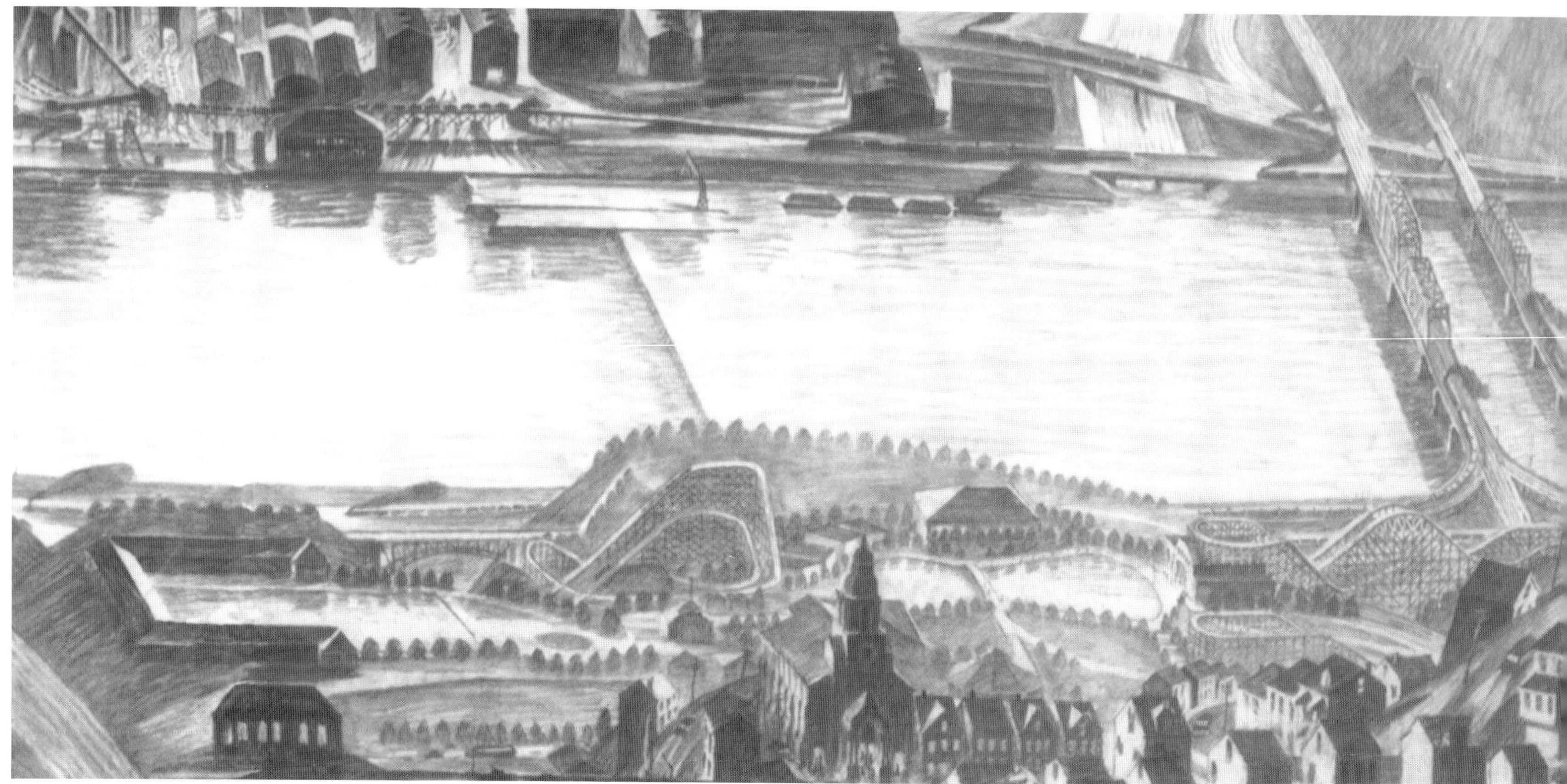

Kennywood Park. University Center Mural. (Photo: Ken Andreyo.)

Kennywood Park management has moved a section of Atlantic City within two car checks of downtown Pittsburgh.

Kennywood

The Kennywood Pool

By 1925, two free trips to Atlantic City weren't necessary as the *Pittsburgh Sunday Post* said that "Kennywood Park management has moved a section of Atlantic City within two car checks of downtown Pittsburgh." Kennywood built one of the largest (350 feet by 180 feet) and most modern swimming pools anywhere. The pool, which cost $150,000, held 2,250,000 gallons of water. It had a colonial style pavilion with a 2,500-seat grandstand built over the dressing room. A 25-foot wide sand beach containing 20 railroad carloads of white sand surrounded the pool on three sides.

Beach guards were instructed to rigidly enforce prohibitions against one-piece suits, jostling and rowdyism, and diving from the rails. The women's dressing rooms contained electric hair dryers and curlers. It cost fifty cents to use the pool and an additional twenty-five cents to rent one of Kennywood's 4,500 sterilized bathing suits. Spectator tickets were ten cents each and children's tickets were twenty-five cents with suit rental fifteen cents.

—CHARLES J. JACQUES JR., *Kennywood*

The Racers

Because they liked John Miller's previous work, they hired him to build a new twin or racing coaster. Brady McSwigan wanted a "snappy ride that wasn't too much for mothers and children to ride."

The new Racer was one of the most beautiful racing coasters ever built. It cost more than $75,000 because Miller didn't use the topography as he had with the Jack Rabbit and Pippin. The highest hill of the new Racer was actually built

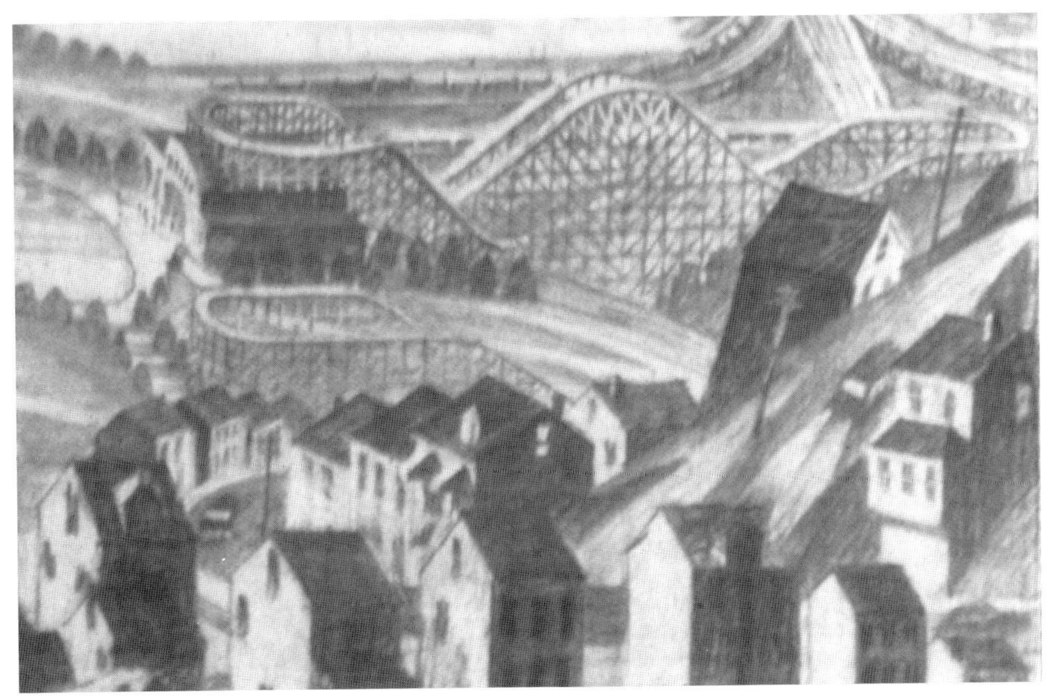

The Racers, Kennywood Park. University Center Mural. (Photo: Ken Andreyo.)

The new Racer was one of the most beautiful racing coasters ever built.

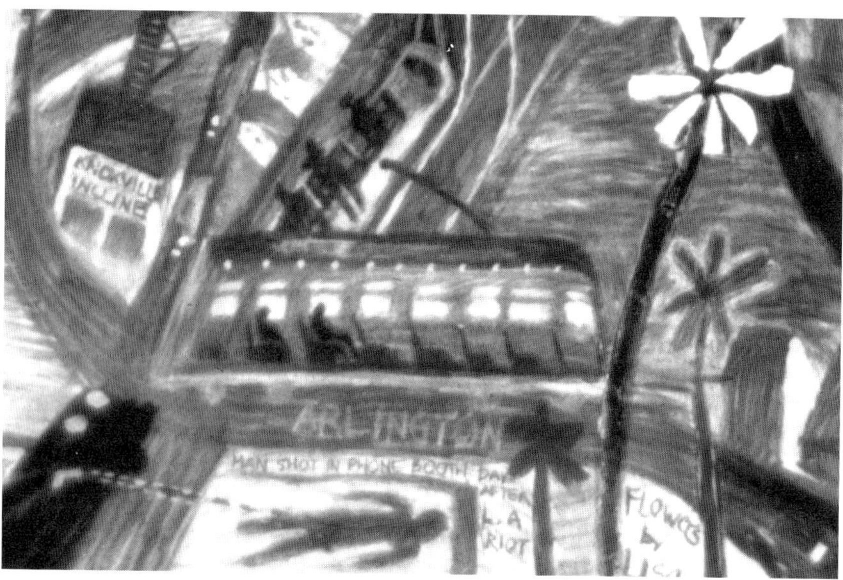

Lisa's Flowers. Heinz History Center Mural.

Just as I was drawing in some flowers, a report came over the radio. . . . A man was shot and killed in a phone booth.

in a ravine and much more lumber was required. Miller designed a reverse curve so that the train that started on the right side of the loading platform would finish on the left side. The new Racer had wheels under the tracks, which permitted banked curves as well as curves on the dips.

—CHARLES J. JACQUES JR., *Kennywood*

18th St. Valley–Birmingham

The Day after the L.A. Riot

On the day after the Rodney King L.A. Riot, I was in my studio drawing Lisa's Flower Store at the corner of Warrington Street and Arlington Road from a sketch I'd done earlier. Just as I was drawing in some flowers, a report came over the radio. There had been a drive-by shooting earlier that morning. A man was shot and killed in a phone booth. The phone booth was at the corner of Warrington and Arlington.

I mixed a slurry of the ugliest color and texture I could make, a mixture of acrylic and charcoal dust that makes a black goo, which is vaguely purple. With this I painted in the drive-by next to the flower store.

—DOUGLAS COOPER

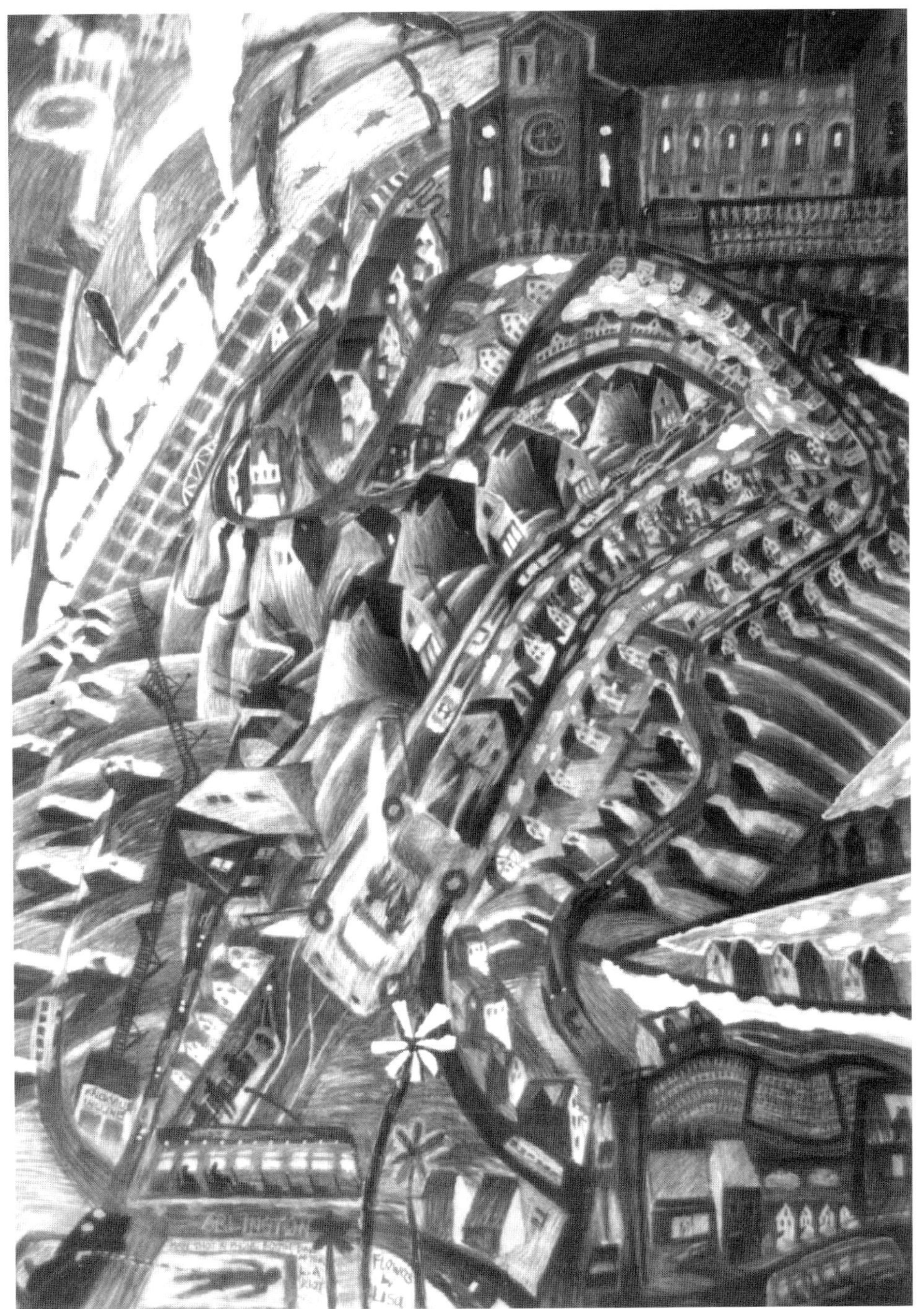

Below St. Paul's Monastary. Heinz History Center Mural.

The phone booth was at the corner of Warrington and Arlington.

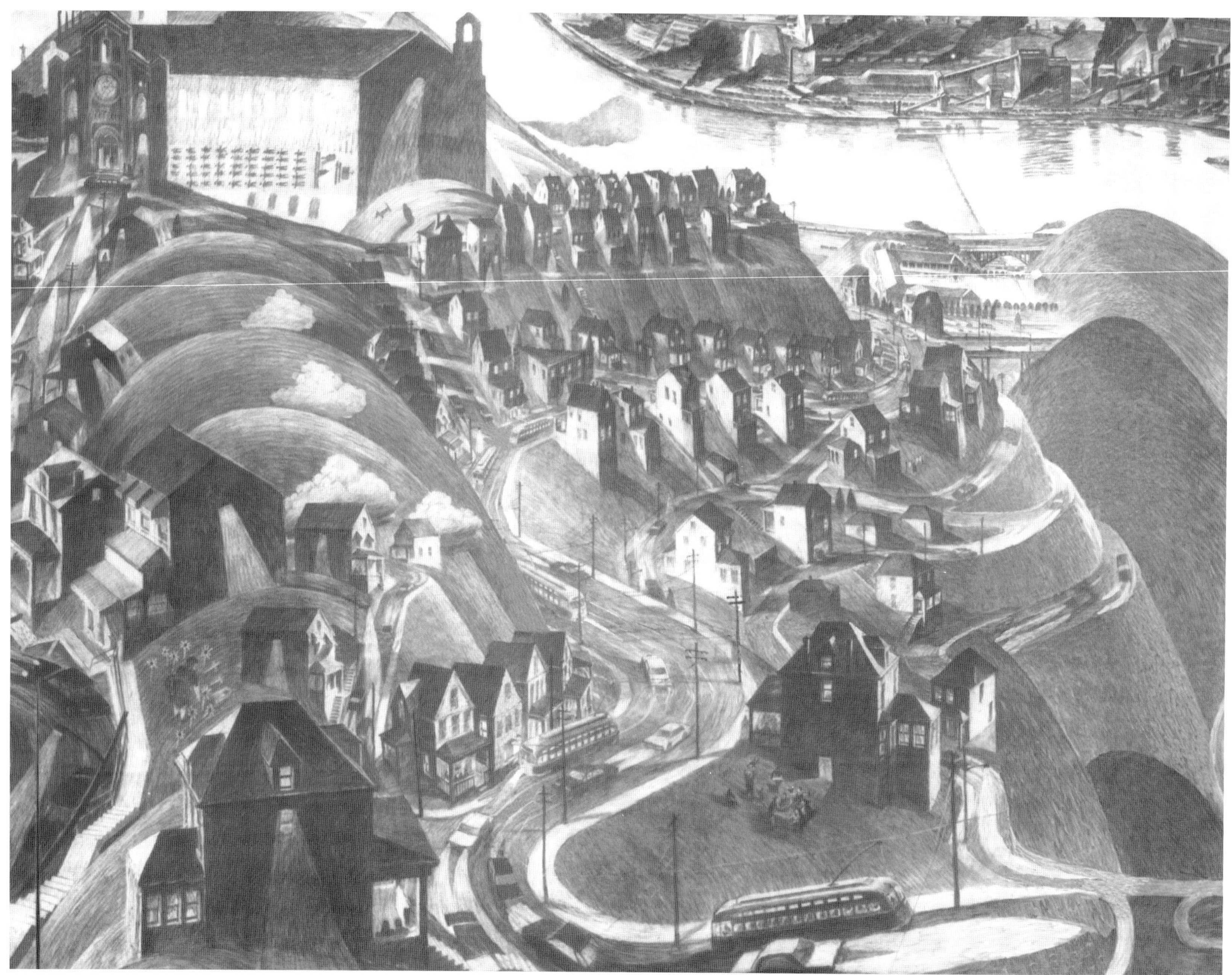

18th St. Valley. University Center Mural. (Photo: Ken Andreyo.)

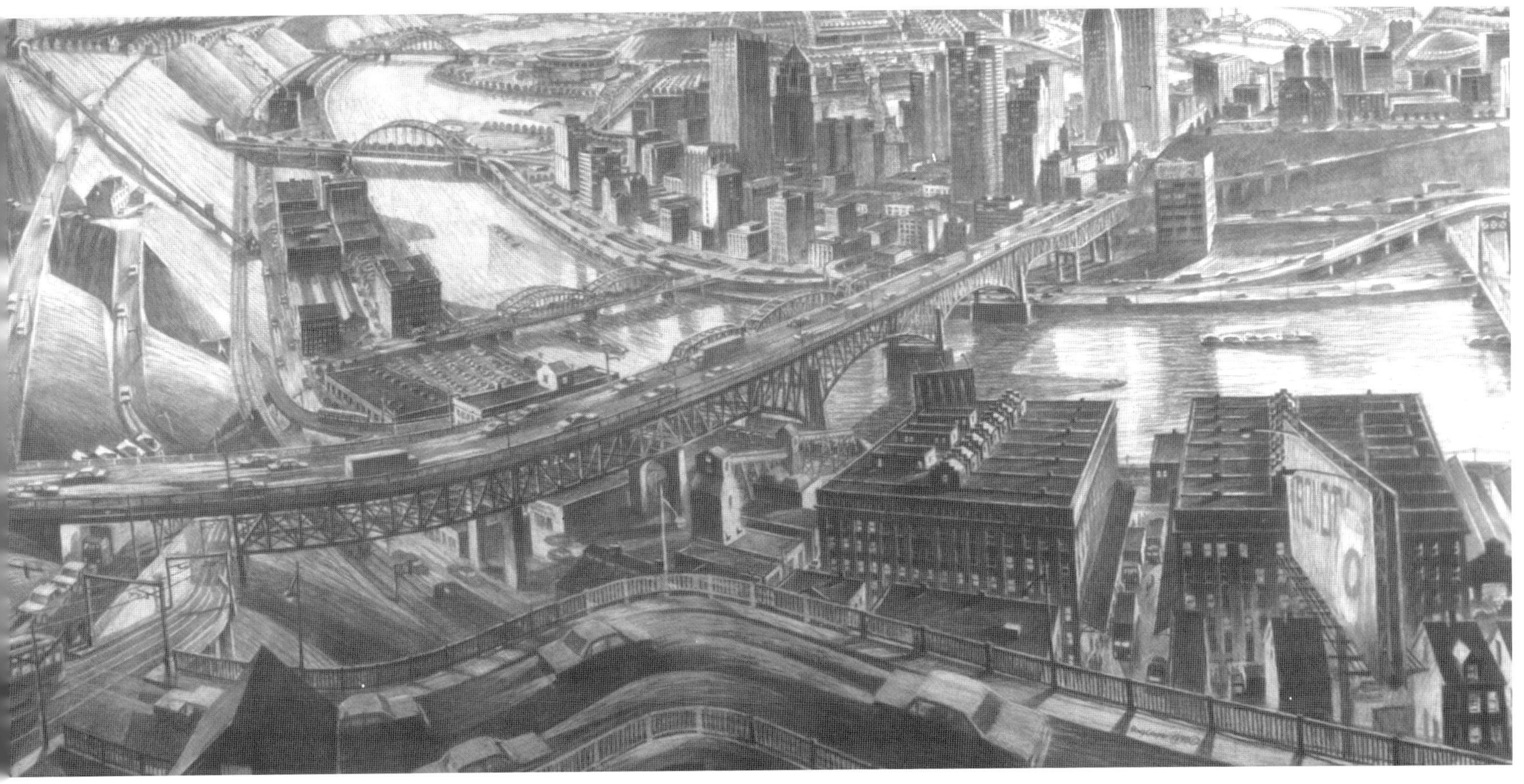

Liberty Bridge and the McCardle Roadway, 1998. 48″ x 96″. (Private collection.)

The bridge had two 420-foot spans with lower chords shaped like segmented arches.

Liberty Bridge and Tubes

The opening of the Liberty Tubes in 1924 seemed to offer a quick penetration of Mount Washington and speedy distribution of automobile traffic to points of the South Hills too far for a walk to the trolley: no straphanging, no jamming-together of houses. But bad ventilation led one day to a panic, and that to a closing until a ventilation system could be contrived. Even after that was done, a bridge envisioned as early as 1910 remained incomplete until 1928.

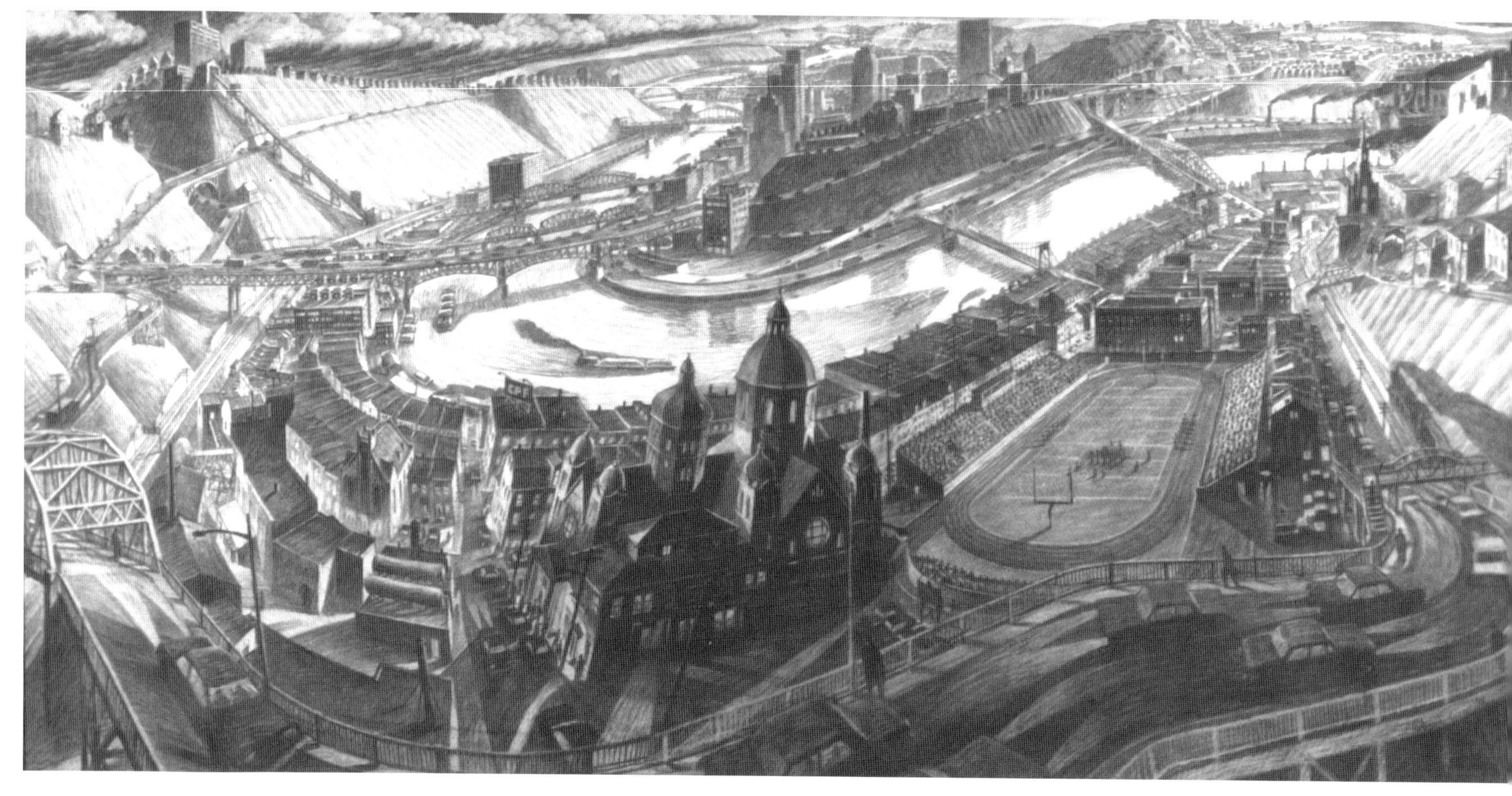

St. John's and the McCardle Roadway, 1998. 48″ x 96″. (Private collection.)

". . . the turquoise colored Byzantine domes of this exotic structure add a note of remote and Eastern fantasy."

The Liberty Bridge, once opened, linked the Tubes with the Boulevard of the Allies as it descended toward town.

The bridge had two 420-foot spans with lower chords shaped like segmented arches, though in fact they consisted of two cantilever trusses and a suspended span. In the 1920s a continuous girder over more than two points of support presented too many variables to be calculated, and the continuity had to be broken. The suspended span, artfully concealed, is at the center of the northern main span.

—WALTER KIDNEY, *Pittsburgh's Bridges*

St. John the Baptist

In the variegated vistas of the Monongahela River Valley near the Point, the turquoise colored Byzantine domes of this exotic structure add a note of remote and Eastern fantasy to the commercial longeurs and the green hills of the Pittsburgh landscape. The juxtaposition of these onion domes with factory chimneys and roofs of mills is almost startling, but by no means uncommon in our Western Pennsylvania valleys. These domes are important as well because they bear historical witness to the presence of immigrant groups that helped to form the past image of Pittsburgh as one of the great workshops of the world. . . . They belong essentially to the world of fable and dreams.

—JAMES D. VAN TRUMP AND ARTHUR ZIEGLER, *Landmark Architecture of Allegheny County, Pennsylvania*

Mt. Washington–Downtown

R.C.'s Game

Bob Skydell first brought me into R.C.'s game. It was a revolving poker game that went from house to house occasionally, but usually met at R.C.'s house. The game was very low stakes, penny-nickle-dime, but was hotly contested. No games with wild cards were allowed. The game kept records dating back to the 1920s, and these allowed players to know and measure their standing against the full weight of history. Around the room were photographs of

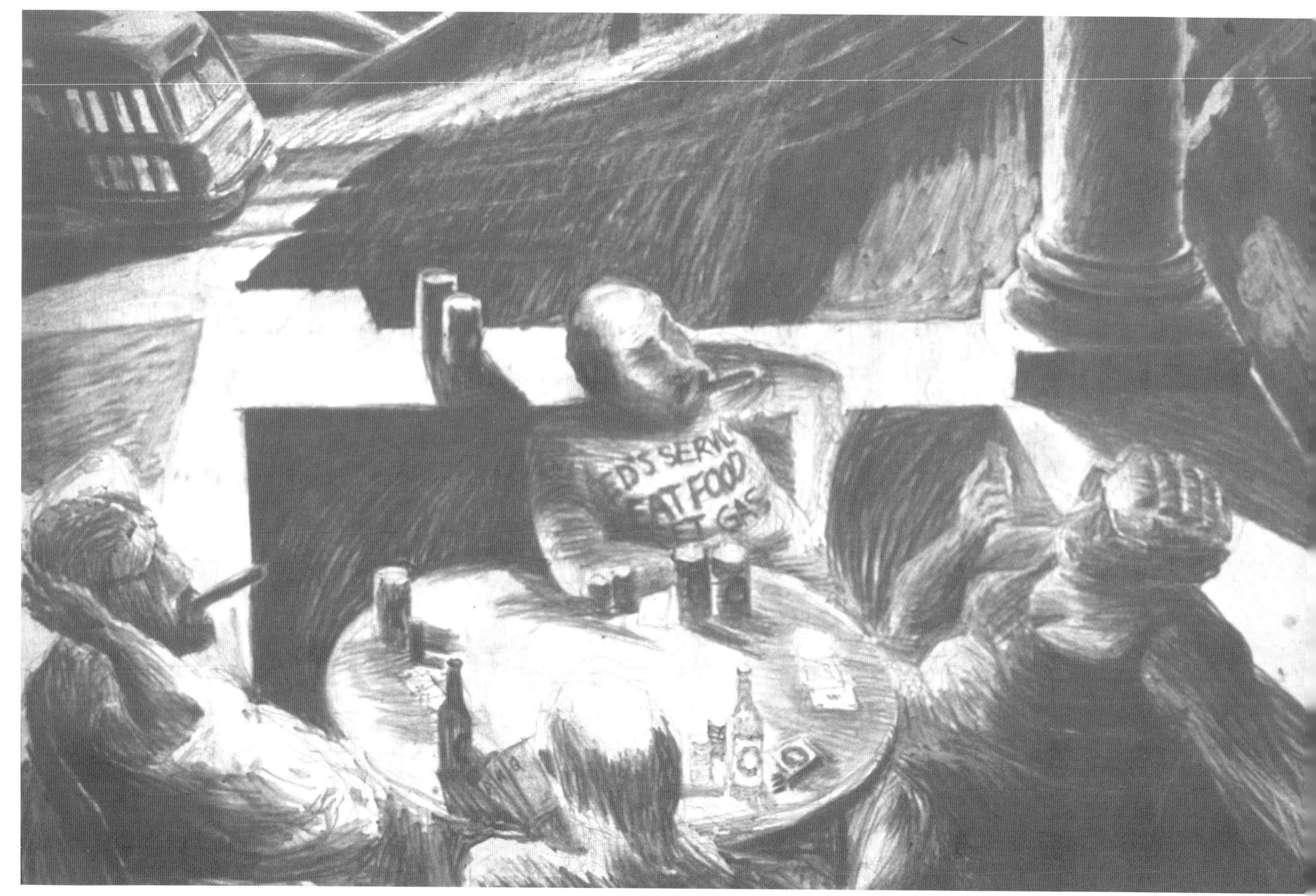

Poker on the Porch. Heinz History Center Mural.

In that moment, it actually seemed possible that shots might be fired over a four-dollar pot.

some of the founding members, wearing top hats. All this tradition had the effect of greatly enlarging the perceived value of the pots. Even at penny-nickle-dime, you could bluff at R.C.'s game.

All of the players had nicknames. There was "D-Jay." There was "P-51," who had been a fighter pilot during the war, and "Black Tom," who was a cop. Once Black Tom brought his piece with him and actually placed it on the table as he bluffed an opponent. In that moment, it actually seemed possible that shots might be fired over a four-dollar pot.

Although he was a good player, R.C. was beset by phobias. One prevented him from ever crossing bridges. This limited his experience of Pittsburgh (and the location of the game as well) to the several blocks near his house. But R.C. was a master of odds. Nailed to the molding around the door of his living room were all of the royal straight flushes that had ever been dealt in the game, dating back to the 1920s. These were displayed fanlike and were signed by all those who had been present on each occasion. As I remember, there were ten or so.

—DOUGLAS COOPER

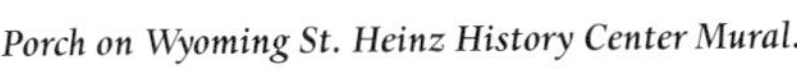

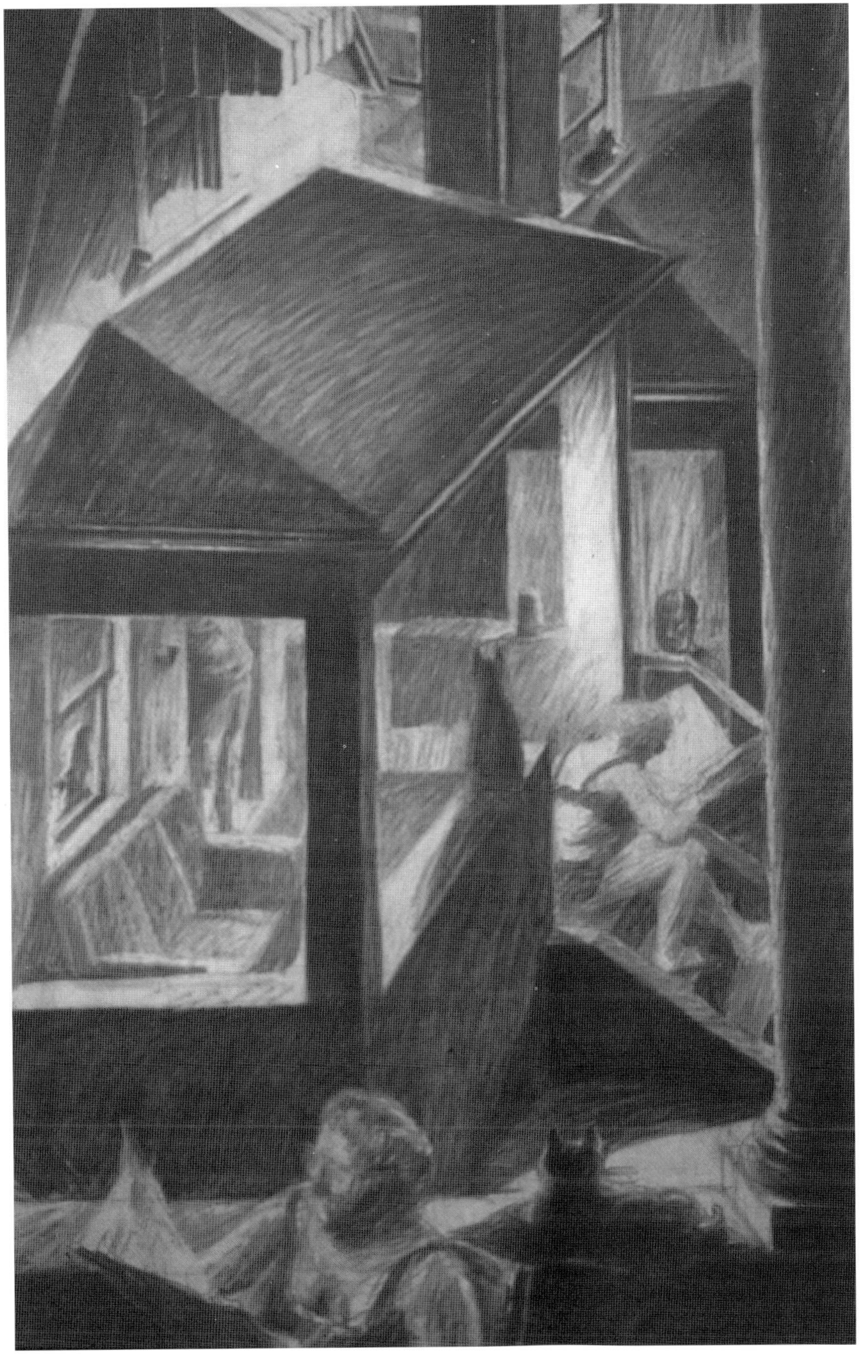

Porch on Wyoming St. Heinz History Center Mural.

It was a revolving game that went from house to house.

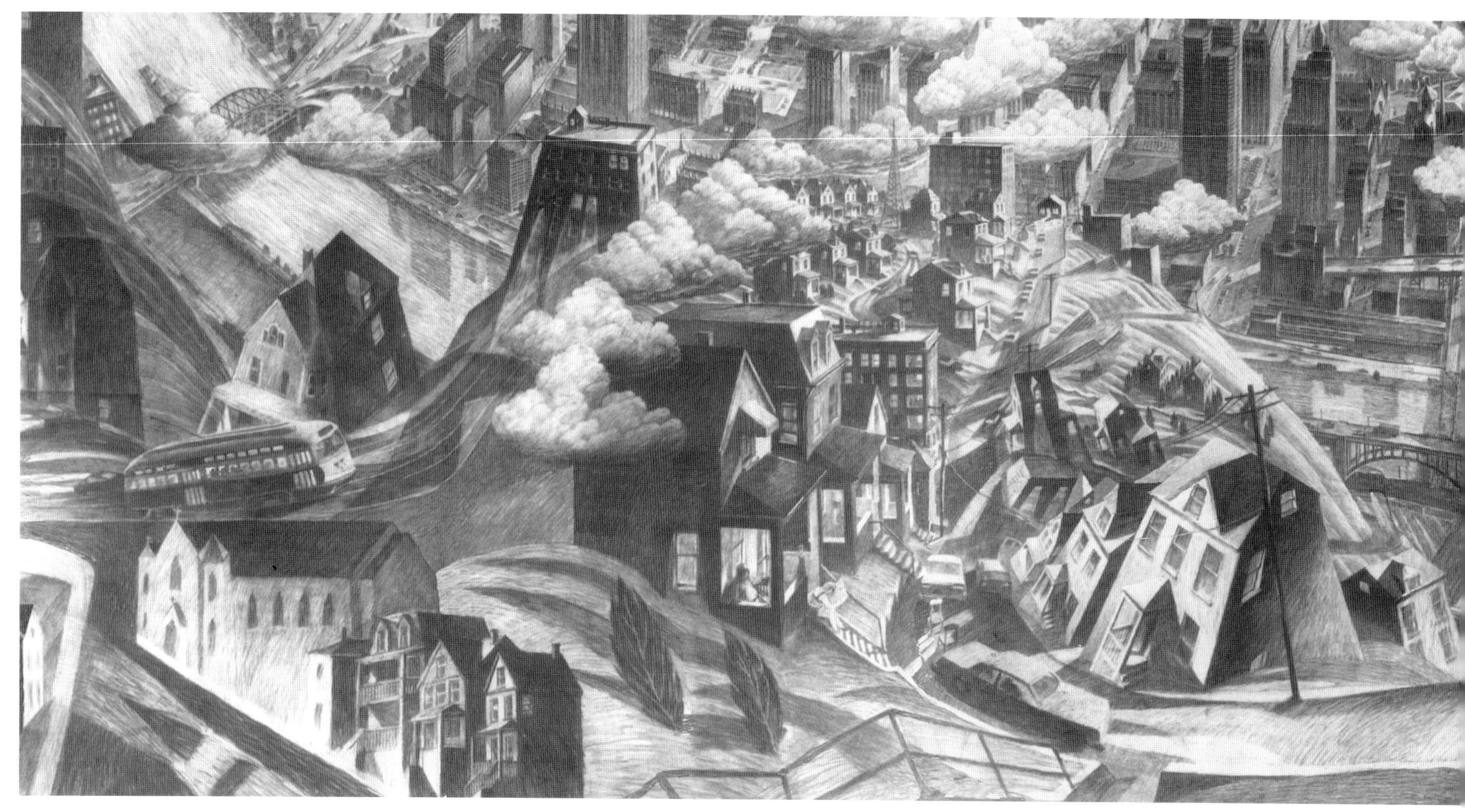

Mt. Washington. University Center Mural. (Photo: Ken Andreyo.)

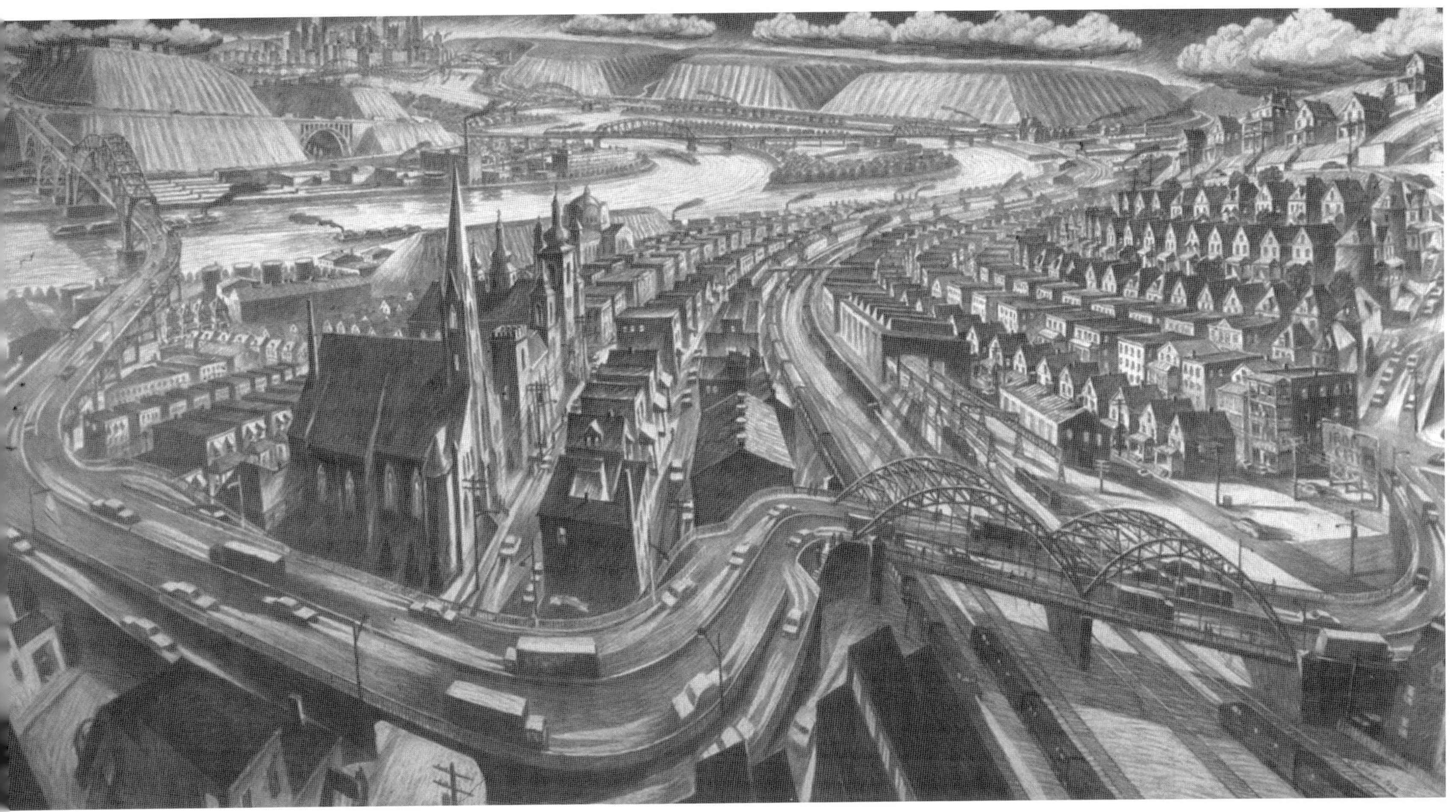

The McKees Rocks Bridge, 1999. 48″ x 96″.

The McKees Rocks Bridge has been called "almost a sample of bridge-construction techniques."

McKees Rocks

McKees Rocks Bridge

The McKees Rocks Bridge (1931) has been called "almost a sample of bridge-construction techniques." The 750-foot-long, two-hinge, spandrel-braced main span is similar in design to the Pennsylvania Railroad's Hell Gate Bridge in New York Harbor. Approach spans include two- and three-hinge deck arches and two distinctive, 300 foot-long crescent-shaped through-arches over the Pittsburgh and Lake Erie Railroad tracks. The structure is nearly a mile long.

The McKees Rocks Bridge connected with the newly constructed Ohio Riv-

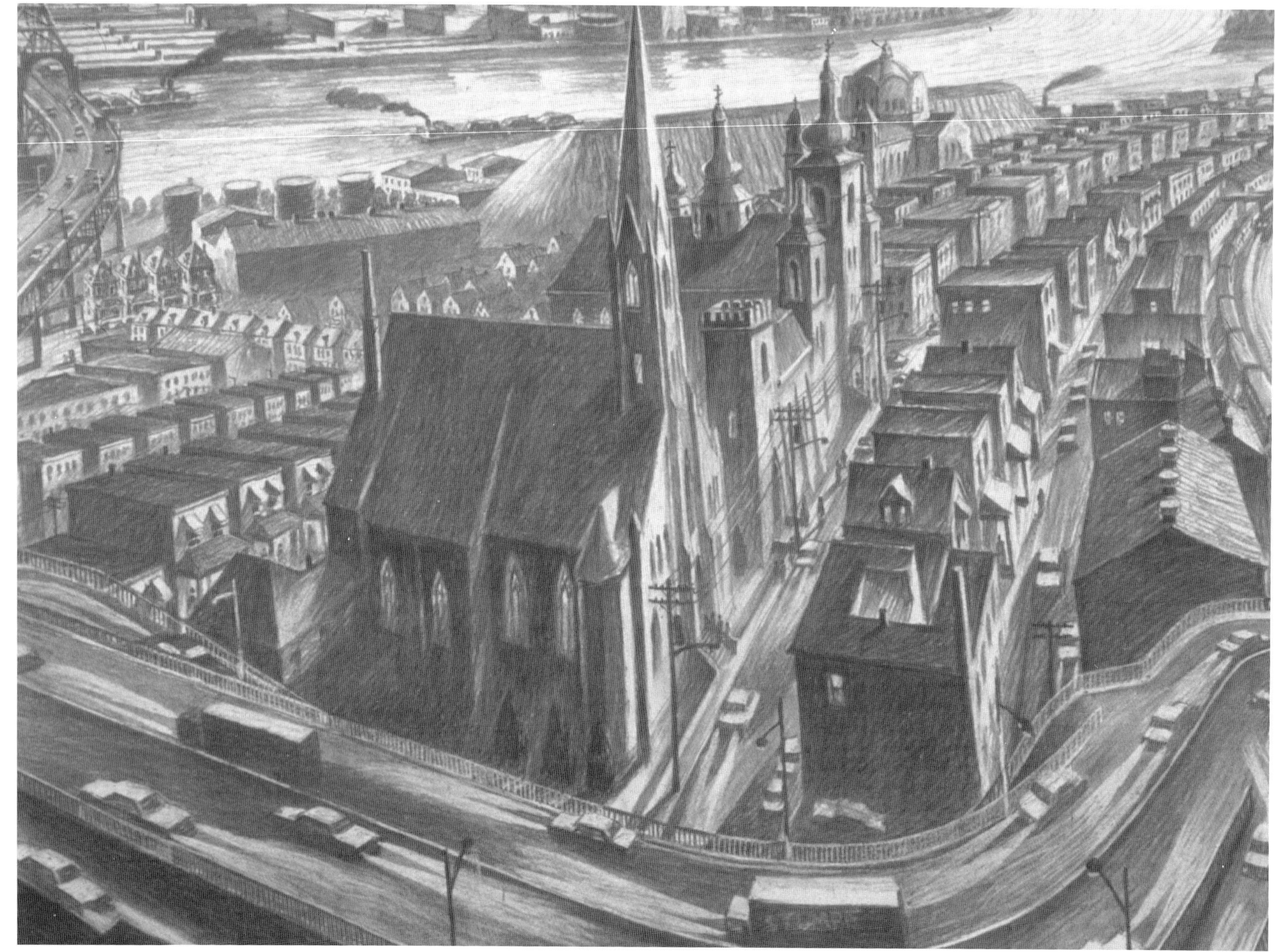

The McKees Rocks Bridge.

The approach viaduct leads over the "bottoms."

er Boulevard, a "boldly conceived" hillside highway that used six reinforced concrete arch bridges to span deep ravines. The Department of Public Works (DPW) designed the bridges so that the steel centering used to make the arches could be transferred from bridge to bridge. The DPW also specified the use of high early-strength cement so that bridge construction could begin in the winter, the first time the material had been used on bridges this size. The innovations enabled the DPW to complete the boulevard spans in just two years

—GERALD M. KUNCIO, "The Golden Age in the City of Bridges" (courtesy of the Historical Society of Western Pennsylvania)

Hill District–Soho

Strayhorn meets Ellington

Shortly after midnight on December 1, 1938, George Greenlee (Gus Greenlee's nephew) nodded and back-patted his way through the ground-floor Rumpus Room of the Crawford Grill One and headed up the stairs at the center of the club. He passed the second floor, which was the main floor, where bands played on a revolving stage facing an elongated glass topped bar. . . . Greenlee hit the third floor, the Club Crawford (insiders only), and spotted his uncle with Duke Ellington, who was engaged to begin a week-long run at the Stanley Theater the following day. "As soon as my uncle introduced us," said Greenlee, "I turned to Duke and said, 'Duke, a good friend of mine (Billy Strayhorn) has written some songs, and we'd like you to hear them.' . . . I knew Duke couldn't say no with my uncle standing there. So Duke said, 'Well, why don't you come backstage tomorrow, after the first show?' It was all set."

. . . Ellington's dressing room was the size of a large dining

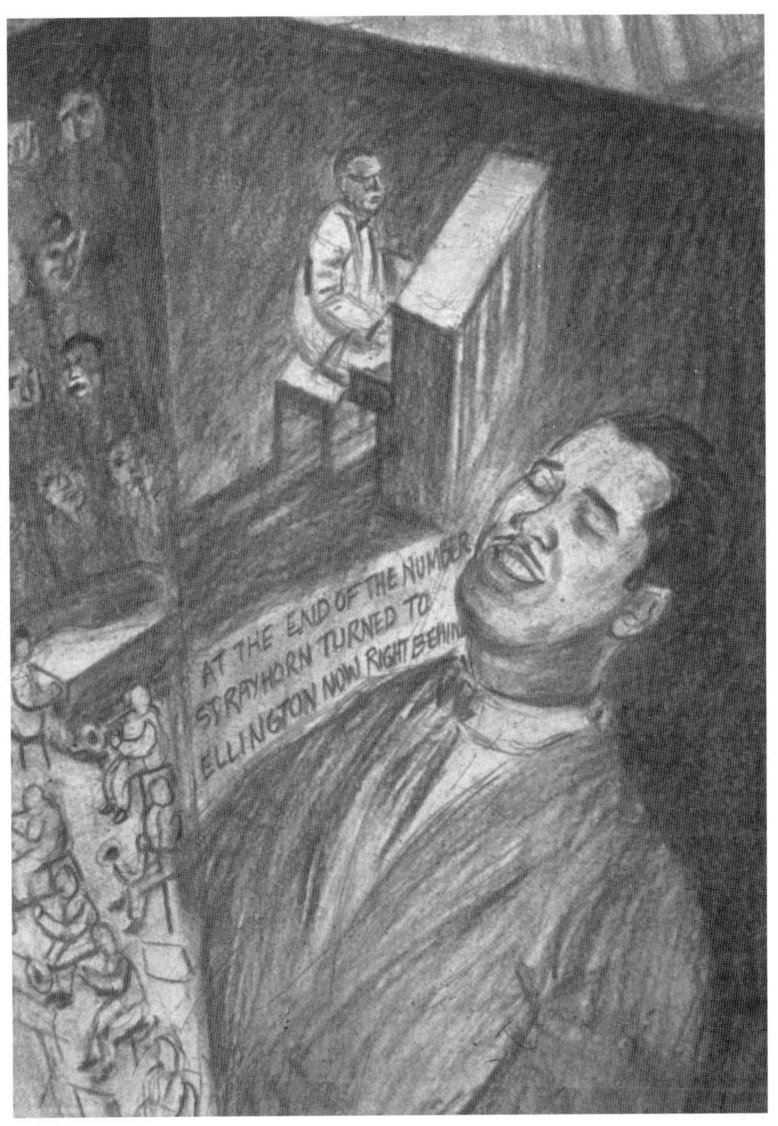

Ellington and Strayhorn at the Stanley. Stage drop for Indigo in Motion, Pittsburgh Ballet Theater, 2000.

Strayhorn began to play his host's melancholy ballad called "Sophisticated Lady."

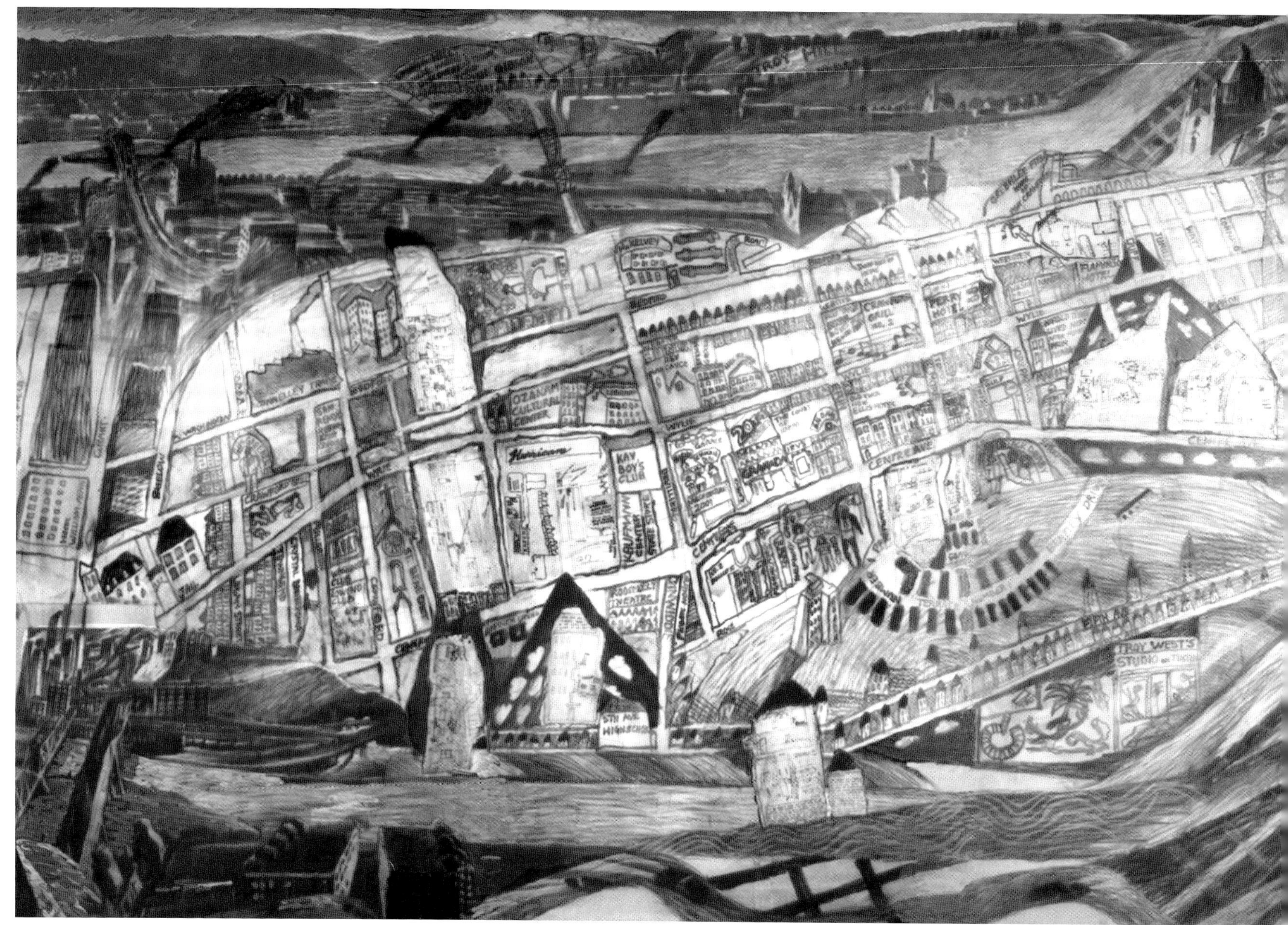
TROY HILL
OZANAM CULTURAL CENTER
KAY BOY'S CLUB
CRAWFORD GRILL NO. 2
PERRY HOTEL
WYLIE
CENTRE AVE
GRANADA
ROOSEVELT THEATRE
5TH AVE HIGHSCHOOL
TROY WEST'S STUDIO

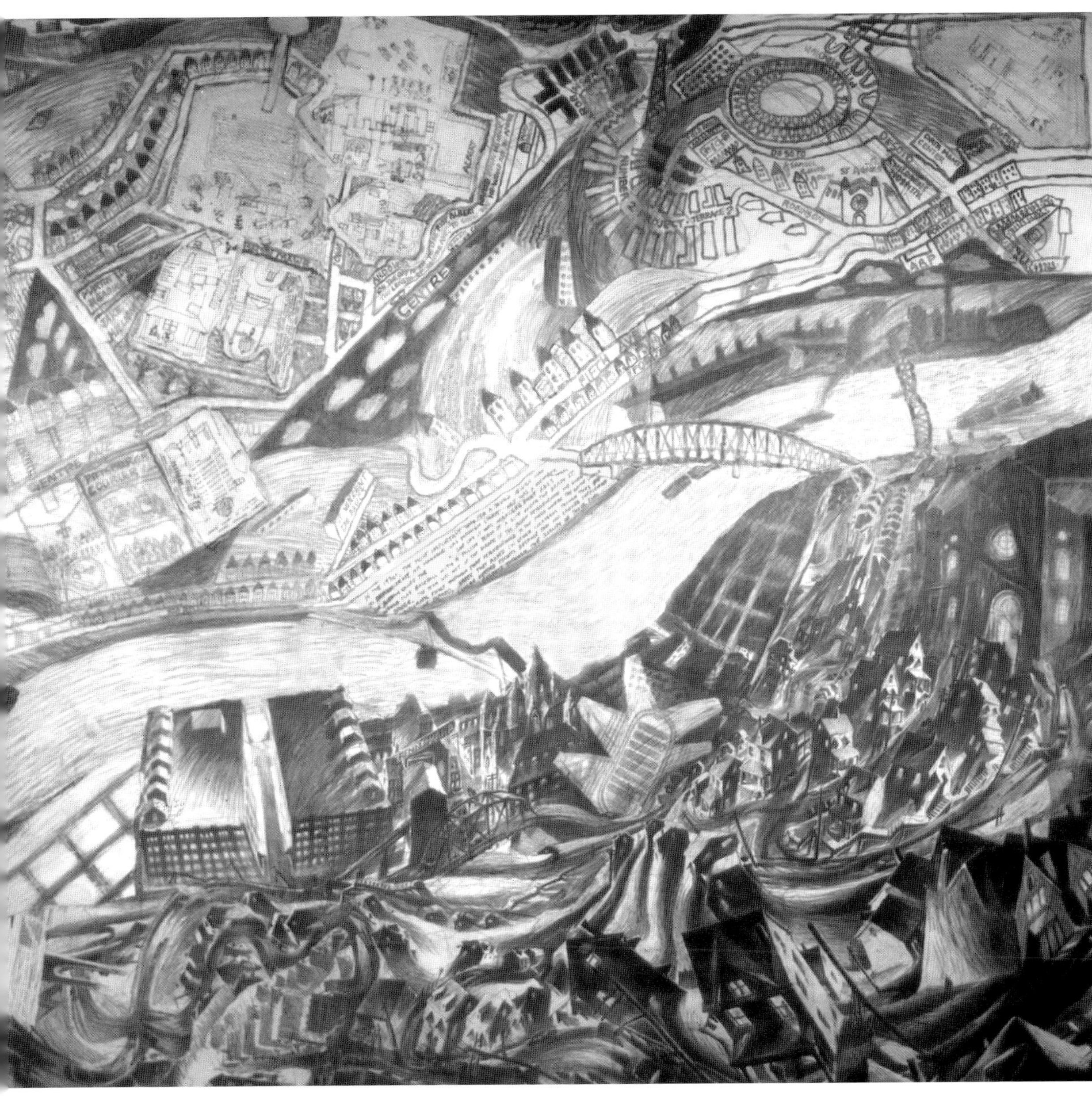

Hill District. 80″ x 162″. *Heinz History Center Mural.*

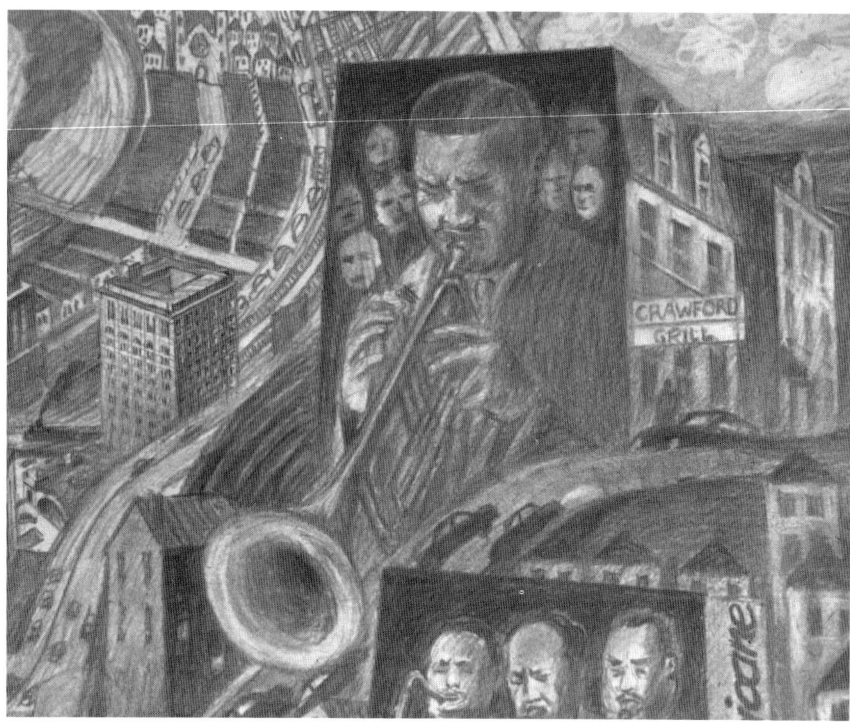

The Crawford Grill. Stage drop for Indigo in Motion.

. . . it was the place to go after a night at the fights or at the ball park.

room and, in fact, was set up like one: several place settings were arranged on the table, and there was an upright piano along one wall. Ellington, alone with his valet, lay on a reclining chair in an embroidered robe, getting his hair conked, eyes closed.

"I introduced Billy, and we stood there," said Greenlee. "Duke didn't get up. He didn't even open his eyes. He just said, 'Sit down at the piano, and let me hear what you can do.' Strayhorn lowered himself onto the bench with calibrated grace and turned toward Ellington, who was lying still. "Mr. Ellington, this is the way you played this number in the show," Strayhorn announced and began to play his host's melancholy ballad called "Sophisticated Lady," one of the few Ellington tunes Strayhorn knew from his days with the Mad Hatter. . . .

At the end of the number, Strayhorn turned to Ellington, now standing right behind him, glaring at the keyboard over his shoulders. "Go get Harry," Ellington ordered his valet.

—DAVID HAJDU, *Lush Life*

Crawford Grill

White sportsmen were frequent visitors to the (Crawford) Grill, and for many it was the place to go after a night at the fights or the ball park. Art Rooney owner of the Pittsburgh Steelers and a close friend of (Gus) Greenlee, and his entourage, often stopped by. . . .

Rooney tells of a late-night rendezvous with Coyne and Greenlee at the Crawford Grill. The three men were sitting in a back room discussing an impending election when a young woman stopped by and whispered into Gus's ear that she wanted some money. When Greenlee refused her, the woman retorted, "That's not the way you talked last night, honey." Greenlee replied, "Last night was last night. When I'm hard, I'm soft. When I'm soft, I'm hard. Beat it." Believing the matter had ended, the three men returned to their agenda when an ashtray came flying by, narrowly missing the senator's head. Greenlee chuckled, but Coyne, rattled by the affair, demanded that they hold their meetings in Oakland from then on.

—ROB RUCK, *Sandlot Seasons*

Brady Street Bridge

In the 1930s, the most important way for a young Jewish man to demonstrate his manhood was through sports. Abe was a member of a top-flight baseball team. One day it was agreed that Abe's team would play a game with a Polish team at a site under the Brady Street Bridge.

The team was met at the edge of the Polish district and given a diplomatic escort to the field under the bridge. Later they played at other locations in the Polish district, now no longer needing the escort because their quality of play had earned them respect.

—STORY TOLD BY ABE LOEB TO DOUGLAS COOPER

Streetcars

Streetcars were orange, clangy, beloved things—loud, jerky and old. They were powerless beasts compelled to travel stupidly with their wheels stuck in the tracks below them. Each streetcar had one central headlight, which looked fixedly down its tracks and nowhere else. The single light advertised to drivers at night that something was coming that couldn't move over. When a streetcar's

Soho. Heinz History Center Mural.

. . . Abe's team would play a game with the Polish team at a site under the Brady Street Bridge.

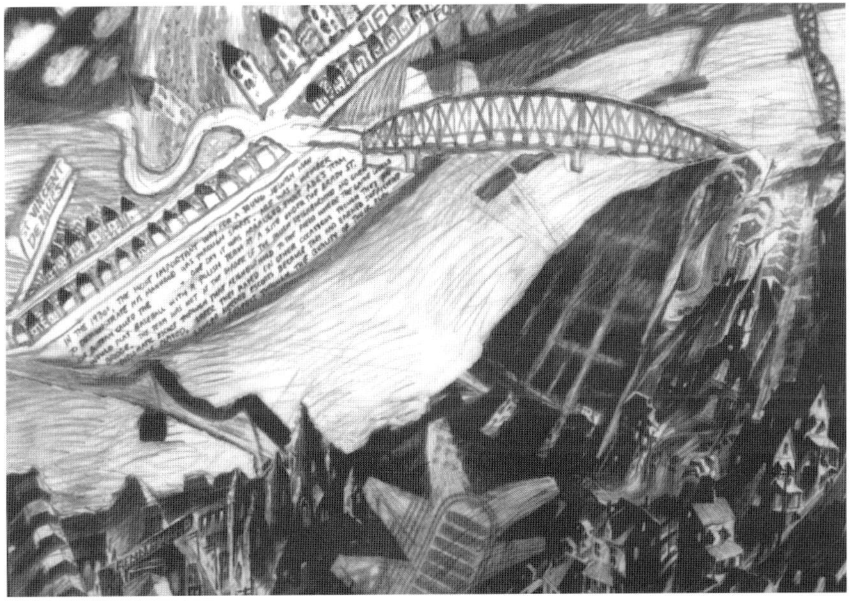

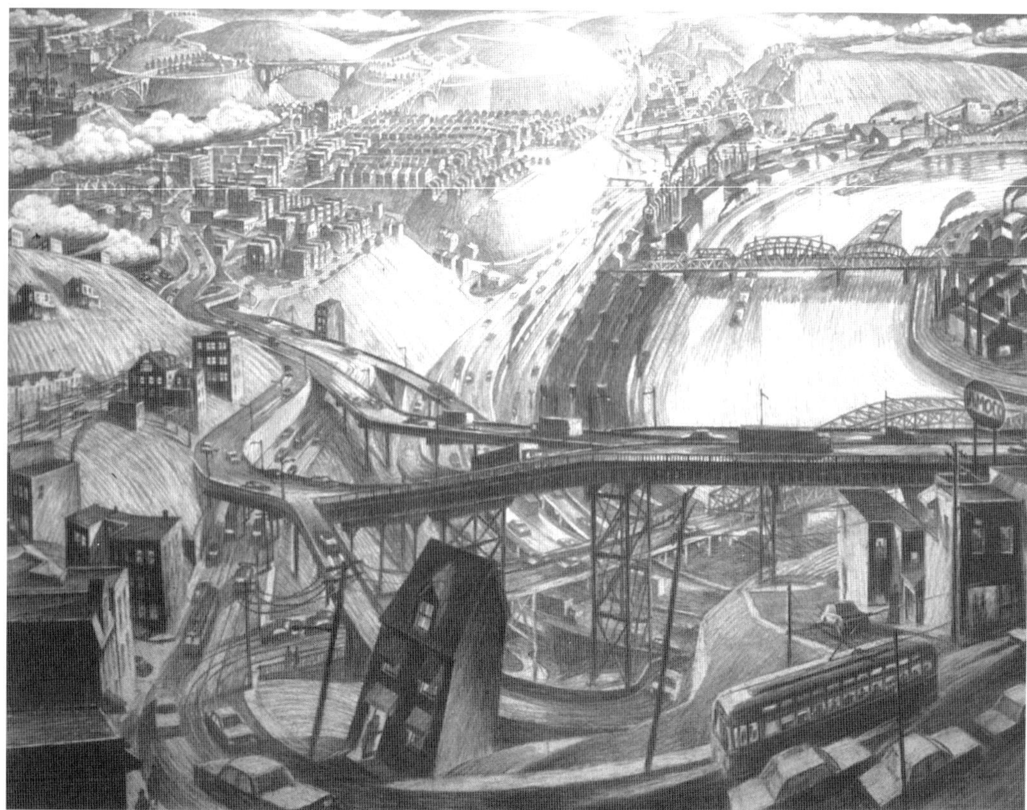

Allies Bridge and Soho Streetcar, 1998. 48″ x 64″. (Private collection.)

Streetcars were orange, clangy, beloved things.

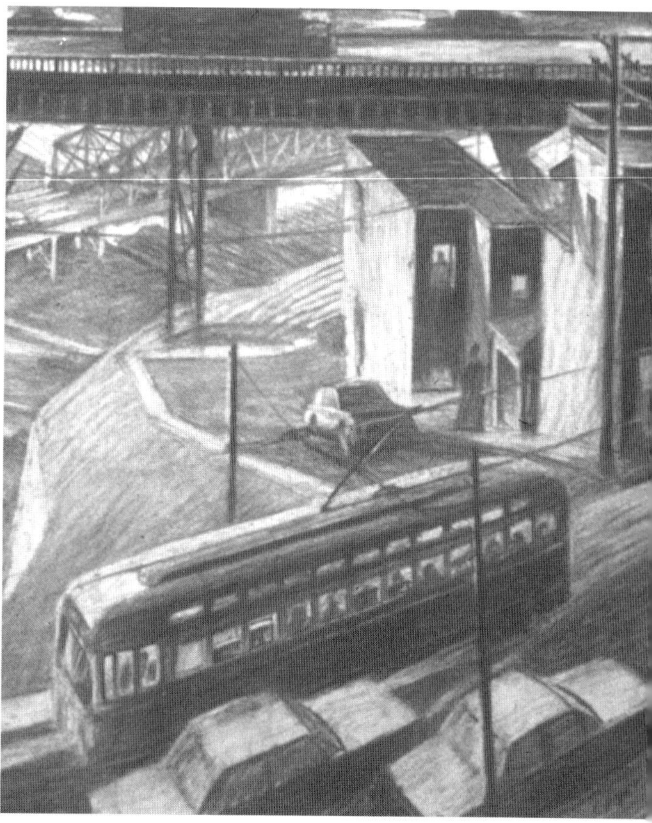

Allies Bridge and Soho Streetcar.

They were powerless beasts compelled to travel stupidly with their wheels in the tracks below them.

tracks and wires rounded a corner, the witless streetcar had to follow. Its orange body bulged out and blocked two lanes; any car trapped beside it had to cringe, stopped against the curb until it passed.

Sometimes a car parked at the curb blocked a streetcar's route. Then the great beast sounded its mournful bell; it emitted a long-suffering, monotonous bong . . . bong . . . bong . . . and men and women on the sidewalk shook their heads sympathetically at the motorman inside, the motorman more inferred than seen through the windshield's bright reflections.

—ANNIE DILLARD, *An American Childhood*

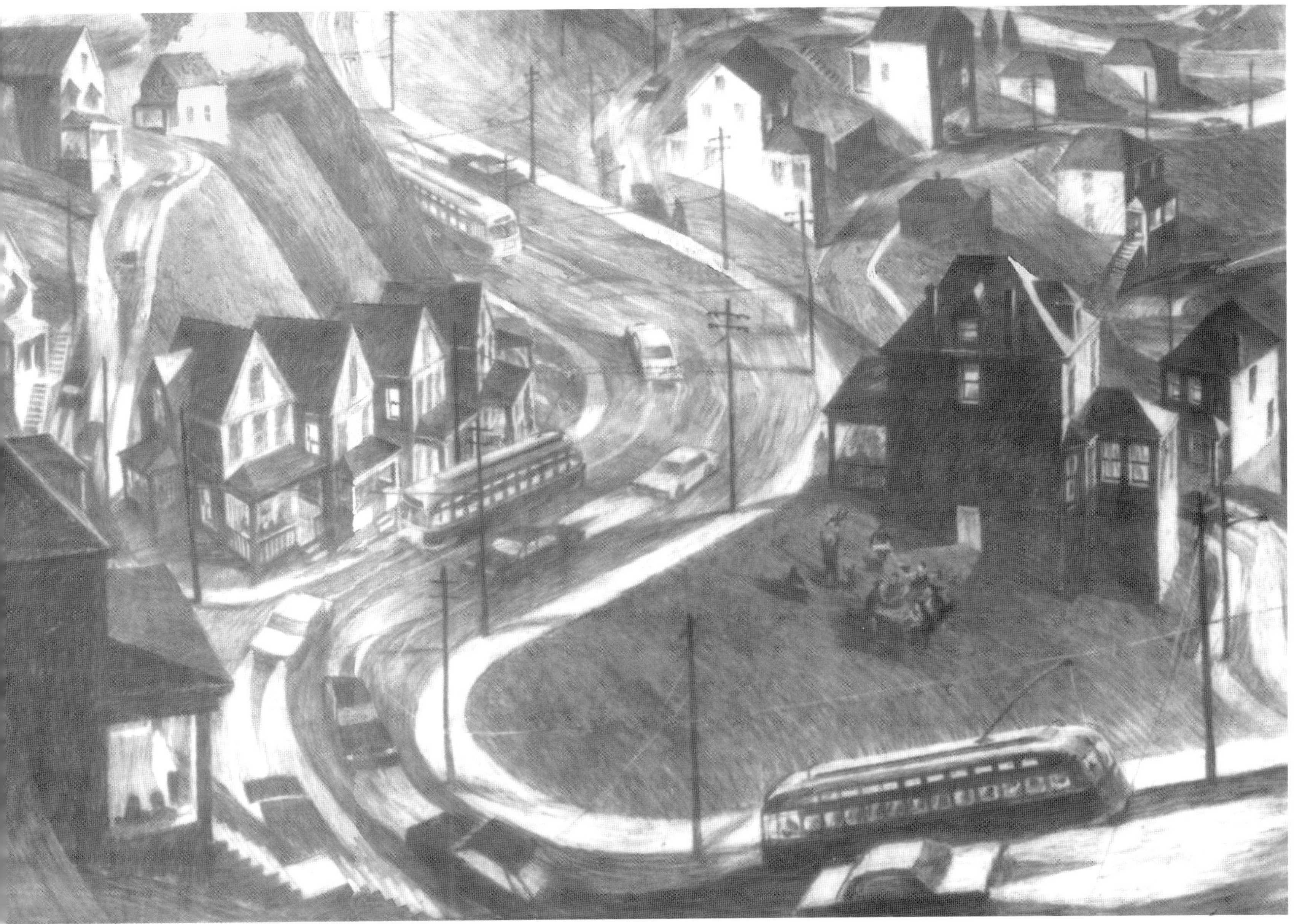

Streetcars in the 18th St. Valley. University Center Mural. (Photo: Ken Andreyo.)

. . . the motorman more inferred than seen through the windshield's bright reflections.

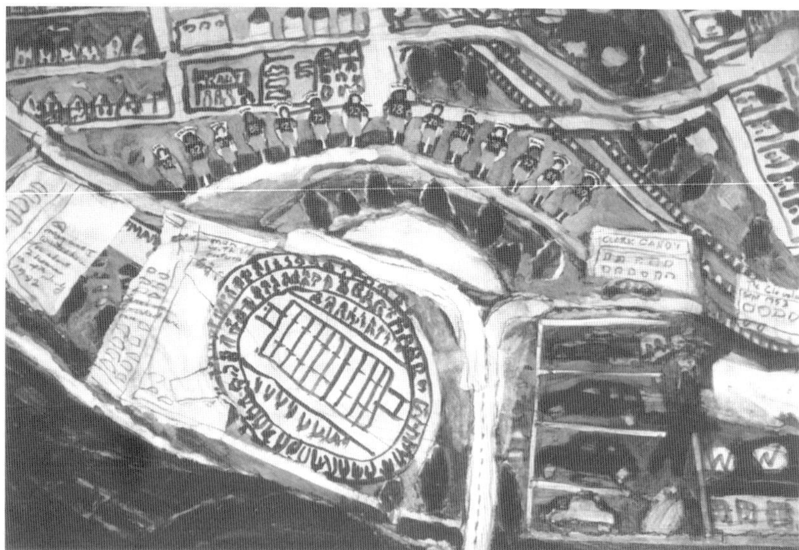

Three Rivers Stadium. Heinz History Center Mural.

Defense? No, deee-fense. Like the Stalingrad Winter.

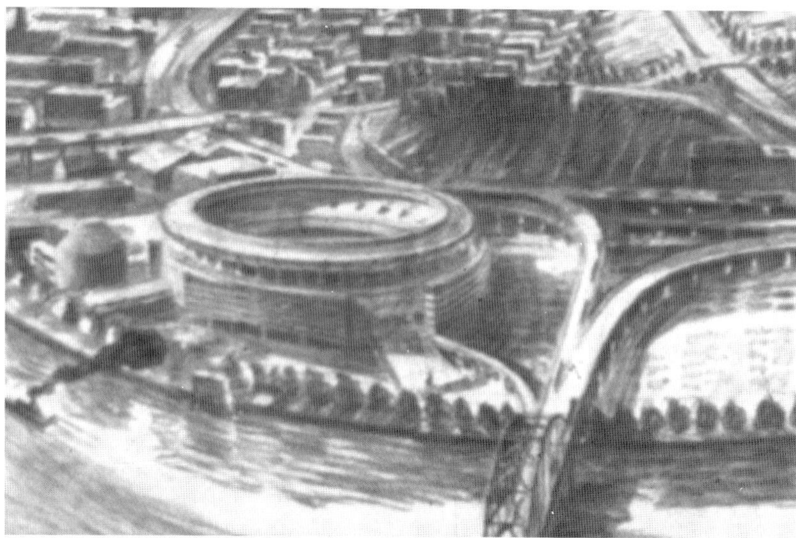

Three Rivers Stadium. Heinz History Center Mural.

After 40 endless years of spilling salt . . . , the Steelers were smiled upon by a benevolent fate.

Downtown-Northside

Deeefense

Pittsburgh, January 4, 1976—Outlined against a ghastly gray January sky, the Four Horsemen rode again. You remember them. Lambert, Wagner, Russell and Holmes.

Al Davis will remember them. They will be in the nightmares of the Oakland Raiders' owner forevermore. The resilient inner core of the Steeler defense played so well that you knew up there on some heavenly vista, Vince and Knute and Granny and the boys were smiling, nodding and nudging one another in the short ribs.

Defense? No, deee-fense. Like the Stalingrad winter. The stuff that cut Oakland's rushing average in half and made Ken Stabler a 42% passer.

. . . Defense. The primary reason the Steelers put it on Oakland, 16-10, yesterday to win the AFC championship in the wildest, gut-wrenchingest, slam-bangingest football game that you, or I, or the 49,103 screaming cases of frostbite at Three Rivers ever saw.

—PHIL MUSICK, *The Pittsburgh Press*
(courtesy *Pittsburgh Post-Gazette*)

The Immaculate Reception

Pittsburgh, December 23, 1972—The God of this game's all-time losers smiled down through a ghostly gray sky yesterday, and in the last desperate seconds of a mean, bitterly-fought football game, did truly wondrous things.

History would have had it no other way. And after 40 endless years of spilling salt and breaking mirrors and walking under ladders, the Steelers were smiled upon by a benevolent fate.

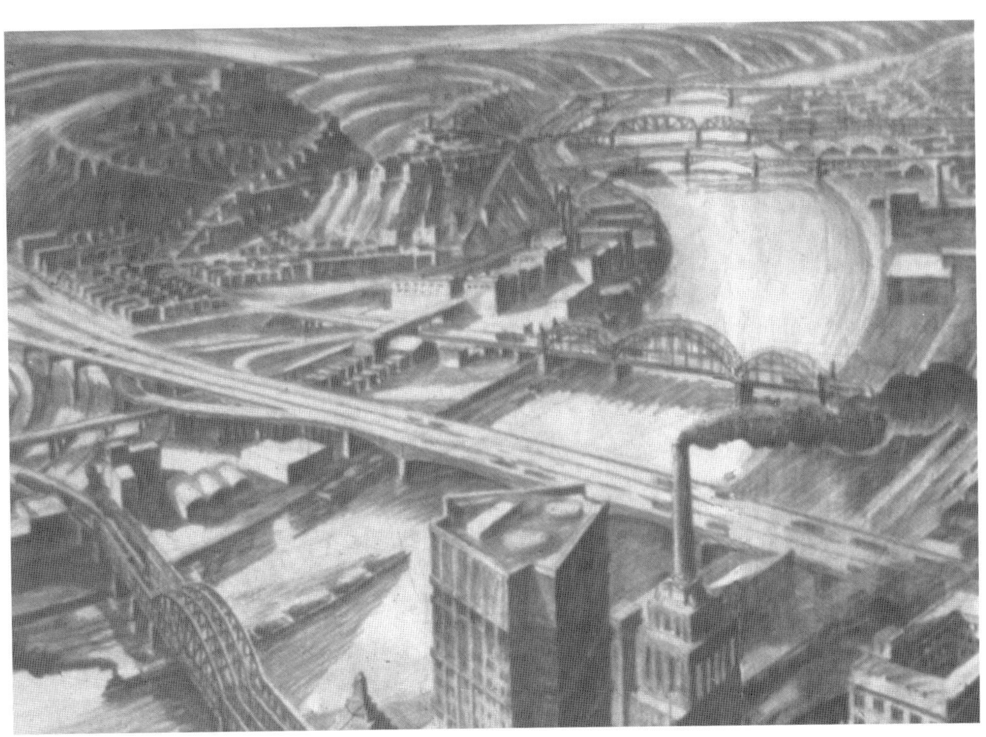

Troy Hill. Heinz History Center Mural.

In its heyday, St. Anthony's (of Troy Hill) . . . drew 15,000 pilgrims to experience the remarkable curative power of the relics.

. . . It was almost unbelievable. It happened this way, and if you can't bring yourself to believe it, don't worry—neither did the 50,350 wild folk who stumbled from Three Rivers Stadium in the kind of daze they might have known had the field suddenly opened and swallowed the Tartan-Turf.

Shackled until the final 1:13 by a Steeler defense that had yielded just 21 points in the previous 21 quarters, Oakland snatched a 7–6 lead when backup quarterback Ken Stabler scrambled 30 yards on a busted pass play to cap an 80-yard drive.

. . . The Steelers worked the ball to their own 40 following the Raider score and with only seconds left, quarterback Terry Bradshaw retreated to pass on a fourth-and-ten play. Evading the Oakland hands plucking at his jersey, he gunned the ball to Frenchy Fuqua.

Fate didn't like his choice. Oakland safetyman Jack Tatum, who had swatted down Bradshaw attempts on the previous two plays, either did or did not deflect the ball off Fuqua's chest.

We'll never know—Tatum said he didn't; Fuqua just leered—but the ball ricocheted off toward the sideline, where Franco Harris whisked it off his shoetops at the Oakland 42, got a partial block from tight-end John McMakin, then outran the Raiders' other safety, Jimmy Warren, to the end zone. There were five seconds left when he crossed the goal line.

—PHIL MUSICK, *The Pittsburgh Press* (courtesy *Pittsburgh Post-Gazette*)

St. Anthony's

It was built by a Belgian in honor of an Italian in a German neighborhood when America was billing itself as the great melting pot, and St. Anthony's

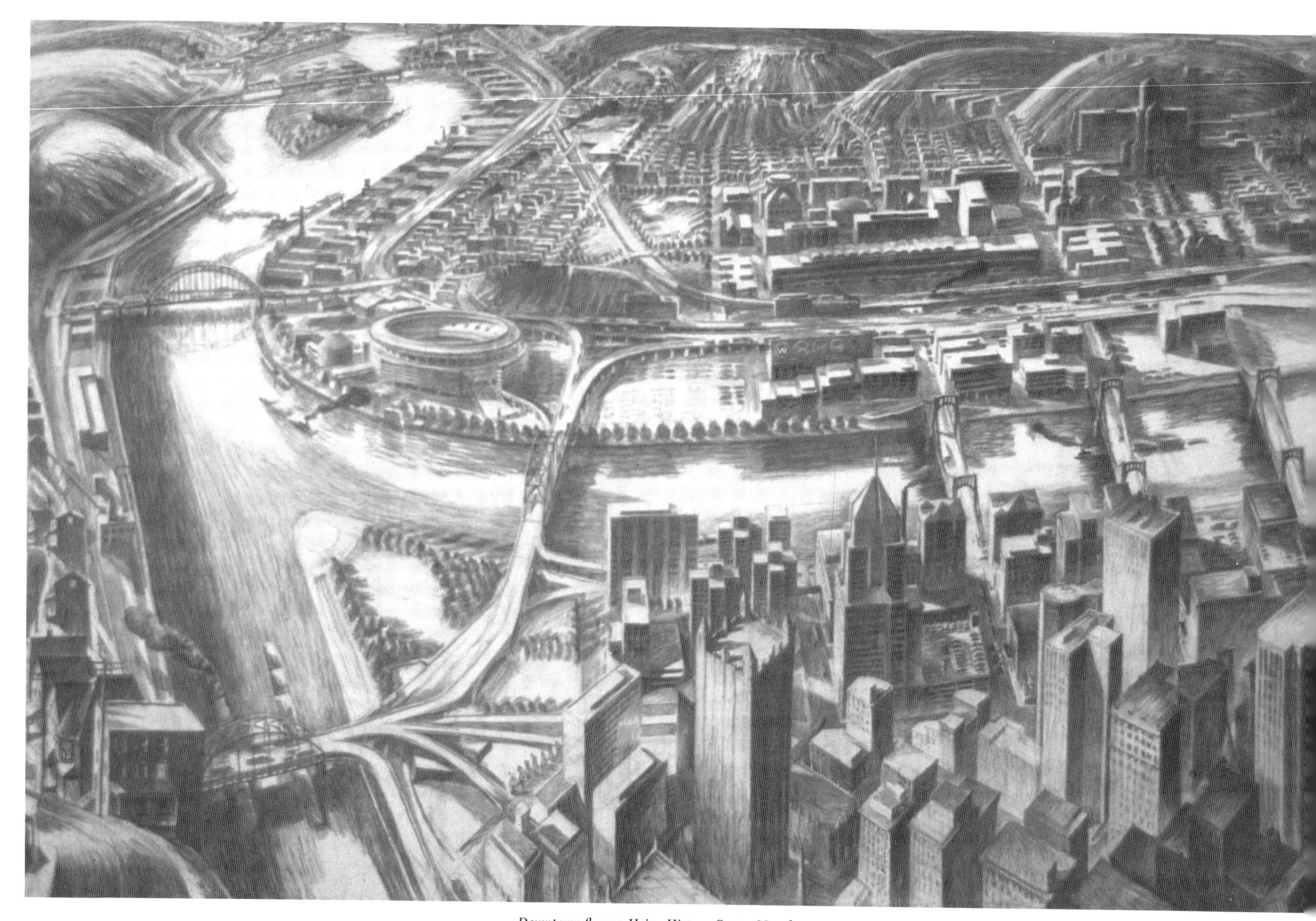

Downtown flyover. Heinz History Center Mural.

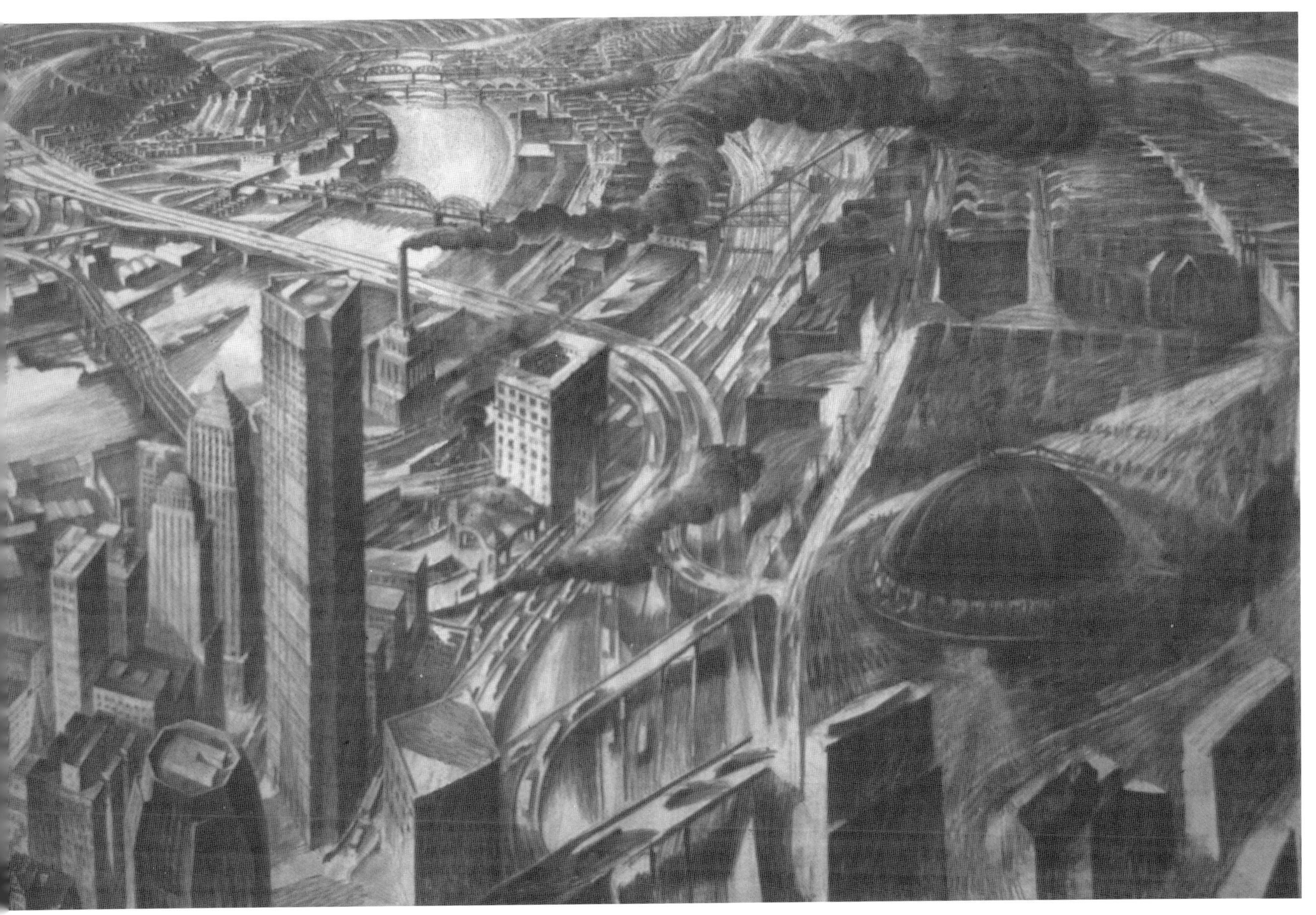

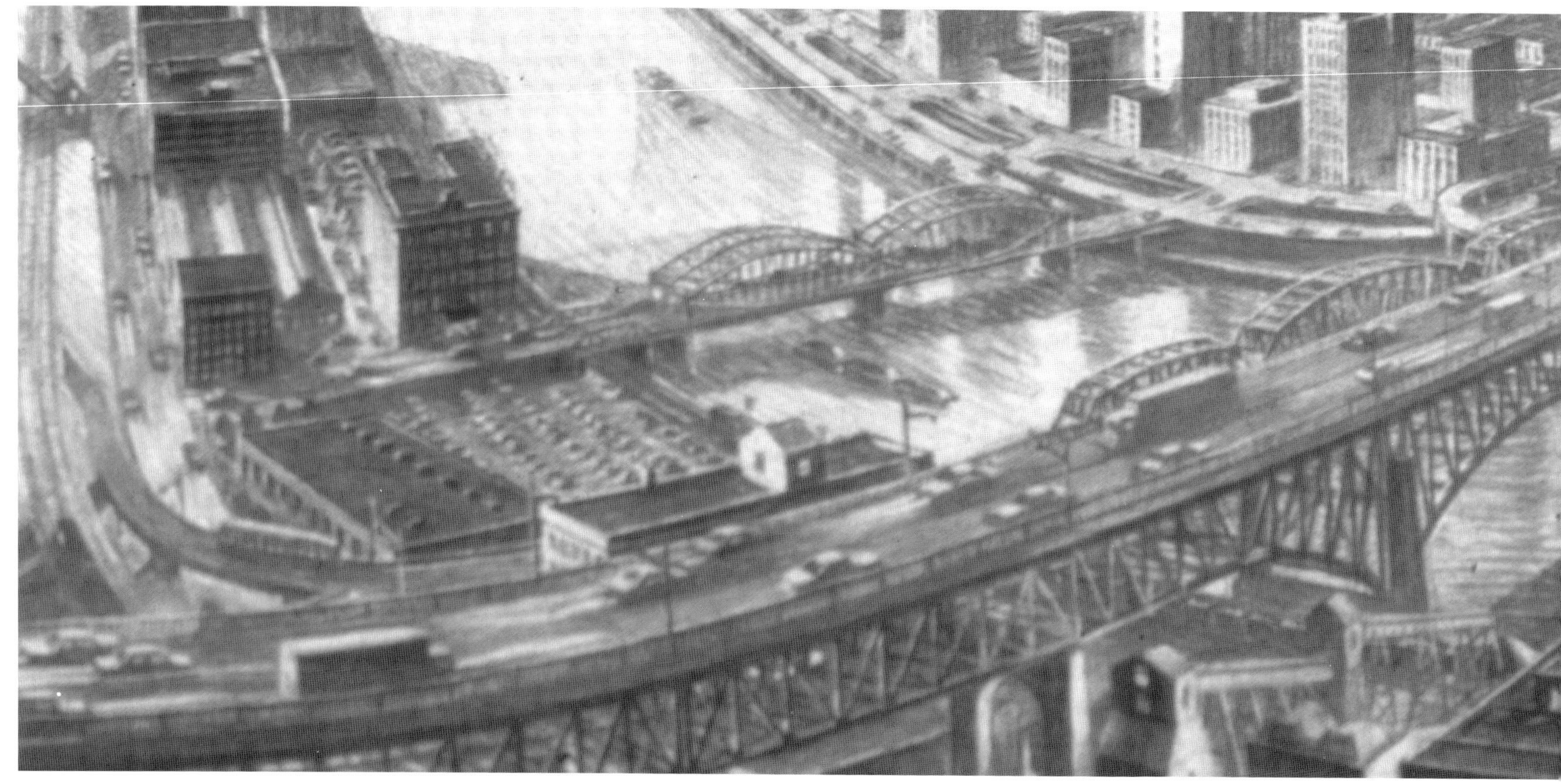

Smithfield St. Bridge. Liberty Bridge and the McCardle Roadway.

In profile, the truss suggests a double-convex lens seen on edge: hence, "lenticular."

Chapel on Troy Hill remains no more probable today than finding the Oakland Original in the Vatican.

Logic might dictate that it should never have been built in the first place. One Suitbertas Gottfried Mollinger, a priest as well as a scion of a well-to-do Belgian family, was named pastor of Most Holy Name of Jesus Parish, Troy Hill's Catholic Church in 1868. While stationed in America, Father Mollinger maintained strong ties with Europe, and when various shrines were being stripped of relics, which found their way into pawnshops, Father Mollinger set out to buy what he could for a new shrine in Pittsburgh. It wound up taking $300,000 of his own money to build the shrine in honor of St. Anthony of Padua and to stock it with more than 5,000 relics and artifacts, including skulls, bones, and pieces said to be of such holy objects as the Manger, the Crown of Thorns, and the True Cross.

In its heyday, St. Anthony's, built from 1880–92, drew 15,000 pilgrims daily to experience the remarkable curative powers of the relics. Indeed the streetcar which brought the faithful up the hill was dubbed "the ambulance" because it carried so many of the lame and the halt, some 3,000 of whom reportedly walked away without their canes and crutches.

—ABBY MENDELSON, *Pittsburgh: A Place in Time*

Smithfield Street Bridge

A lenticular, or Pauli, truss operates on a very simple principle: its upper chord is an arch, which thrusts outward; its lower chord is a catenary, like the draped cable of a suspension bridge, which pulls inward. The horizontal forces cancel each other out, and vertical forces are transmitted to posts and hangers, and counters within the truss absorb dynamic and off-center loads. In profile, the truss suggests a double-convex lens seen on edge: hence, "lenticular."

—WALTER KIDNEY, *Pittsburgh's Bridges*

Sixth St. Bridge

People jumped from the Sixth Street bridge into the Allegheny River. Because the bridge was low, they shinnied all the way up the steel suspension cables to the bridge towers before they jumped. Father saw them from his desk in silhouette, far away. A man vigorously climbed a slanting cable. He slowed near the top, where the cables hung almost vertically; he paused on the stone tower, seeming to

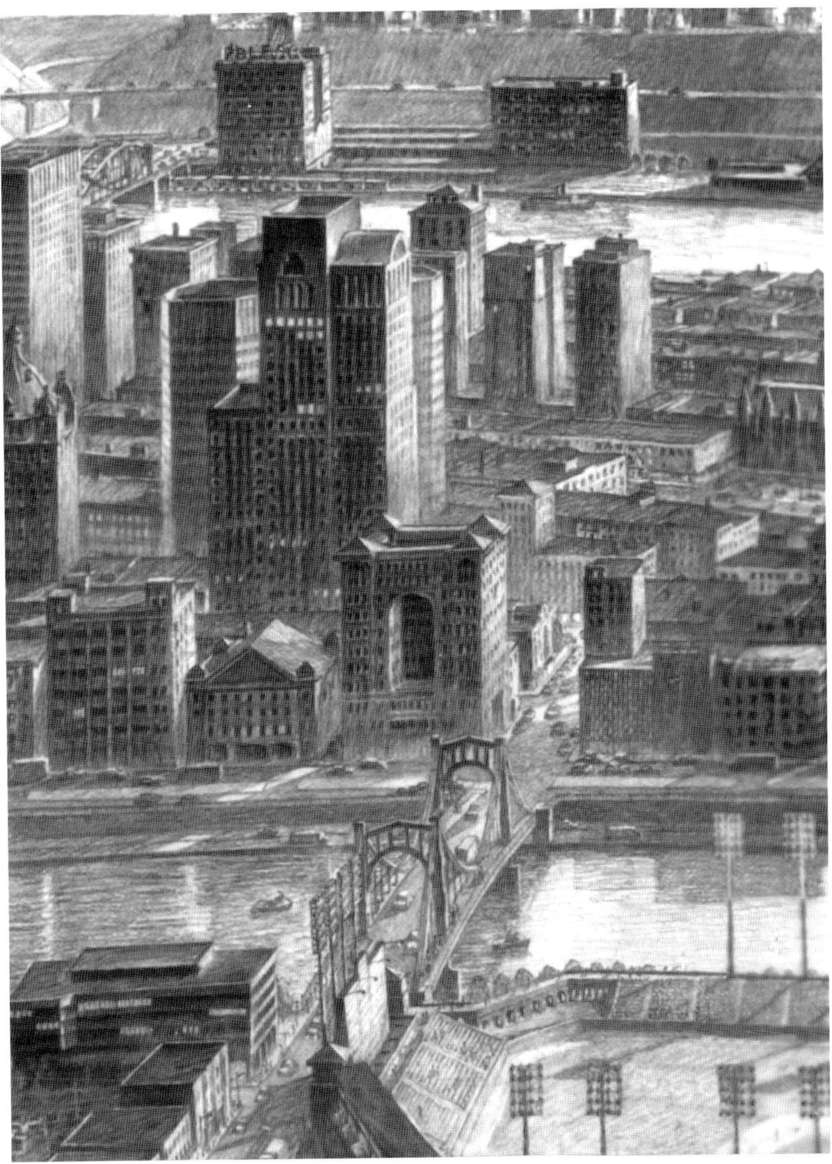

Sixth St. Bridge. Mascaro Mural. (Photo: Ken Andreyo.)

People jumped from the South Street Bridge into the Allegheny River.

sway against the sky, high over the bridge and the river below. Priests, firemen, and others—presumably family members or passerby—gathered on the bridge. In about half the cases, Father said, these people talked the suicide down. The ones who jumped kicked off from the tower so they'd miss the bridge, and fell tumbling a long way down.

Pittsburgh was a cheerful town, and had far fewer suicides than most other cities its size. Yet people jumped so often that Father and his colleagues on the fourteenth floor had a betting pool going. They guessed the date and time of the day the next jumper would appear. If a man got talked down before he jumped, he still counted for the betting pool, thank God; no manager of American Standard ever wanted to hope, even in the smallest part of himself, that the fellow would go ahead and jump.

—ANNIE DILLARD, *An American Childhood*

The Underground River

The Monongahela, the Allegheny, and the Ohio Rivers form the borders of the Golden Triangle at their confluence near the Three Rivers Stadium in the city of Pittsburgh. In the summer Pittsburghers attend the Three Rivers Arts Festival and the Three Rivers Shakespeare Festival. It's all so triangular. So neat and three-sided. And it's all wrong.

You see there's a fourth side to the equation, a fourth river that no one has ever seen, even though every day thousands of us bathe in its waters and drink from its depths. This massive body of water flows along under the Allegheny and Ohio Rivers from a spot north of Warren, Pennsylvania, until it surfaces again in the Ohio River near Beaver, Pennsylvania.

The underground river consists of a river bed, largely of gravel, brought to its present location by the Wisconsin Glacier, a million years or so ago. It is actually a homogenous layer of course sand and fist-sized round stones, very porous, with loads of space for water to flow between the stones. It is constantly replenished by water from the upper Allegheny River.

Pittsburgh's "underground river" is what geologists call an "aquifer," but it differs from other aquifers, most of which are irregular and wide-spread and do

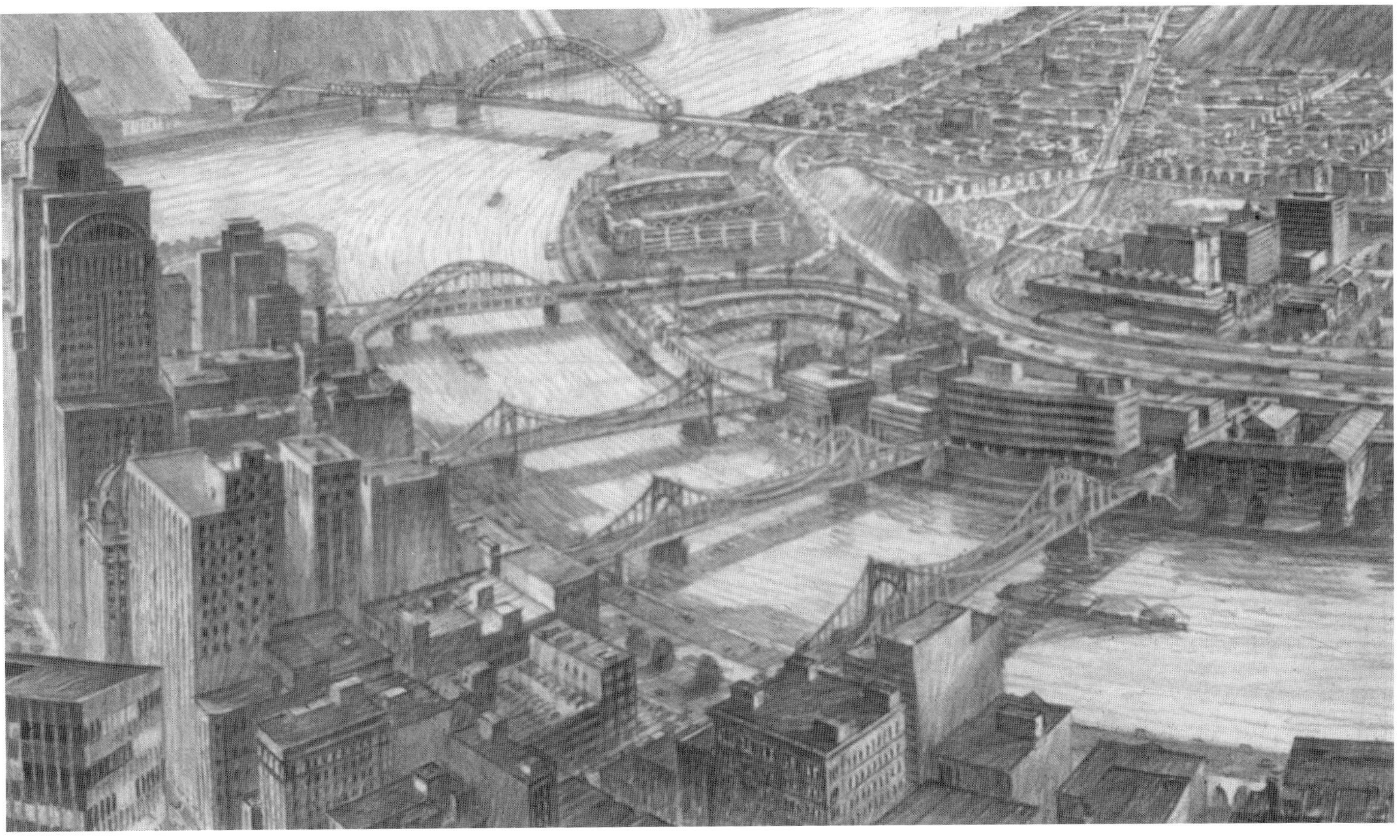

Looking toward the Point. Turning Gulf, 2000. Urban Design Associates.

It's all so triangular. So neat and three-sided. And it's all wrong.

not follow a channel. The regularity of our underground river's flow makes it more like a true river than other aquifers.

—STEVE TREVOR HADLEY, *Only in Pittsburgh*

The Gulf and Koppers Towers

Egyptian architect and urban planner Hassan Fathy complained in the 1960s that western architects failed in their buildings' summits to marry earth to heaven, as their eastern counterparts had done with domes and minarets. But both the Gulf and Koppers buildings enjoy if not proper marriages, at least happy relationships with the sky. . . . Koppers' tower is verdigris, copper (what else?) green in the form of a chateau. Gulf's pyramidal point is lit in weather forecasting tones at night: red means fair; blue is precipitation; a solid color means rising temperatures; flashing, falling temperatures.

—BARRINGER FIFIELD, *Seeing Pittsburgh*

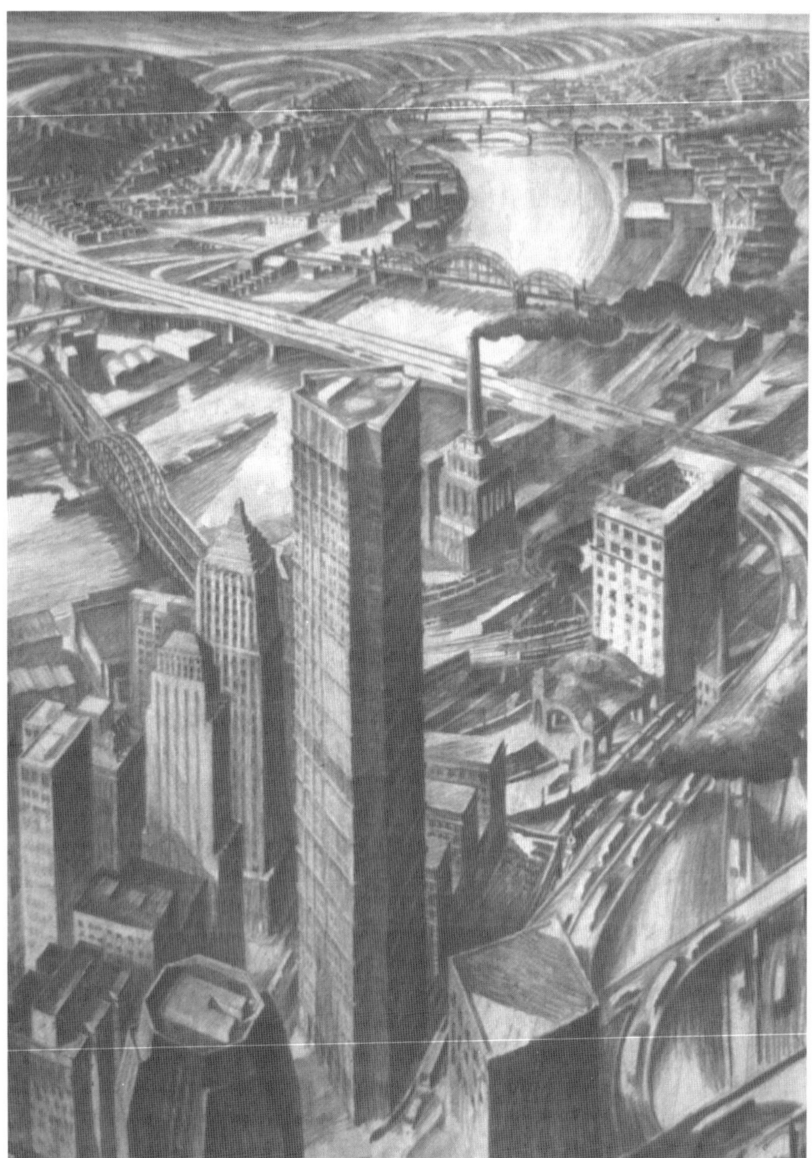

Towers on Grant and the Old Pennsylvania Station. Heinz History Center Mural.

This site has always been a traffic nexus.

The Site of Pennsylvania Station

This site has always been a traffic nexus. The East Busway, which uses part of the old railroad right of way, terminates here, forming a link with the Amtrak station, the downtown subway, and hence the rest of the light-rail system. Here Penn Avenue, the original route from the east, enters the Golden Triangle; and here the railroad's predecessor, the 395-mile-long Main Line Canal, had its terminus.

The canal, which reached Pittsburgh in 1834, was an extraordinary work—a massive manipulation of nature, as Forbes Road had been three quarters of a century earlier. Immortalized by Charles Dickens in American Notes, it included a 1,100-foot-long covered aqueduct over the Allegheny and a final canal tunnel under Grant's Hill. It boosted trade, but the canal never paid its way; the railroad fulfilled its functions after 1852.

—BARRINGER FIFIELD, *Seeing Pittsburgh*

A First View of the Point

As I got down before the canoe, I spent some time in viewing the rivers, and the land in the Fork, which I think is extremely well situated for a fort, as it has the absolute command of both rivers. The land at the "Point" is 20 or 25 feet above the common surface of the water; and a considerable bottom of flat, well-timbered land all around it, very con-

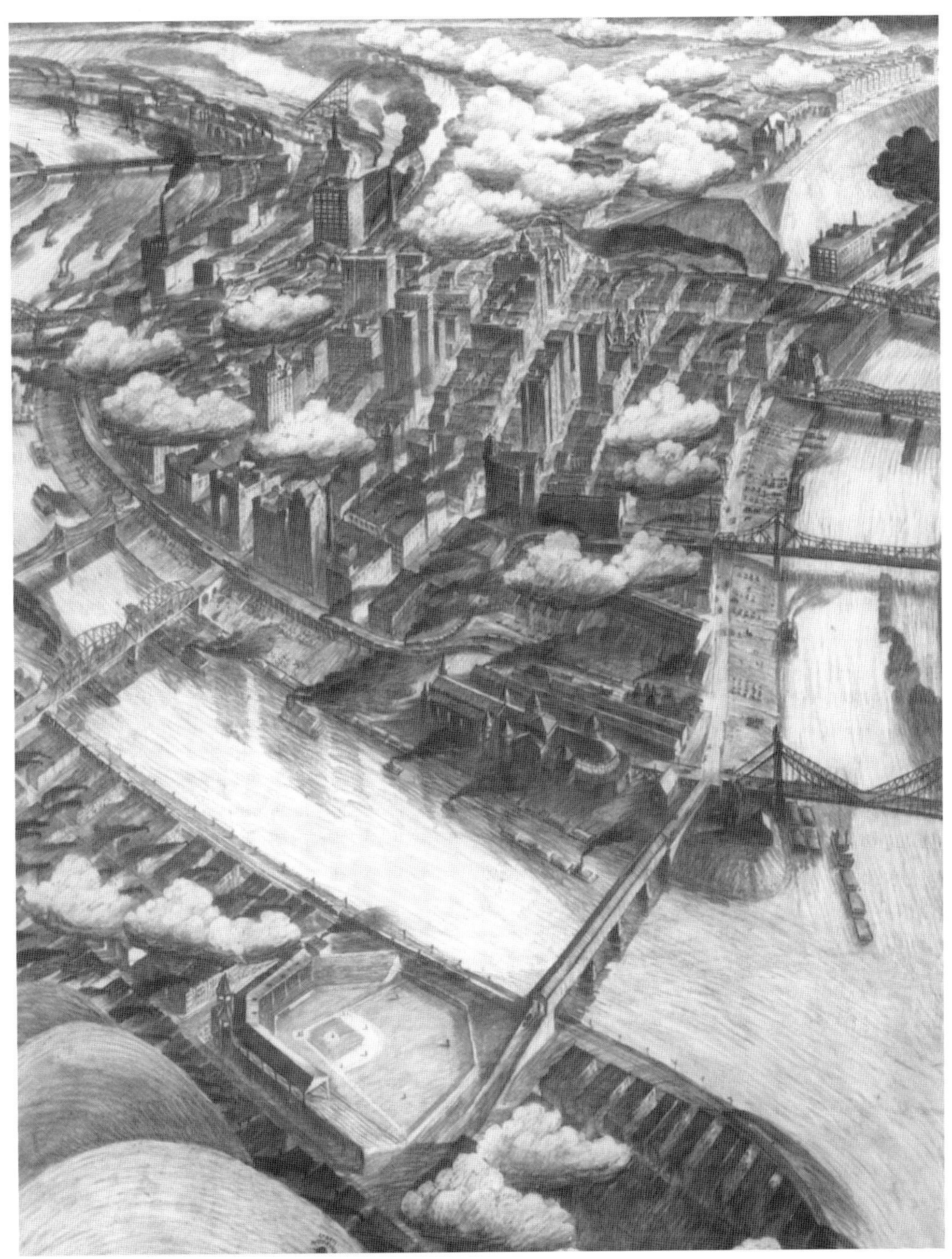

Downtown, circa 1900. University Center Mural. (Photo: Ken Andreyo.)

I spent some time in viewing the rivers, and the land in the fork.

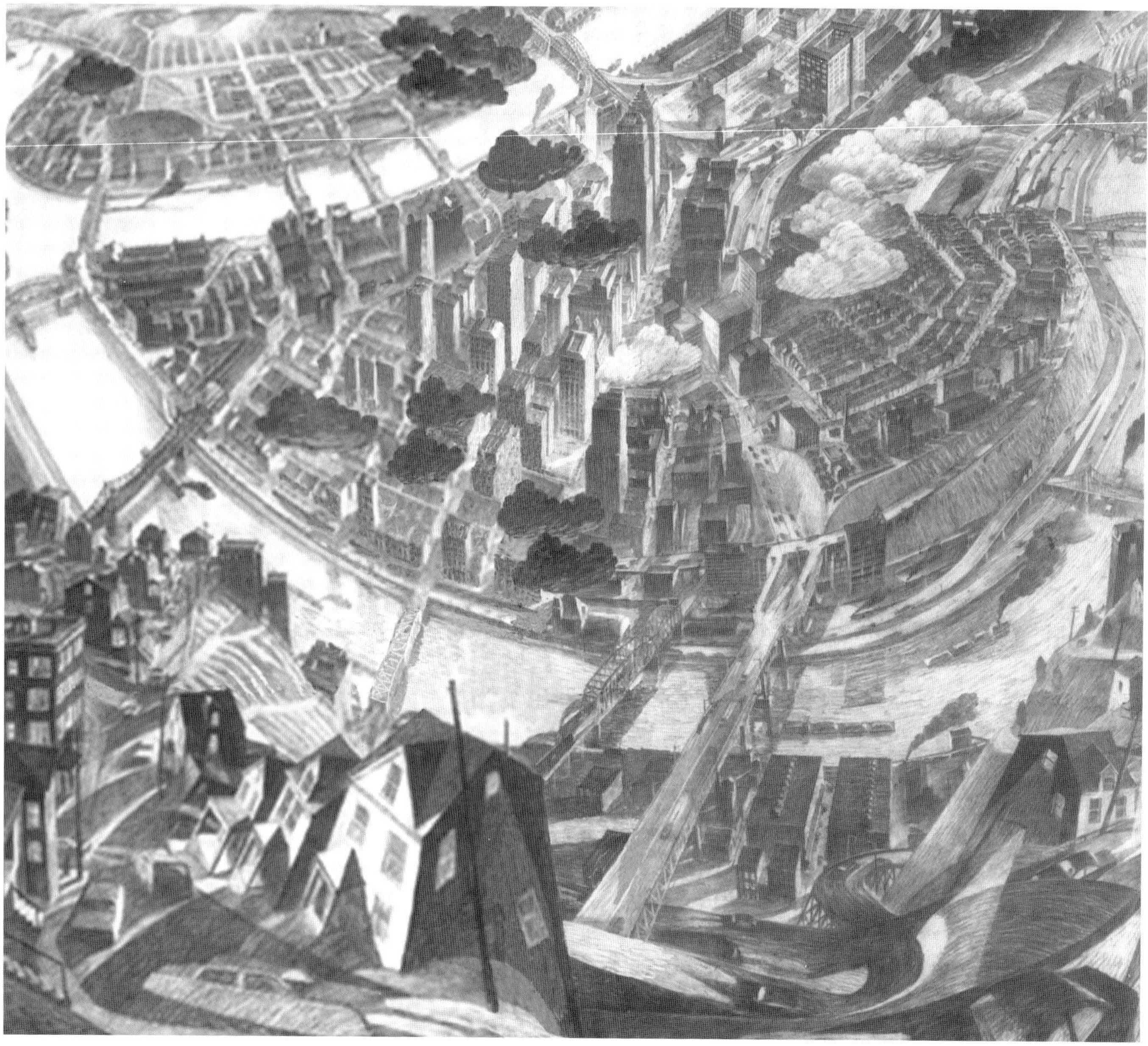

Downtown, circa 1900. University Center Mural. (Photo: Ken Andreyo.)

This town in future time will be the place of great manufactory.

venient for building. The rivers are each a quarter of a mile or more across, and run very near at right angles. The Allegheny bearing NE and the Monongahela SE. The former of the two is very rapid and swift running water; the other deep and still, without any perceptible fall.

—GEORGE WASHINGTON, 1754, *Wilkinsburg Journal*

The Future Town

This town in future time will be the place of great manufactory, indeed the greatest on the continent or perhaps in the world. Our distance from either of the oceans will make the importation of heavy articles very expensive. The manufacture of them will become more of an object here than elsewhere. It is prospect of this that men of reflection which renders the soil of this place so valuable [sic].

—HUGH HENRY BRACKENRIDGE, 1786

Bibliography

Bell, Thomas. *Out of This Furnace.* Pittsburgh: University of Pittsburgh Press, 1976.

Blair, Peter. *Last Heat.* Washington, D.C.: Word Works, 1999. [Winner of the 1999 Washington Prize].

Byington, Margaret. *Homestead: The Households of a Mill Town.* Pittsburgh: University of Pittsburgh Press, 1974.

Chabon, Michael. *The Mysteries of Pittsburgh.* New York: Harper Collins, 1989.

Davenport, Marcia. *The Valley of Decision.* Pittsburgh: University of Pittsburgh Press, 1989.

Dillard, Annie. *An American Childhood.* New York: Harper Collins, 1989.

Fifield, Barringer. *Seeing Pittsburgh.* Pittsburgh: University of Pittsburgh Press, 1996.

Graham, Laurie. *Singing the City: The Bonds of Home in an Industrial Landscape.* Pittsburgh: University of Pittsburgh Press, 1998.

Groat, Dick, and Bill Surface. *The World Champion Pittsburgh Pirates.* New York: Coward-McCann, 1961.

Hadju, David. *Lush Life: A Biography of Billy Strayhorn.* New York: Farrar, Straus & Giroux, 1996.

Hadley, Steve Trevor. *Only in Pittsburgh.* Cincinnati: Education Publishing Resources, 1994.

Jacques, Charles J., Jr. *Kennywood: Roller Coaster Capital of the World.* Jefferson, Ohio: Amusement Park Journal, 1982.

Kidney, Walter. *Pittsburgh's Bridges: Architecture and Engineering.* Pittsburgh: Pittsburgh History and Landmarks Foundation, 1999.

Kuncio, Gerald M. "The Golden Age in the City of Bridges," *Western Pennsylvania History* [Historical Society of Western Pennsylvania] (summer 1999).

Loftus, Tom. "Not Working Is a Tough Job," *Mill Hunk Herald,* no.12 (fall 1982).

McMillan, Tom. "When Prince Was King." *Pittsburgh Post-Gazette,* June 11, 1985.

Mendelson, Abby. *Pittsburgh: A Place in Time.* Pittsburgh: Cathedral Publishing, 1999.

Musinsky, Gerald. "On Russian Hill," *Mill Hunk Herald,* no.16 (spring 1985).

Ruck, Robert Lewis. *Sandlot Seasons: Sport in Black Pittsburgh*. Urbana: University of Illinois Press, 1993.

Sanger, Martha Frick Symington. *Henry Clay Frick: An Intimate Portrait*. New York: Abbeville Press, 1998.

Serrin, William. *Homestead: The Glory and Tragedy of an American Steel Town*. New York: Times Books, 1992.

Tinker, Reverend Harold. [Interview]. "A Map of Memories." [Television program].

Toker, Franklin. *Pittsburgh: An Urban Portrait*. Pittsburgh: University of Pittsburgh Press, 1986.

Van Trump, James D., and Arthur Ziegler. *Landmark Architecture of Allegheny County, Pennsylvania*. Pittsburgh: Pittsburgh History and Landmarks Foundation, 1967.